What people a

M.E Myself and I –

There is only the one story! We have it in the fairy tales, and the great myths and legends. We have it in all the great novels and literary works. And we have it here in Nicky Alan's extraordinary book! An extraordinary book by any standards! And that one story is the story of the rise of the hero within each one of us as we face the challenges and difficulties that we must overcome on our Spiritual path to full Enlightenment. All the requisites for a best-selling novel are here! Except this is all real! All this is actually part of the life journey of Nicky Alan herself! And just one of those horrific and devastating events in her life would be enough to shatter and destroy most of us! But not Nicky! Nicky's book is a true record of how it was and is for her. Speaking from her heart, Nicky reaches out to each one of us with compassion and love as she openly and honestly shares her most intimate life details: the horrific, demoralising and degrading suffering, the betrayals by those closest to her; the injuries and injustices done to her; the violence perpetrated upon her starting at such a young and tender age; the debilitating pain and immobility; the loneliness and the isolation; the depression; the thoughts of suicide; the attempts to block it all out; the loss of absolutely everything in her life and the constant ongoing onslaught of one disaster after another.

Through such an amazing course of events and synchronicities, Nicky eventually found the secret! The secret of total trust in the universe! The universe knows exactly what is going on, the universe knows exactly what each one of us needs at any point in our life, and the universe delivers for our own highest good.

This book is a refreshing and real story. Horrific, but real. Nicky's faith in the angels and in a superior guiding force has been tested to the full. Her sufferings have made her the strong, compassionate woman she now is, a shining light, a beacon of hope to the world. A reassuring and comforting voice to us all, as we continue on our Spiritual path. We are never alone. We do not know the whole plan. We just have to trust, follow the signs and take note of the synchronicities Spirit sends us.

Nicky's gift for writing is obvious from the very start of the book! This is obviously what she is meant to be doing! This is her unique contribution to humanity. And this contribution will continue to serve humanity in its darkest hours long after Nicky herself has passed on to the higher vibrational levels of the Spirit worlds. For this book is timeless. Timeless in its strong message of hope to us all. Strong in its message to us all that we can overcome the challenges and difficulties to become the hero of our own story. And Nicky should know! She has had a lifetime of challenges and difficulties. Here in this amazing book, her own catharsis, she lays bare her soul, stripped of all ego, as she struggled through so many dark nights of the soul. But we must first come through the darkness before we can come into the light. And the result? The amazing, compassionate, inspirational, caring and beautiful soul that is Nicky Alan!

You will not be able to put this book down, guaranteed! Because we see a potential Nicky in all of us! Any one of us could have been Nicky Alan. But how would we have coped?
Eileen McCourt, Spiritual Author and Teacher

This book will be great for people, and their families, that are suffering from M.E., fibromyalgia, depression or any other debilitating illness, but will also appeal to others whether they are spiritually minded or not. Nicky's connection with Spirit and the Angels and the messages she receives will astound you.

As a retired police detective she always asks for 'evidence' that what she is being told is true.

This book tells the story of her life, peaking as a successful celebrity psychic medium. This all came crashing down after a road accident left her with M.E./fibromyalgia. This illness led to her losing everything she owned including her home, and she was left feeling completely worthless and suicidal.

It tells how her connection with Spirit and the Angels helped her heal herself, and by sharing this experience she hopes that this story will help others.

Lindsey Cox, Retired Police Officer

An autobiography that will take you on a journey of tears, inspiration and hope. I could not put this book down, it's so much more than a diary of Nicky's life. If you are going through a tough time or a bereavement, this book will help you get through the dark days and give you comfort in knowing your loved ones are always by your side. I always thought a gifted psychic would have a rosy life with 24 hour communication to those upstairs! Well how wrong was I!

At times I found it shocking to learn what Nicky has gone through. From a tough childhood, bereavement, bankruptcy and a debilitating illness she is still standing, remains positive and has utter faith that this is her journey. This book made me realise that angels and spirit guides are always by your side, you just have to call them in.

A corker of a book and one I will pick up again when I am having a tough time!

Annie Conlon, TV Producer

What a ride! I've experienced every emotion possible reading this book. Firstly an immediate identification of suffering with this invisible illness, and the honest and no-holds-barred portrayal of desperation it brings to your door. The grief and relief that somersaults through the journey is described. If you want unbelievable drama sprinkled with miracles, undeniable proof that everything happens for a reason, this is the book for you. That having courage and reason to trust the process with faith and patience will set you free. This will always remind me never to give up, to sit in my own truth and not to be silent.

Anne Lloyd, Holistic Practitioner

Recently I have had the absolute special privilege of reading Nicky Alan's book, *M.E Myself and I – Diary of a Psychic!*

Not only is this masterpiece a hugely potential best-seller, it is the life of a very special lady laid bare, with raw emotion and honesty for all to see. Nothing is held back and her style of writing packs one almighty punch in the solar plexus and heart!

From start to finish I was taken on her incredible journey of happiness, success, positivity and guidance to heartbreaking sadness, illness, depression and loneliness.

One of the many things that really shines is her spirituality! A very powerful channel for our beautiful spirit realms!

Nicky has given everything of herself in this book. I have laughed and sobbed in equal measures!

A definite page turner and I highly recommend it!

I really hope you enjoy it as much as I have.

Joanne Barry, Angel Reiki Master

Wow! I have just finished reading Nicky's new book. I can honestly say that I just couldn't put it down. I cried and laughed so much throughout. Love the fact she says it how it is! This was refreshing and real! Her faith was tested to the limit but she still managed to get through it. Such amazing knowledge and so inspiring! And the synchronicities were unbelievable! All in all a brilliant read!

Helen Wright, Pain Relief Practitioner

M.E Myself and I – Diary of a Psychic

A Miracle Journey Surviving Chronic Illness

M.E Myself and I – Diary of a Psychic

A Miracle Journey Surviving Chronic Illness

Nicky Alan

6TH
BOOKS

Winchester, UK
Washington, USA

JOHN HUNT PUBLISHING

First published by Sixth Books, 2020
Sixth Books is an imprint of John Hunt Publishing Ltd., No. 3 East St., Alresford,
Hampshire SO24 9EE, UK
office@jhpbooks.com
www.johnhuntpublishing.com
www.6th-books.com

For distributor details and how to order please visit the 'Ordering' section on our website.

Text copyright: Nicky Alan 2019

ISBN: 978 1 78904 451 5
978 1 78904 452 2 (ebook)
Library of Congress Control Number: 2019948272

A CIP catalogue record for this book is available from the British Library.

Design: Stuart Davies

UK: Printed and bound by CPI Group (UK) Ltd, Croydon, CR0 4YY
US: Printed and bound by Thomson-Shore, 7300 West Joy Road, Dexter, MI 48130

We operate a distinctive and ethical publishing philosophy in
all areas of our business, from our global network of authors to
production and worldwide distribution.

Contents

Dedications

I dedicate my first book to the Angels and my Spirit Guides
who were relentless in their mission to bring me back to sanity.
I thank my fur babies Teddy and Mia for being my Earth
Angels and keeping me going.
As I had always planned, I also dedicate this work to my dad
Alan, who held my hand and soul through the whole journey.
Dad, I did it!
Finally, I honour every single soul who is bravely battling
chronic and mental illness. Keep fighting, come what may.

Preface

Worldwide there are as many as 24 million sufferers of M.E. and Fibromyalgia who I hope will be inspired by reading this book. They have been lost as I have in a system that has forsaken us all. I want to reach the 'Millions Missing' and let them know that they are not alone. My book is also aimed at anyone who has suffered loss, mental health issues, suicidal tendencies or disability. I hope that spiritualists and a curious public interested in angel and spirit phenomena will enjoy the miracles that the unseen can bring. Self-help fans or lovers of journeys of the human spirit will hopefully find enlightenment through my story. Most importantly I want to show the world that no matter how dark life gets, there is a spark that will eventually lead you to the light.

With Love, Nicky x

Acknowledgements

I want to thank my friends who not only stood by me during my darkness but also had the patience and the love to help this book come into fruition by continually believing in me. Special thanks go to Josephine, Claire, Lindsey, Helen, Jo, Leigh-Anne and Jay for wiping up my snot and pushing my wheelchair!

Bless you, Helen, Jo, Anne, Eileen, Lindsey, Verity and Annie for being my book guinea pigs!

Finally I want to say a huge thank you to my graphic designer Verity Rock who instinctively knew and shared my spiritual vision. Verity, you rock!

My world is a better place knowing I am loved by such magnificent people.

Author's Note:
All names highlighted with * have been changed
to respect privacy.

Prologue

As I lay looking out on to the sun-bleached Devonshire valley, I felt that familiar yearning to be walking through it. Houses were cheerily dotted along the hills that led to the Dartmouth Estuary promising human life and interaction. In essence any normal person would have let out an exhilarated sigh. They would have smiled and thought how lucky they were to be seeing such an awesome sight in such a beautiful location. Well no, not I. I resented those people busily leading their lives. To me they might as well have been aliens residing on the moon. I had not seen anyone apart from the postman for months.

I looked out to the swaying eucalyptus trees and allowed the silent tears to continue their steady stream down my cheeks. My eye sockets complained at this familiar motion continually working overtime, nothing stemming the pain. They sang out in a voice that joined the rest of my body chorus. Every nerve fibre, joint, muscle, tendon, bone and sinew roared, demanding attention.

The insomnia drove me to near insanity along with the most demoralising depression.

I was pretty much starving most of the time, as to even think of preparing food was about as possible as climbing Kilimanjaro on roller skates. I had bailiffs knocking at my unanswered door and merciless bankers demanding money. The people who I thought were friends turned their back or simply got bored of me. I was 44 years old living like a 95-year-old invalid.

My soul, body, mind and spirit were slowly dying and, my God, did I welcome death every single day. Death's sublime taste of freedom from this eternal imprisonment was all I could yearn for.

The thought of residing in heaven was my only reprieve. I had nothing left, nothing to live for.

I was lonely, terrified of my non-existent future and grieved my old successful life. The rawness of loss never left me. It just continued to stab me with a hot sharpened poker whenever I thought about it all.

The fight had gone; the battles of my mind and body raged on with no imminent victory.

I was standing on the precipice, facing an abyss of darkness, uncertainty and fear.

How could I step back and prevent falling into a void of blackness, and change direction?

I couldn't as far as I was concerned. I drew the curtains, got back into bed and dreamt of suicide.

Chapter 1

Seventh Heaven

I can remember it as if it were yesterday. It was 2010, I was standing next to the late psychic medium, Colin Fry, on stage at the Beck Theatre in Hayes. Thousands of people were applauding us as I took a humble bow. I was so proud of myself. The spirit people had been kind to me that night.

The messages to the chosen audience members were strong, full of magnificent evidence, and I was joyous in the knowledge that I had reached masses of people with proof of the afterlife.

Ah, yes, at this juncture I should tell you that I am psychic, have been since the day I was born. For me, seeing dead people and angels is pretty much as natural as breathing. So this isn't only my story of being dumped with an impossibly debilitating condition; it has a little twist. You see I can't say that I am a hero, battling against the odds to survive and thrive. That bit was pretty much orchestrated by entities that most people do not see or even have a clue exist. I am not some fluffy spiritual nut that believes in everything with wings. If anything I was the most sceptical angry 'anti-spiritualist' you could ever meet once the accident happened. In the next chapter you get the full picture, but let us start on a high, as after this there was nothing but serious, catastrophic lows. This book is not intended to depress you by any means, however, it shows the stark reality of how my condition can ravage not only your body but your mental health and soul.

After book signings and a vodka and tonic, I sleepily walked back to my dressing room totally elated. I had come exceptionally far as a professional psychic medium.

I was maintaining my family legacy where seventh sons of seventh sons spread back through our generations. I found that

3

once fully in the energy of the spirit world and angel realms there was no stopping my swift development and rise to becoming a highly acclaimed international medium.

At that point in my life, sitting in the dressing room looking into the mirror, I smiled and can remember clearly how lucky I was and how much I had achieved. I had enjoyed two seasons of *Angels* on Sky TV working with Gloria Hunniford. I had also done many other TV programmes as well as guested on radio shows all over the world. I had regular magazine work in all of the mainstream spiritual magazines and a column in one. I had finished my book *Heaven Calling* and I had publishers waiting for me to get the book out there.

I was being asked left, right and centre to do many other TV shows that were respectful to spiritualism. I had been asked to travel globally on tour. I had a beautiful following of people in their tens of thousands who not only were spiritually comforted by my knowledge, but were also willing students in my sell-out workshops, seminars and retreats. I was at the top of my industry and demand for me was high. I was wanted and needed, which made me feel whole.

Most importantly I was the slimmest that I had ever been. (Girls, you will understand that bit!) I was single, I felt strong, attractive, independent, self-assured, and confident in my capacity as a medium, and the world literally was my oyster. I was in seventh heaven and couldn't be happier.

How far I had come from my old life! I felt truly blessed.

Blessings.

Interesting word.

We are told to count them, embrace them.

I took them for granted.

I never took the time to count every single one of them. At the time though, I didn't realise. I thought that everything was on track and I was following my divine path. As I took each step I never really embraced how I was doing. I never took a breath and sat in my own energy, making sure everything was OK. I swallowed down the murmurings of the demons from my past. I got swept along on a whirlwind of celebrity parties and a roller coaster of the 'Nicky Alan' ride.

I never stopped to realise that I had traded my 'Detective' armour for the 'Nicky Alan' armour.

I was a detective in Essex Police prior to being a full-time psychic. I had forged a very effective armour over my heart and soul to stop anyone knowing my failings and my innermost fears. I so loved that armour! It kept me safely cocooned. Yes, I felt amazing and strong and invincible, but that was because I was wanted. What I failed to realise at the time was that I was just wanted for my gift, not for who I really was. I was leading a life of deception I suppose, that I was deceiving myself of my own truth. The regular demon that gurgled its way to my mind would remind me that if everyone knew me without the armour I would be discarded. So I thrived on the rapturous audiences. I adored the emails and messages that came to me from all over the world telling me how amazing I was. This esteem blanked out the inner failings that haunted me every day. I continued my existence partially blinded, valuing the words from the public as I had none of my own to give.

Abuse in my adolescence had firmly created a true lack of self-worth and esteem. But as long as everyone saw the bright shiny armour, why should I care?

That lack of self-worth made me choose the first mistake that led to my downfall.

On my fortieth birthday I started a relationship with someone who started the decline of my 'perfect' life.

I will not mention his name as it is akin to saying the name Voldemort! Let us just refer to him as 'Dick'.

I do not wish to give any energy to this person, but what I will say is I should thank him really, as he started the snowballing events that changed my life forever.

On reflection, despite him being an exceptionally poor choice, I desperately needed to be loved and that's why I let him in. He was there, so I grabbed him with both hands despite knowing in the pit of my stomach that it was so wrong. At that time, the voices of reason, the small divine voices that were telling me to stop making the decisions I was choosing out of weakness, were firmly put in their place, ignored, imprisoned and the key to their freedom deftly thrown away.

Through his actions I became estranged from my brother and sister. (More of that later!) I, in my weakness, failed to see the truth of it all, and promptly mourned the loss of them and my nieces and nephews in that small dark pit where the monsters resided.

He also managed to manipulate friends around me, which I failed to see at the time.

I had lost my sense of self. I had lost the ability to listen to my guides and divine friends who were trying to appraise me of the situation. I only listened to them when I was working for the public.

But of course, everything materially was peachy, so why should I worry about myself?

Why not carry on in denial, feigning true happiness?

Why indeed.

We all do it, we all take the easier option as change brings about an inherent fear in all of us. I am as guilty as the next person for failing to see what made me truly happy. I had no intention of treading the treacherous path of finding redemption and freedom. Happiness and love to me were way beyond my reach, so I always settled for second best. I didn't deserve happiness, that had been beaten into me from way back. I was walking along a rope bridge refusing to see it burning away at each end, slowing leading to the biggest fall of my life.

So I continued in my 'seventh heaven' existence, gripping on to my career and success with all of the strength that I could muster. Completely oblivious, completely in denial.

This is a story of loss.
This is a story of finding true faith.
This is a story of survival and the strength of the human spirit.
This is a story of miracles and amazing synchronicity.
This is a story of redemption and self-discovery.
This is a story that I hope will reach the hands of the desperate, stuck in their darkness, and who on reading it will find their way back to the light.

Chapter 2

This Is Me

All of my past students will tell you I am a stickler for writing soul journals.

Soul journals help us record our meditations, dreams, messages from the spirit world and most importantly our feelings. It is an excellent way to monitor your spiritual development, and also a fantastic therapy tool for your soul transition as you journey along the lessons that the Spirit World and Angel Realms bring.

So my soul journal is really the heart of this book. It has also enabled me to record every single thing that took place. I sometimes look back and read random pages and am still blown away by the synchronicity and miracles that happened.

But we are not at the miracle stage yet, not even close.

I think this is the best time to give you a picture of who I used to be, as after the miracles took place you will see who I am now. You will not believe how I have changed. In fact I still compare the old me to who I am today and it shocks me!

My first trauma was when I was sexually assaulted by a man when I was seven years old. He dragged me into the men's toilets at my local park and showed his son what you do with girls. In those days, the 70s, victim care by the police was shocking, pretty much non-existent. My dad was angry, but I thought that he was angry with me. I felt dirty and scared. The man was never caught. God only knows what his son grew up to be like. I don't think I ever truly recovered from that incident until a lot later on when the miracles started. It never occurred to me why I had an obsessive phobia of damp toilets and changing rooms after that incident.

My next trauma was when my darling dad Alan died in a road accident when I was nine. My brother Richard was five years old, my sister, Sarah, nine months old. I can still remember the cold February morning when my aunt told me that I would never see my dad again as he had gone to Heaven. He was my world, I adored him and followed him everywhere.

That day when I looked into my mum Evelyn's once bright cheery blue eyes, I noticed the death of her spirit. Her soul had been diminished by the loss of the love of her life. Her eyes had a haunted, vacant expression which told me instinctively that the light that once shone so brightly had been extinguished. It was then that she sought solace in alcohol, a salve that never abated.

Three days later my dad drove by me when I was walking along with my aunt.

He slowed the car down and said to me, "I'm OK, Nick, don't worry."

I was hysterical, why had I been told he was dead? I ran home telling the whole family what I had seen. My paternal side, especially my granddad Fred, knew I had seen the spirit of my dad. However, the maternal side of my family just looked on with sympathy in their eyes assuming this was my stage of denial in grieving.

From then on I knew that I was different. I saw and felt things that I soon learned other people couldn't. I always felt like I didn't fit in, so I assumed the persona of an intimidating, loud, bubbly character to make people like me. I used humour to make people laugh as I saw this as an unspoken acknowledgement that I was liked.

This persona was pushed even further when my mum married, four years later, what I can only describe as an animal.

He was a violent beast of a man, who periodically beat my mum and then me. I watched my mum's light diminish even further over those years during the 80s.

The man had an obsession with me. It was pure hatred. I pretended to be strong, my words vicious towards him as I received one beating after another. He would also touch me inappropriately. He would tell me how useless I was, how ugly I looked and how pathetic I was. He played my mum off against me. If she wouldn't take a beating he said that he would go upstairs and kill me, so I would then find her covered in blood on the floor in the morning.

I had always been a tomboy. From my dad's life insurance (which he upped a few months before his death as he knew he was going soon!), my mum bought me my dream, a pony. I spent my days galloping about on him. If I was not riding I was climbing up mountains, kayaking, hiking and abseiling. I needed to be in nature all of the time. It also gave me an escape from the arsehole that had inched his way into our home.

I had always wanted to be a police officer and he hated that. My anger boiled away inside of me towards my mum for being too weak to leave and for me staying to protect my brother and sister.

My 'armour' was intact by the time I was fifteen.

I was letting no one near me. I didn't want anyone to see how scared, vulnerable and angry I really was.

Unbelievably, during those years of misery, I came away with eleven O levels from school, my mission to join the police my only goal in life.

Four months after leaving school I joined the Essex Police Cadets where my career took off.

I used to try and get back home to make sure my brother and sister were OK. I tried to time it when the animal wouldn't be in. On one occasion he was in the house and I ended up getting stabbed by him as I laughed in his face saying that I wasn't scared of him.

It was incredibly embarrassing being a victim when I was a Police Cadet. Another time he punched me so hard down the stairs that I thought I had broken my neck. At that point I had to report to my Superintendent periodically to discuss the domestic issues that had arisen and that I was safe.

My mum told me one day that all of my possessions were at the end of the road and I had to come and get them. Because I had had him arrested, I wasn't allowed anywhere near the address. I picked two dustbin bags of stuff up. The rest of my childhood acquisitions, I assume, were taken to the dump.

It never occurred to me that this incident would stand me in a permanently vulnerable state, and would shape my belief that I would always be abandoned by the ones I trusted and loved the most.

The trial for his assaults, which were a number of Actual Bodily Harm assaults as well as one for Grievous Bodily Harm, was a joke to be honest.

He was put on a suspended sentence and told to pay me damages. Even though I knew he worked, he stated that he didn't and so was ordered to pay £5 a month which he never honoured.

By this time I was a Constable in Essex Police living in North Weald, Essex. He had put a threat out to kill me so I had to have regular police 'drive-bys' by the patrol on duty and any calls from my address were to be a grade one (immediate) response.

I could never show how broken I was to anyone as I thought I would lose my job. I swallowed down the pain, the abandonment by my mum, the anger, the bitterness and all the other dark demons that haunted me.

I turned that vulnerability into a loud, party girl. I worked hard and I played exceptionally hard. I was always the last girl standing at any function and refused to see that I really did need help. If there was a man to be snogged or flirted with I was there, desperate for any attention. I had a very unhealthy view of sex, seeing it as a way to get a cuddle afterwards.

Don't get me wrong, I did have the best years of my life in my twenties. I adored my job and loved working on crime units, vice units and eventually as a detective on CID and then Major

Investigations. I was in my element. The culture around policing in those days was work your socks off on duty then play hard with your police 'family' during your time off.

As a detective on Major Investigations, I mainly carried out family liaison duties for murder victim families and rape victims. I was obsessed with death from birth; murderers fascinated me. I was on many occasions standing next to the murder victim as I investigated their death. They sometimes gave me visions and thoughts that would help their perpetrators get the justice that they richly deserved.

I had been in a long-term relationship from 20 to 29 but that faded. I wasn't happy but I couldn't find the source of what was wrong. In fact, truth be told, I refused to face what was wrong.

My mum had divorced the animal and was with another man who would never be a father to us, but who made her happy. They moved to Spain. I visited as much as I could, but I look back and realise that I still harboured a heartbreaking grudge against my mum for putting us through eight years of pain.

I really did pull away from family values to be honest. I saw my brother and sister now and then, but the cracks of our past started to create invisible ravines that could have only been bridged by talking and making the effort which we never really did.

Sadly I was medically retired from an injury on duty in 2003. My reason for being was my police career. Eighteen years of service as a police officer and nothing to show for it. I was beside myself. I had lost my 'family' and my security. I lost my reason for being. I felt abandoned once again. That is when I went through my first breakdown.

The only anchor that was keeping me going was my career, and now the rope had been cut and I was left floating in a dark abyss of fear and resentment.

I started drinking heavily to block out the pain. The demons from my past started to creep back. I was losing my ability to cope.

When it all got too much I sought help for the first time. I found the most amazing man, Pete Evans, a brilliant psychotherapist. I connected with him straight away which is vital when you have so many barriers up. If you can't connect with your therapist you won't share your truth which doesn't help anyone.

I spent two years with this man and I put a lot of ghosts to rest including the bitterness I had towards my mum. I realised that she was just as much a victim of our past as I was. I also binned alcohol, cigarettes, sugar, fats and yeast from my diet in an effort to cleanse myself. After a year I started drinking again but in a healthy way. (Well that's what I thought!) I tried the best I could to eat healthily and stayed off the fags.

Halfway through my therapy, the spirit world dragged me into their world. (That story is for another book!) They had called upon me for a different type of duty where they were my new bosses. I had been doing readings and psychic parties in the evenings after work in the police, so I had had a lot of practice. I proceeded to march forward on an uncertain path as a full-time professional psychic medium. I soon found it a wonderful blessing though, leading to a new way to comfort and support humankind which was obviously my true destiny.

Before I knew it public demand for me was high. After one week of doing readings at my friend Claire's salon in Rayleigh, I had a six-month waiting list.

I was serving over 80 spiritualist churches throughout the country. I was doing a lot of TV consultations, paranormal investigations and theatre shows. I had radio interviews all over the world and was on such a high with my new career that I forgot to take care of my inner child as I had been taught by Peter.

My new persona was Nicky Alan, and any frays in my inner turmoil that hadn't quite been firmly clipped into shape were abandoned. They were left in the little dark crevice in my soul, unanswered and untended. I gave my whole self to helping other people and not helping myself.

I can't put into words how humbling and truly rewarding helping people through my natural gift made me feel. To transform people and their lives through my knowledge and ability to connect to the angel realms and the spirit world overwhelmed me.

My career grew from strength to strength. I still partied hard after work. I used to love the karaoke nights I had with the girls. I slowly relapsed into not having a particularly healthy diet and continually drank Red Bull to keep my energy up for shows. I knew deep down that I had depression but just ignored it. I was in a long-term relationship with a man who had alcohol issues. I knew he was bad for me but I didn't care; I adored him when he was sober.

It is SO easy to take the simplest option and just go with the flow hoping that you will find your happiness. I was floating along waiting for things to change for me. I had no courage to make any personal changes out of fear and abandonment. I had friends around me that I knew weren't real friends, I didn't care. I eventually had the courage to leave my partner and I would say they were the best times I had, as a single woman. Those were the years I was in seventh heaven.

I figured, if I was helping people and giving my all for the spirit world, surely they would reward me in time.

They did reward me, but it took years for me to see that. Instead what I saw when it all happened was that I had been persecuted and punished for being such a failure. I saw nothing in my mind but the Angel Realms and the Spirit World forsaking me. They were discarding me because they finally realised that I was no good, just as it had been drummed into me during my adolescence.

As the car came skidding towards me, I had no idea what was

to come, and as I have said many times before, the events that were to take place after that impact still leave me breathless.

Chapter 3

Crash and Burn

Do you know those dreams when you wake up with a start, with shallow breath, sweating and your heart racing? Well on the morning of Monday, 23 January 2012, I had one of those dreams. It was so real. I could see me letting out a scream but it was silent as a car came smashing into me. The only problem was that's all I could see. No other information. Not when, how or where.

I have often wondered throughout my life why I have these prophetic dreams. Sometimes they are of global disasters a couple of weeks before they have happened, other times the night before. But there is nothing you can do about them. Who would listen?

I asked this once of my main guide Julianus (more of him later!). He said that it was just the fact I was at one with the Universe and any spikes through the natural equilibrium I would experience through dream state or meditation.

It was exactly the same for celebrity deaths and sometimes murder victims telling me of their plight. I would have murder victims come to me, I would then see the murder on the news and knew that I could help. But I know as an ex-police officer, psychics are just a box that needs to be ticked as being spoken to on a murder investigation to cover tracks. Psychics are never taken seriously.

So when I told Dick at the time about my dream I remember exactly what he said.

"Well when is it going to happen then?"

"I don't know."

"Is it in our car?"

"I don't know."

He didn't reply. What should I do, stay indoors forever?

We had planned to drive to Devon that day. We were in the process of buying a holiday mobile home and I had been doing a lot of work at the Lupton Trust, a community location near Brixham.

So to drive, or not to drive?

We drove.

After arriving at Lupton House, we realised that we were hungry so we decided to go the local pub for something to eat. I was in the passenger seat. It had been raining and was just after 7pm. We indicated to turn left into the pub driveway and the young girl behind did not even see us. As I looked out of my window I saw her screeching towards us in a brake lock. All I can remember at the time was frantically trying to get my seatbelt off and get to the driver's side as she was heading straight for me. I also had flashes of my dad running through my mind as he had been killed from a side-on impact.

The sickening crunch came. Luckily the main impact was the rear door and rear wing. I was in the most peculiar position on impact. I was half leaning across the centre console. The handbrake had driven into my ribs. My shins had smashed against the centre console, and my neck was strained against the seat belt that I had failed to release.

Instantly my jaw felt like it had been punched by a hammer. My back was screaming and my ribs felt like they were being plucked out of my skin by an unseen hand.

Thank the heavens, a couple of seconds behind us there was a police car. Very shortly after this the paramedics arrived and got me into the ambulance under gas and air. Very interesting substance that gas, I have to say!

After all the usual tests I was released in the early hours of the morning diagnosed with severe whiplash and soft tissue damage. But something didn't feel right. The pain was indescribable for just soft tissue damage.

I was taken back to where we were staying and promptly fell

asleep, no doubt aided by the morphine.

In the early evening I remember waking up and hearing the murmured tones of Dick and my friend. I can only describe how I felt as being encased in a fog of pain, and complete and utter exhaustion.

I tried to sit up but millions of spiteful burning hot needles flamed through my body. My eye sockets screamed out in protest with the movement of my head and the light of the bedside lamp. Despite the pain, I tried to slide out of bed, and realised that I couldn't walk through sheer agony and exhaustion.

I had to be carried to the toilet, and can honestly say that I felt like death.

I then started to get other symptoms. I found that I had to have the curtains closed as the light was like molten lava on my eyes. I asked everyone to whisper around me as sound smashed through my skull like a sledgehammer. I found that I couldn't hold my bladder very long. I also had the most alarming thing start to happen. I couldn't pronounce words and had to stop and think about what I was going to say. I also stuttered and words came out in the wrong order. I felt permanently nauseous and had a tummy upset with everything I ate. I had no balance and kept falling over; my coordination was horrendous.

I couldn't concentrate either. If I watched the television through my squinting eyes, I would have absolutely no idea what I was watching. I couldn't process the words or actions, and forgot what I had just watched. My short-term memory was appalling. I started to panic, but everyone around me just said it was the medication I was on.

I really can't describe the pain to you. Every joint in your body feels swollen and throbs with dull pain. Your muscles feel like they are full of lactic acid, every movement takes your breath away. Then the nerve pain starts, vicious hot stabbing pains shooting through your whole body. The weirdest thing was that my skin hurt to touch. It felt like the whole of my skin was bruised and any light touch was like a Chinese burn. My hair follicles hurt so whenever my hair moved my scalp felt like it was on fire.

I would get tracers in my eyes whenever I looked in a different direction and blurred vision. When my eyes moved I could almost hear them shifting and feel the pain slicing into my sockets. I also had random spots on my scalp which, if I touched them, felt like I was driving a drill through them. The following day they would disappear but then turn up in a different place on my head. My nails hurt on my fingers and on my toes. There was not a millimetre on my body that was pain-free. None of the medication touched it. I would just rock in a foetal position longing for sleep to escape the agony.

I felt like an outsider watching the drama of my life unfold. I felt that I was standing helplessly by, completely impotent.

During this time, Dick had picked up a rescue dog that had been abandoned. He was a tiny little shih-tzu cross. I named him Teddy as he looked like a live teddy bear. In later years I would realise that he was an Earth Angel brought down to me. That beautiful soul saved my life on more than one occasion. I had saved him and my God did he save me right back!

After a few days I returned to A&E as I was convinced that they had missed something exceptionally serious. On further examination they found nothing. They stated it was most probably shock and gave me stronger drugs.

The pain never abated, the exhaustion continued. I was terrified. I felt like I was worsening every day. Each morning I would wake up with new and different symptoms. I felt like there was a puppet master cruelly standing above me pulling strings of torture.

I had no energy at all. When normal people say they are tired, they have no idea what exhaustion really is. I found it hard to breathe. The exertion of my abdomen moving and my lungs inflating was like running a marathon. I did not wash and

I did not get dressed, I just laid down in bed like a coma patient watching one day fall into the next. Teddy was then joined by Mia, another rescue dog. She was a shih-tzu that had been rescued from a puppy farm. I have never seen a dog in such a horrendous condition mentally and physically. Those two dogs were a joy to me. They stayed on the bed with me as we all clung together reeling from our own traumas, supporting each other.

I realised that I had to cancel everything for the next few months. This brought into play money worries, and the fact that I was letting people down who had waited so long to see me. I had staff to pay, two homes to pay for and I was suddenly not earning. I convinced myself that I would only be off for a little while, I would bring the money in soon.

At that point I felt slightly safe as Dick was very supportive and helpful. It never occurred to me to wonder why my brother and sister hadn't shown up to see how I was. I never wondered why I hadn't heard from my mum regularly. I just put my complete trust and life in Dick's hands.

The best analogy I can think of is an innocent child taking the hand of a dangerous stranger. I took that hand and refused to let go. But as the weeks turned into months, I realised how stupid I was to trust the person closest to me. In the fog of permanent sleep and teeth-gritting pain, I was totally unaware of the abandonment taking place around me.

Steps were being prudently taken by the only person I relied upon. He was helping me to survive this apparent misery that I found myself in. He was washing me, feeding me, changing me and doing all of the housework. I thought of him as my hero.

Well that's what I thought.

Those steps he was taking, those slow baby steps, were to secure his exit.

I had absolutely no clue. Do you know that song by Pink Floyd, *Comfortably Numb*? That's what I felt like, numb and comfortable being off my face on painkillers. Comfortable in the knowing that someone was looking after me in my desperate time of need. The medication enabled me to be in complete denial of my situation. Even if I tried to think of how to take my life forward, my brain told me that creating thought and coping mechanisms were simply too bloody exhausting.

The only discomfort was when the painkillers wore off and I came rocketing back into the world and my reality. I wanted to smash the girl's face in that had created this. Anger, self-pity and desperation were my familiar friends during this time. I found no positives as I lay in bed every day. I stank of urine and body odour but had no way to get to the bathroom and wash unless Dick decided to pop his head in and help me.

In this hazy fug I didn't realise how much time Dick was away from me. I could sleep all day and night, and not know when he was there. I had no clue what day of the week it was. My life was just day, night, take medication. If I tried to get up my limbs would shake, promising imminent collapse. I honestly thought that I was dying.

The doctors were useless. They had no empathy at all for what I was feeling. They just kept pumping me with more analgesics. I was on long waiting lists for rheumatology, neurology and the pain clinic. I was basically left to get on with it. I remember collapsing on the floor in the doctor's waiting room. I had no energy to get up and was lying on the floor crying my heart out. The doctor looked at me as if I was auditioning for a major film.

The look of 'hypochondria' blazed in his eyes.

They have no idea what pain and exhaustion on this level is like. You only understand it if you have it yourself.

After six months the fog started to thin as I realised bills needed paying. It was at this point that I should have surrendered. This was the point I should have faced facts and realised that I was seriously ill. The armour was starting to shine through its tired tarnish. My ego told me that I had to get back into the material world and make money. I was in denial of my illness and knew that I had to get money in fast. I had no respect for my body. It was hurting and I was ignoring it. It was telling me that it was too exhausted; I saw that as me being a victim and a failure. I blamed myself for being ill and convinced myself to get my arse in gear and stop feeling sorry for myself. How I hated myself back then!

Dick was supposedly working but I soon found out that he wasn't. Everything I had worked for was at stake. This was the only thought running through my mind as I forced myself out of bed. If I had trusted the Universe then, this would be a very short story. If I had let go and let everything around me just flow knowing that I was going to be OK, I would have saved myself a lot of heartbreak and pain. If I had reached out to my oldest friends, I would have found an easier route.

But we never do take the sensible route, do we?

I didn't realise what was happening around me. I didn't realise that I was going to kill my body. I didn't realise the second that young girl hit me, my life had changed forever.

Chapter 4

The Long Road Down

So, rather stupidly, six months on, trying to get a grip of this perpetual pain and exhaustion, I started to work again. I had no respect for my physical body at all. I am ashamed to say that I was filling myself up with morphine, and to aid their delivery was washing it down with endless cans of Red Bull, and sometimes vodka to get the tablets to really kick in. I was in complete denial of my illness; convincing myself that if I ignored it, it would go away and magically disappear.

I remember doing a show in Norfolk that year. I cried all the way up there as the drive was excruciating. I sat in the passenger seat rocking in a foetal position like a forlorn baby. The organisers even put a settee up on the stage as I couldn't stay standing for too long. I always had a bubbly personality and was very loud so I laughed off the fact that I had to sit on a comfy settee to do my evening of mediumship. What was I thinking? I was thinking that I was the only breadwinner, and had to pay the bills and the wages of my staff. I was thinking that if I cancelled my shows I would not be liked anymore.

So I dragged myself to every event, got through it with a smile then went home and slept until I needed to get up to do my next bit of work. I even honoured a holiday that we had booked a while ago to Thailand. I did feel slightly better there, but then alcohol and painkillers are a great mix!

They always say that when you are down this is when you know who your true friends are. Boy did I find that out!

The 'friends' started to dwindle as I left voicemails unanswered and the phone on permanent silent as I rested my tortured body. I had no energy to engage in conversation with anyone.

The only other thing that I was doing was going to the doctors trying to get a diagnosis, as I honestly thought I had cancer or some other disease. Truth be told, any diagnosis would have been met with relief so I knew what I was fighting.

The only person who was around me the most was Dick. I never realised it at the time, but I was totally isolated apart from who I saw at my public performances and readings.

As I lay in bed month after month, he obviously realised I was a lost cause.

As I have already said, I had no idea what was happening as I literally spent every hour sleeping and trying to manage my pain. Whilst I was suffering he was up to no good. Very soon I was about to be the victim of his hateful and selfish behaviour. I was oblivious.

We had decided to have Christmas in Devon in the mobile home as a change of scenery. To me it was just a different bed to lay in, with the change of background sounds being the waves and seagulls.

Wednesday 19 December 2012
Sometimes when you are a spiritual worker you really don't know what is spiritual and what isn't. I sit here in the caravan looking at the sparkling Christmas tree and out to the fog laden sea, feeling absolutely awful yet again. I have flu whilst everyone else is ferreting away at Lupton getting ready for the Green Christmas fayre up there. Dick is up there all hours, so I sit here alone pretty pissed off. My health hasn't let up at all. I had brief respite in Thailand. I wonder was it because I had no stress? The Heat? Not working? God knows. I'm lost as I really don't know what I want. When I sit in Lupton I feel I want to be there. But then other times, I don't want that to be the one and only thing in my life. Other times I want to leave Essex, then I want to stay. Then I think perhaps I should move somewhere hot. Then I think shall I just stop work for a few months and then I think I will lose the house. It's all jumbling around in my head and there seems to be no resolution.

Am I ill because of a spiritual or physical ailment? Does the medication help or hinder? Are others harming my energy? Am I a target of ill will? I just don't know what I should be doing. What I do know is, that I have to get well. It is a joke how I feel, nothing brings pleasure. I have no real life. It consists of sleeping, feeling depressed. Then I have a moment of enjoyment at a Christmas dinner, then payment time, full on flu. I have been permanently ill now since the road accident.

What is the lesson?

Or is it just stop fucking working for a while? But everyone else has to work? They don't get ill because of it. Be nice to just take a couple of months off knowing that the bills would be paid.

Christ if Dick got paid for the hours he puts in at Lupton we would be sorted.

I can't commit to that. Rightly or wrongly I don't want to lose my home. I don't want to lose my way of life (well the one I should be having!), I don't want to live in a caravan. My perspective keeps changing. Spiritual people around me say so what if I lose my home! No if it's my spiritual lesson, then I'm afraid I'm going to fail it miserably. I have made some very bad decisions regarding buying the car, caravan which I am truly paying for now. It's done so I can't worry about the past but, materially, I need to get back on track pretty quickly as financially all is not good at all.

I need peace, stress relief and to find myself again. Yet again I've set myself loose into a whirling river with no foundation. How often am I going to keep doing it this lifetime? Something needs to give. But if I rest I lose money, if I don't rest I stay ill. WTF?

I need answers.

Some of the answers I may already know but are they marred by the state of my energy? Am I reading into things as a self-destruct mechanism or is the truth so obvious that I'm reeling away from it?

Perhaps counselling is the way forward again, but then that's pennies! Bloody nightmare! My spiritual faith is yet again being tested. I feel so 'unlinked'. The last show at Lupton was awful. I was so ill, gulping cider vinegar, honey, vodka and Red Bulls.

I need to love myself. Heal myself. Acknowledge what I need and have the strength to go forward. I can't keep stuck through fear of change or confrontation. I am so, so tired. So very fatigued every single day. I have to deal with so much pain. I just find I never have a few months of complete health and happiness. So is that spiritual or just that I'm going to be like this for the rest of my life? I need to write, why have the magazines closed down? I am swimming against the current permanently. I need to let go and let the tide just take me and go with the flow. Because, quite frankly this ceaseless current I'm swimming against is killing me...

What do they want from me?

This was the time when I started to reach for my soul journal more than I had ever done before. I can't really apologise for the bad language as it is the transparent 'me' and what I was going through at the time. When I write the excerpts from my journals into this book, I am so shocked on how blinded I was from the illusions of human life and people. I just want to smack the old me in the face and say, "What the hell were you thinking!"

Why didn't I notice that my magazine work had dried up at the blink of an eye for a reason? Why did I not stop then and there working when I collapsed halfway through a show at Lupton? Before the show I was shaking with exhaustion, and every nerve and fibre in my body was screaming in agony. I was going against everything I had ever told my students. Never work if you are feeling under par or in a low energy.

I had already had my limit of morphine, so I chucked three co-codamol in my throat swished down with a vodka Red Bull. The energy in that room was horrendous that night. I struggled to connect with every spirit person and was working as if my life depended on it. By half-time I dragged myself to a room and promptly collapsed. I was in a cold sweat, shaking like a leaf and gasping to get air into my lungs. My lungs felt too exhausted to work so I was then experiencing anxiety, and at the time had a huge panic attack. My limbs were on fire, and I knew then and there, that this was it. I could no longer fight this ridiculous monster that had a grip on me. I had no more to give and could not sanction this way of working, using drugs and alcohol to get me through.

I took more painkillers and despite people telling me to not go on, I did.

I finished the evening knowing that I would not step foot on a stage again for a very long time. But the lion part of my ego said, yes, I would.

I went home and cried my eyes out. I was in the mobile home that I had dreamed of having. It was right by the sea in Goodrington, Paignton. I remember listening to the waves crashing on to the craggy coastline, feeling the most terrified I had been for a long time.

I see a completely different person in these excerpts, a person I no longer recognise in any way, shape or form. But for you to experience my true journey, they must be included in my story.

0026 hrs Tuesday 1 January 2013
Thank Christ 2012 is over! One of the worst years of my life! I have just stood on the decking ALONE again and watched over the bay at all the fireworks and Chinese lanterns. It was quite magical! To hear the cheers and whoops across the bay was really something.

When you wish upon a star...
So here it is.
PLAN
HEALTH
Complete Rest
Lose weight
Improve fitness very slowly
Positive mental attitude. Be in nature. Meditate.
It's all about ME!
LOVE

Deal with relationships!
Say goodbye to the old
Embrace friendship time
Reach out. Don't isolate
Make friends a priority
WORK
When I want to!
Finish book
Do angel board/cards
DO NOT OVERDO IT!
Go with the flow, no pressure, no planning
LIVE!
Do what I want
Fight the debt
Try and dive
Have lots of play time
Get house done
Do volunteer work at animal sanctuary
These are my initial plans, but no. 1 comes first as without
that I have nothing. I have spent a year flat. In pain, unhappy,
depressed, fatigued, no energy, no excitement, no optimism,
NOTHING!
This year I have nothing to look forward to apart from going
yet again back to the fundamentals which I keep missing out,
ME.
If it means I've got to start again, so be it.
I never want to be in the darkness again.
I can't take another repeat year so things must change. If nothing
changes I will be in the same rut I have been in, in the last 365 days.
So, Nick, the rock bottom can get deeper, are you going to sink even
further? Are you going to continue living like a 70-year-old or a
42-year-old? Get your passion back. Get off your arse and change.
All those messages of hope going out in the lanterns. Mine is in my
thoughts.

Angels and loved ones, please help me.
It's a tough journey but I want to know that I'm not alone.
I need help and guidance to show I'm on the right path.
I will check off each point that I succeed in.
It will be MY life.
I desperately hope that I have the courage to change. I desperately
hope that I read this next New Year and smile, thinking, wow how
fab my life has turned out! Come on Nick xxxx

Funnily enough, none of the plans I made on that night even began to come into fruition. I also had nowhere near a smile on my face the following New Year. My life was to get worse, far worse.

I remember that New Year's Eve very well. I sat on the decking of my holiday home and watched the Chinese lanterns casting their light into a velvet black sky out towards the sea. I watched the fireworks and heard the cheers of people welcoming in the New Year.

I was there alone, he was sleeping.

I had the biggest sense of foreboding and knew that this next year was not welcome at all. I was on the precipice looking down into a deep dark emptiness and I knew that I was going to fall into it.

I shakily stood up and looked up to the sky.

"Whoever is up there, you must help me," I said through streams of tears.

"I am on a long road down and I know that I haven't even begun to tread its tarmac. I'm in your hands as I cannot do this any longer."

I waited expectantly. No one answered.

Chapter 5

The Fear

Fear is so powerful. Fear stops us from making positive change and gives us tunnel vision when we need to see with clarity. It can keep us imprisoned for many years. That fear was crawling its way into my consciousness, closing me down. It was whispering all of the potential outcomes of my predicament. I knew that I couldn't work so how was I to pay the mortgage? Dick was getting more and more distant; I could feel his coldness permeating the house.

I tried to justify it by thinking how hard it must be for him to care for me. I blamed myself for his distance. It's something I had always done. If someone wasn't happy around me or had distanced themselves, I always felt that I had caused the problem. In my eyes, I was always in the wrong. I would tick all of the boxes of self-loathing, not even thinking for a minute that it was the other person that had the issue! So with my lack of self-love and self-belief, I tried to be as nice as possible to him, terrified that he would leave me. We didn't even sleep in the same bed. There was nothing there, and as far as I was concerned I didn't blame him one little bit.

My only joy were my two little ones, Ted and Mia. Mia had come on leaps and bounds. She was starting to act like a normal dog after months of shaking and hiding under anything she could find. I watched Ted show her where to eat and drink from. He would wait patiently for her to go to the back door, and walk with her into the garden to go to the toilet. She followed him everywhere. They were inseparable. I would smile when every morning and night he would wash her ears and her face.

Our pets aren't just domesticated animals. They are our salvation. They are brought down here to guide us, love us unconditionally and help us through the storms. Why do you think they have such short lives with us? Because they deserve to go back home to the Rainbow Bridge, their layer of Heaven, rather than fight it out surviving in this world. When their job is done helping us, they go home. My last dog Meena waited until my birthday the year before, until she could hold on no more. She had guided me through my breakdown and comforted me as I found a new life in being a professional medium. I remember the night of my birthday; I had been sleeping with her on the settee bed as I knew she was going to be leaving me.

I said to her, "Darling, I know you are in pain, I am ready now for you to go home. So when we go to the vet man in a couple of days, it's OK for you to go. Thank you for helping me through a very difficult time. I love you so much, more than anything."

As I said these words through my tears I almost felt the sigh of relief whisper through her body. I meant every word. My dogs to me were the safest in investing my love. The only way they would leave me was through no fault of their own, it was just time for them to go home. At the vets, she passed away. The hurt was unbearable but later on I knew she was fine and safe as she turned up with my dad in a dream wagging her tail and running around like a nutter!

So during those days of loneliness and pain, Ted and Mia would look at me as I lay in my bed and I would literally swoon looking at their cute little faces. I would chat away to them telling them all of my fears as they patiently listened.

I could feel my body getting weaker. It felt like my mind and soul wanted to just give up as it was too exhausted to carry on functioning. All of these worries were swirling in my mind when I was awake which these days was very rare. I literally could sleep for weeks. When I was awake I had a sinking feeling of impending doom. My depression was overwhelming me. The doctor had doubled my antidepressants. I literally was a walking chemist with all the crap I was taking.

I couldn't shake it, this sickening fear washed over me whenever I let it in. It's like when you hear the electricity in the air before a storm is about to arrive. You know that it's coming, you can feel it, but you don't know when. I would lose myself in crap TV and try to fend off this sense of impending darkness. Every time the feeling came back to me, I jolted with the sheer intensity of it. I felt that I was on a runaway train and could see the broken bridge ahead. The fall was imminent.

Sunday 6 January 2013
Sometimes I could strangle him. I look at him and want to smash him in the face! Staying up till 2, mooching into work at 1.30 pm, then back at 5 and he wonders why I get the hump. We are totally living beyond our means without a fucking penny. In Devon he is up and out at 9, here in Essex it's a joke!

I'm still so weak, ill in pain and totally fucked off. I weigh 16 stone 8 lbs and am unfit! I have been drinking no alcohol at all so we shall see.

My hand is hurting so much writing this. I have the pain management clinic tomorrow. I am going to let them have it!

Saturday 12 January 2013
I'm still exceptionally fatigued. I could literally sleep for England. It's a joke. I generally get up between 1 and 4 pm. Then do something little, then its dark, watch the telly, go to bed. My life is a joke, but it's all I can do. I tried a normal day the other day after the pain clinic which was a joke. She was more interested in if I could see her dead mother! I walked the dogs and went to Sainsbury's and cooked dinner. It killed me. I slept all day the next day! The pain clinic are sending a letter to my GP for a full MOT again. So hopefully we can get further down the road. It's so hard. I have a week off until I'm working again at celebrity Mike Reid's house. No pressure then!

I tried meditating today. I managed to get to my old meeting place. The spirit door opened and I was aware at the top of the stairs was a bridge of a ship. I wouldn't walk up there though. I sat on the settee, had floating visions of Nan, Granddad and Dad but nothing solid. I then went out of the patio doors intending to go look at my own soul. I remember the rock path, seeing Granddad Fred and that's it. Next thing I know, I wake up! God knows how long later, music finished. Sleeping again! I suppose I need to rest. Fuck me I'll be resting until I'm dead!

Something has got to give at some point. I need to get some improvement, but as soon as I try to do something I pay for it. When I was out the other day there were weird synchronicities, especially Earth Angel voices. Before the hospital appointment,

"If you don't show you're being proactive, then they won't."

In Sainsbury's,

"You just got to keep on going."

The number 333 everywhere. A robin staring at me opposite the pain clinic. My spirit song played twice, "Nothing's gonna stop us now." So I'm trusting.

To be honest at this point I really wasn't trusting anything. I was holding on for dear life hoping that a valiant rescue would be imminent.

The signs and synchronicity were there, I was just misinterpreting them. If I took time to close my mind and listen, I am sure they would have guided me along. I was too exhausted though. I was in such deep crisis I was blocking every way for them to come in and help. I know now that they were preparing me, they were warning me for what was to come. By adding the feelings of doom with the signs I was receiving I should have connected the dots, but I didn't.

Earth Angel voices by the way are people around you who say something in your vicinity which you are supposed to hear. You are either inspired by the angel realms to be in their space when they say the words or they are briefly inspired to approach you out of the blue and say something that is vital for you to hear.

I remember when I was worried about doing the programme *Angels*. I was worried I was going to be made an idiot. The fear was creating all sorts of projected catastrophes in my mind.

A lady was standing next to me in the vegetable aisle when I was in Sainsbury's one day. She just turned to me and said,

"You have to remember you're special and you should reach out and show people about what you know, trust the process."

She then turned away and carried on shopping. That is an Earth Angel message. They are a bit freaky but wonderful to experience. On her words, I agreed to do the programme.

Back to the real world. I then had another let-down. It turned out that the solicitor I had appointed had done absolutely nothing with my road accident case so I had to find a new one. How can a solicitor leave such an important case to a bottom drawer? I had no energy to fight or make a complaint. I needed to find another solicitor. I was banking on any payout to help me keep my home. It would also help me to stop work. I eventually found a local solicitor that someone on Facebook had recommended. Why they recommended him Christ only knows. I remember the company when I was in the police. The defence solicitors had been very impressive. I was to learn, however, the accident claim side of things was so under par it was ridiculous.

Stupidly, despite collapsing at Lupton, I still tried to work to keep the money coming in. The work was rare and only once a week if that, but it kept the money vultures away, just about. I would do group readings in people's homes so that I could sit in a comfy chair whilst I was working. I loved helping these people and delivering valuable messages, but all I could think of was the minute that I would finish. I would collapse in the car and go into a deep sleep on the way home. I would then not leave my bed until the next time I had to drag myself to someone's home.

I felt grateful for Dick taking me to these events. It didn't even cross my mind to question that he was happy to take me despite me being so ill. It never occurred to me that he should have worked longer hours and left me in bed. As usual, being an empath, I was trying to be the saviour and the survivor. As usual, I was so desperately grateful that he was with me, I didn't see the wood for the trees.

Tuesday 22 January 2013
I cried into the early hours of the morning. Then suddenly an energy within me started to vibrate and talk. I don't think it was family, it felt higher. Don't think it was Julianus. This is what happened last night.
"Right enough is enough. Stop feeling sorry for yourself. You have been ill all year but we can still blend with you! So get on representing us! Start your telephone readings, moderation will not damage your body if doing readings at home and it will help get the second book done. It will be called THE OTHERS. Introduce us to humankind and show us through darkness and light. Educate them from our side. YING and YANG. Light and DARK. ANGELS and DEMONS. Trust! Trust! Move on! Start writing!"
Wow. So today I started to write the next book, it is flowing like Heaven Calling *did. Then I get a phone call. It's from a girl who had had very dark energy in her home and she was telling me with my help the house was now full of angels, and her spirit family. Exactly what I am writing about in this book! My soul feels revitalised, like I have something to focus on. So I'm trusting more and coping.*

Now I realise why the angel realms came and spoke to me that night. They were desperately trying to get me to focus on a goal, to start writing. They also knew what was coming and knew what I needed to do. They were showing me new ways to work with this lifestyle change. I was so far in denial though, there was no way I would change my work and accept this new way of living. It also didn't help that I had abandoned taking my book *Heaven Calling* any further because I was too ill. It was the last thing I wanted to do, deal with publishers on top of everything else!

Three days later, three days after the anniversary of my accident, the next bullet of my descending life shot sure and true into my heart leaving it perpetually bleeding for a very long time. A cruel twist of events would see me sink further into the abyss. The runaway train had hit the part of the bridge that had broken. The freefall was about to take place and all I could do was hurtle downwards, desperately hoping for a soft landing.

Needless to say, I didn't write another word for *THE OTHERS*.

Chapter 6

Betrayal

The day arrived. Dick was going to do some work down in Devon and was going to take the train.

He never got there.

He disappeared into thin air.

After two days the police got involved. The embarrassment of having my house searched and my holiday home visited by police was mortifying. That selfish pig of a man left no note and so I was left alone trying to cope with all of the police questions and my illness.

I stayed in bed day after day wondering how he could leave me knowing how ill I was.

It didn't take long to realise why he had done a disappearing act.

I had hobbled to the kitchen to feed the dogs and I heard the letterbox rattle. My stomach lurched as I thought it may be letters from the bank, as I had not paid the mortgage that month.

It was worse than that.

I opened the letters and I slipped to the floor shaking. Old credit cards that I had kept in my locked filing cabinet appeared to have been resurrected. Thousands upon thousands of pounds had been cashed. Obviously without any credit payments the interest was sky high.

My heart was in my throat as I frantically searched through my filing cabinet. All of the cards had gone.

I called each company and all of the credit cards had been maxed out. I also found bank accounts opened in my name where overdrafts had been used to the full.

I can only describe it as my mind flatlining. I had noticed with M.E. your ability to cope with stress is non-existent. Through the exhaustion, if anything comes along where you have to make an extra effort to cope, forget it. You just go into a massive anxiety episode and withdraw.

That's exactly what I did. I had no one around me to help. I languished in bed all day and all night embracing sleep as my escape. The 'friends' that I thought I had dissolved away, especially the ones connected to Dick. The ones that I knew I could count on, I refused to talk to. I didn't want to share my burden with their busy lives. All I saw was a broken miserable wreck in the mirror and was terrified they would abandon me for being such a failure. I know my oldest friends are going to swear when they read that bit, as all they wanted to do was help. I just wanted to disappear. I felt that I was no use to them anymore being a fragile burden rotting in bed. I also had this ridiculous burning pride. I would rather languish than ask for help. I was my own worst enemy.

I had also discovered that the arsehole even had the thought to sell my Virgin air miles. Everything I had worked so hard for was slipping through my fingers. I was in such severe debt, which I had never had before. I had no idea how to attack this new problem, I was terrified.

As the credit card statements flew through the door I knew I would have to contact them again.

After talking to them all, they stated that the debt was with me and I should have been aware that he had taken my cards. How the hell was I to know what he was doing when I was ill in bed? They didn't care. Funny isn't it, when you are in credit the banks and credit companies are your best friend. When you are in dire straits they treat you like a convict, passing down penalty after penalty completely devoid of any compassion.

I even managed to get the credit card slips that he had fraudulently signed, it still didn't matter.

I was coping with chronic illness, severe debt and had lost my partner. Most people break on just one of those traumas. I had racked up three so far.

I was told that the only way to get the debt taken from me was to have him arrested. He was still missing, but after a visit to the police station he was now wanted for fraud and theft.

He had been cashing the credit cards through his friend's company. The friend didn't even bother to let me know he was doing it. All of the betrayal started to sting like an annoying wasp.

During this time I had fleeting thoughts of just taking a whole load of morphine. I had plenty of it, so really it could have been a simple process. I was appalled with myself for having such thoughts, but they started to creep in more frequently than I would have liked.

He had managed to split my connection with my family and friends. I had never felt so alone in all my life. Looking back I wondered why I hadn't heard from my brother, sister or mum. I wondered why no one had popped in on the friend side of things. He had very cleverly isolated me so he could do his bidding.

The bank had agreed to give me a crisis break for six months from paying the mortgage so at least that was covered. If I wasn't able to work, I couldn't pay the mortgage, so this house that I lived in, that I had worked so hard for, was slipping through my fingers.

In February 2013, I was finally diagnosed with severe M.E. and fibromyalgia. It is disgusting how someone with my condition is treated as a hypochondriac as I mentioned earlier.

Doctors, consultants and specialists viewed me as a person who could not be diagnosed with anything else, so last resort, M.E. and fibromyalgia.

That's what it felt like.

There is no cure.

There is no respect for the condition.

You are labelled, you are given a cocktail of drugs, you are told to go home and get on with it.

Over 350,000 people in the UK suffer with this debilitating condition, in the US 10 million and 3-6 per cent of the worldwide population fight this disease. The old 'yuppie flu' name given to this condition back in the 80s still sticks. We are treated as if we just have a bit of pain and a bit of tiredness, and we need to get over it. We are known as the 'missing millions' ignored by society and shunned by the medical profession.

I became a research nut on M.E. and fibromyalgia but drew a blank. There were certain diets and holistic approaches but truth be told at that time all I could do was swallow pill after pill washed down with Red Bull, and carry on doing my thing. I was too exhausted mentally and physically to even think of trying to help myself.

My workload limped along, but the finances were starting to suffer. I lost my staff, I lost my support. I had no requests for feature writing and the media phone calls had stopped.

I had just racked up my fourth loss, my career.

I lay in bed just eating biscuits as I was too weak to prepare or shop for any food. The sheets were never washed as I didn't have the strength. The dogs were fed, they had a big garden to run around in, so even though I felt guilty that I couldn't walk them I knew that they were being looked after.

I cannot begin to describe how many tears I shed during those days. I was helpless, alone, vulnerable and the fear that swept through me took my breath away. I would retch on my empty stomach, shaking in a cold sweat lost in my own misery and defeat. A new symptom had emerged, a problem with my body temperature control. I was either freezing cold or sweating with hot flushes.

They say things can only get better. They did for two weeks in April but then they got worse. If I had known what was to come, I think that morphine would have sailed down my throat and not touched the sides.

The next hit was the new solicitor I had appointed. He told me that because I suffered with depression before my accident they may not be able to pursue a claim for my condition following the accident, as a lot of the symptoms were similar to M.E. and fibromyalgia. I just couldn't believe what I was hearing. He was another solicitor who was obviously in line with most of the law society's attitude about M.E. as a 'malingerer's disease'. The fact that I was bed bound most of the time and had symptoms that I had never had before the accident was apparently irrelevant. He stated it also didn't help that I had sustained a back injury in the police some twenty years' previously.

Oh happy days. I couldn't cope with this news and filed it away into my 'cannot cope anymore with this' box and withdrew even further. That was one big mistake that was going to hit me like a train in the future.

Unbelievably I continued to work. How I did it I have no idea. Again copying the excerpts from my journals I want to scream, "For God sake, Nick, just surrender!"

But nope, I just kept pushing and pushing. I was not going to lose my house.

Be warned, the language gets uglier the more desperate I get!

Sunday 10 March 2013

This really is the most trying time of my life ever! It's certainly on a par with my police retirement. The weird thing is, that this time I know it's OK. I just know I'm going to get through it.

The M.E. was ravaging me. I was bed bound day after day. I felt my soul was dying, in fact everything was dying. Dick who I thought was well, spiralled into a whirlwind of lies, deceit and disappeared stealing thousands from me and my friends. You couldn't make it up could you! Fuck me! I will be like Van Gogh. Someone will find these after I'm dead, print it and I'll be posthumously loaded! Lol. My arm is hurting writing this but I will carry on! I am broken that my sister didn't invite me to her wedding. My mum of course spent her time at Sarah's rather than here. So I have been tried, tested and rung out. I have a massive debt problem from not being able to work as much. The 2012 shift has shifted!

So I need to surrender, hand it all over to the big guys and push on. I am for the first time ever going to live my life this year free from the shackles of being 'Nicky Alan'. I will do enough to get by, but I need to get well. I need to stop and finally live my life without mediumship being the be all and end all. I have been dedicating myself to the public that can be fickle. If I'm not on the scene they go elsewhere. Simple. I now dedicate myself to me and my friends, the people that love me and have rallied around so unbelievably it truly is jaw dropping.

Spiritually it's all there and all of my loved ones up there are here. The advice was being brought to me when I was with Dick. I remember the day when he had left me yet again alone and the door banged and the radio turned itself on and the song Black Heart *played and then the radio switched itself off again. Why did I ignore the signs? I was too weak to deal with Dick. I honestly believe the dark waters that ran deep within him were zapping the life out of me as I feel stronger, calmer, positive.*

Last night Sophie came round. We had a fab night but then she started to channel through all of the family, here's kind of how it went.

She described Aunt Rene, Nan and Granddad Cookie, Duncan, Dad, Meena and Nanny Dolly!

They were all there and my pulsating diamond! It was alternating between white, blue and green. Nan had her arms open wide and it seemed like she was pulsing the energy out of me. She kept saying,

"Look for the light!"

Sophie then smelt smoke and Dad stood in front of her. Nanny Dolly said I had to cherish what I already had. Nanny Cookie said that justice would come but the scales were currently unbalanced. Aunt Rene said I would end up by the beach.

I then asked Dad:

"What's happening next?"

"Prepare yourself, shit's gonna hit the fan."

"Shall I keep the caravan?"

"Yes."

Sophie then saw Koi carp which is Dad's sign it's him. Then granddad Cookie stood in front of her.

Soph then said, "I can see a book. You must write."

Meena Moo was there wagging her tail all the time, so was Julianus and my spirit brother. Dad then came back. I asked,

"What about Mum?"

"She's your mother!" (As in nothing is changing there.)

"Where am I going to live? Here? Devon? Abroad?"

"Stop thinking! Just stop! Take it easy, Nichola!"

"Will the money be OK?"

"Stop thinking!"

Dad then kept saying about me losing my keys to the house. I think that was all of it. Bit worried about the shit hitting the fan and the key issue. I'm glad they are all around, makes me feel safe. Dad then walked off and whistled for Meena who trotted off behind him, so she is well looked after.

Sophie is my friend and was my hairdresser. She is an amazing medium but doesn't want to take it further, she just has random outbursts where she starts flowing with messages from the dead! So infuriating as I would have loved to have helped her develop her ability.

My aunt Rene had said I would end up living by the beach; was I going to be moving then? Or was I going to end up in the caravan?

There was a sliver of relief that Dick had gone. It was something that should have been done a long time ago. It was his exit that made me sick to the stomach.

I still had phone calls every night from the police asking if I had heard anything. In the end I just let the phone ring out.

Again I didn't really absorb what had transpired in this reading. I know from years of doing readings that when the whole family rock up, they are there to let you know that things are going to get rough. Funnily enough I chose to not delve into the fact that they had all turned up.

If I had looked into the fact they were there a little further, I might have just allowed myself to prepare a bit better for what was coming.

Chapter 7

Suicide Or Bust

Monday 18 March 2013
Today has been the worst day I have had since Dick disappeared. It doesn't help I had to work Friday. The evening was amazing, Christ only knows how I did it. Then I had to work Sunday, lovely day with the workshop only 12 people. Today my body has moaned about the work. I have been extremely dizzy, in pain, tired and tearful. Perhaps the reality is kicking in. Many people around me have been truly remarkable.

I have the debt interview tomorrow. Pete from the Centre for Natural Health is giving me acupuncture treatments for free. I then have the Dr on Thursday, neurologist at Broomfield. So, a productive week. Felt very sorry for myself today, so I suppose I have to take each day as it comes. The weather stays cold, wet and dark which doesn't help. I long for the sun, just need to find someone to look after the babies. I know that work is making me worse, so I definitely have to stop for a few months. A boring existence. I feel very, very sad that Dick isn't here. I also want him to at least get in touch. It's like a time bomb ticking away. No one knows where he is.

Monday 25 March 2013
I don't think I've felt so desperately scared, alone and powerless in all my life. It's nearly 2 am. I have just worked till 11.45 pm to people please. I hate the intimate evenings at the moment as I have no energy and feel the endless pressure of having to reach everyone in the audience. I'm sick of chasing money. Christ knows what will happen when I stop all of my commitments. I would say workshops and telephone readings and places like Dartford are my best option and hopefully writing. I keep needing help but can't ask for it. I have been so ill, overdone Friday then worked Saturday. Been in bed since I had to get up today.

The debt is a joke. Alone again. Having to fight again with no husband to help. When the fuck am I going to get it right? The pain, the illness, what the fuck do I want to spend a whole life struggling for? For what? To hobble about like a 90-year-old with no life?

Today a man came through who killed himself. He was sick of the pain he went through so he ended it. I know exactly how he feels. My house needs cleaning, I have no milk or shopping in. I'm saving every penny I can and I'm sick to death of being a fucking misery. I would get sick of me as well if I was my mate. But most of them don't get it.

I don't want to go out to dinner. I want a volunteer to help me hoover! Lol. Everyone has their own lives to lead, they can't keep running around for me. Even my hand is in agony writing this.

I'm so alone. I just don't seem to learn my lesson. I just fuck it up time and time again. I'm sick of myself. I'm 42 and fucked financially, emotionally and physically. Some pretty big things have to change in the next couple of months because if they don't I really don't know what to do. I am surrounded by misery. My highlight is being able to get to the shops or walk the poor babies. I know other people are worse off, but I can't help it. Dick has left me in the shit. Kicked me while I am down. I see NOTHING to look forward to. I'm in a very dark space. I don't see any way of getting out of it at the moment. Six months. If nothing changes, exit might be a good strategy. End it. What's the fucking point dragging myself through every day? What the fuck for? To see if I get less pain? To see if I can manage to get to the shops? To work when I'm feeling shit just to pay fucking bills? What the fuck for?

No family. Friends who have all got their own lives. I don't value myself, am sick and tired of being sick and tired.

I fucking hope to Christ that I look back on this and say, "Wow that was my real rock bottom. Thank God my life is brilliant now."

I want to look back on this and smile knowing it has got better and completely changed.

25th September. That's 6 months' time. Let us see what has changed by then. 20th would be more apt, same date as Meena died. Never thought I would be writing this. Perhaps it's my path, to go back early. My only anchor, work, that's gone. Health gone. Family gone. Life gone. Wealth gone. Security, gone. Laughter, gone. Credit, gone. Savings, gone. Love, gone.

Everything just blown up in my face. All gone. What the fuck have I done to deserve all of this shit?

I must have been some sort of arsehole in a previous life or have had to learn some pretty tough lessons this life.

Something has to give. I feel angry, resentful and I feel well and truly done. Lost my sense of humour on this one. Waiting for the Tramadol to kick in. I'm not drinking can't stand it. How I'm not smoking Christ knows.

GOD HELP ME. PLEASE.

Monday 1 April 2013
April fools! More like a year fools! I think that this is all a cruel sick joke. I really do miss Dick dearly. I also worry about him every day. I have had a very painful, exhausting week and have had certainly more lows than highs. Now and then I get the odd sign, but nothing magical. One day at a time. I was at Mike Reid's house doing readings for his family. Very interesting what came out. Yep still fucking working.

It seems I have to toughen up. I have been drawn to liars, losers, hangers-on, false promise arseholes. Pretty much the lot. Time to toughen up and be truthful with myself and others. Otherwise I will end up alone or with another grade A fuck up!

I'm so lonely.

My friends are brilliant but they can't be here all of the time. I am so weak and useless. I can't lead a normal life which is driving me insane.

I know people are thinking I'm exaggerating or am some sort of hypochondriac. It's getting on my nerves a bit. It's a shitty, all-consuming disease that I can do fuck all about. I must get better though, as why would I be chosen or used to teach and show such an amazing gift if I couldn't do it?

Something will come out of the wash. It has to.

I cannot go on for the rest of my life watching TV and dragging myself out now and then.

The poor babies hardly get out. I feel a twat for moaning as there are people dying of cancer and God knows what, but it's a disease just like other people's stuff. I see people on Facebook moaning about pathetic stuff, they want to try being in my shoes! I feel quite bitter sometimes I have to say. I just need a medical person to help me, understand and get me on some sort of programme so I at least feel I'm working towards something.

I hope to God that I read this in a year's time thinking, "Christ how bad was that?"

It's during times like this that you know who your friends are. Funny how most of them all fuck off when you are spiralling down. I know that I haven't been the best friend in the world to people. Always putting work first. But even though I feel lonely, I always tend to want to be alone! Perhaps that's the depression! I can't make any goals at the moment. I'm just doing one day at a time. Baby steps.

I was on the brink. There was no doubt about it. Do you remember the film *An American Werewolf in London*? There's the scene in the cinema where the cursed are suggesting how the man bitten by a werewolf could kill himself before he fully turns? Well that was me. I would fantasise about the easiest way to do it and get it over with. It was like my comfort blanket that by September the 20th, it would all be over. I would no longer have to lead this nightmare life. I would look at my piles of tablets relishing the thought that they would take me away to oblivion forever.

On writing these excerpts I could now see the anger stage of the grieving process kicking in. I was angry with my situation, my illness, the world and everyone in it. The police hadn't located him or arrested him, so the banks were still refusing to budge. There was still no word at all from Dick which was infuriating. It also amazes me how I write how much I miss him in these entries. What the hell was I thinking? I have no doubt that if he had come back with a half decent excuse I most probably would have forgiven him. That was how unhealthy and codependent I was. His abandonment simply fuelled my self-belief that I was never wanted after a while. It corroborated my false sense of self, that I was worthless and unlovable. That's the beauty of soul journals, they show you how you can change and look back at a weaker and more vulnerable self.

The letterbox continued to rattle to the tune of unpaid bills, and now a new development, debt collection agencies. They were merciless. I just ran away from all of it. I had no clue how to approach these people and didn't have the energy or the coping mechanism to deal with it.

I then started to think of my dad's death a lot. If he hadn't died I would have had two parents coming over and caring for me. Instead I had a mum miles away in Hayling Island sitting at home with her lazy partner. I hated the lot of them and resented everyone else's lives.

I ranted and raved to anyone that would listen as I sat alone in my bed. I managed to get out to the shops at the end of my road to get food in on very rare occasions. I would silently cry as I asked for the key to the mobility scooter in the supermarket. I felt old, ashamed and exceptionally sad. It took me ages to get the courage to get on a scooter. I would hobble around the shops grimacing in pain. I was smelly and dishevelled. I'm sure the security guards watched me as I looked like some would-be homeless shoplifter! On one occasion I just sat on the floor in the shop, I couldn't move another muscle. The staff were very good as they flapped around me. It was then that I knew I had to use a scooter. It felt like defeat. I hated the taste of acceptance that I may be disabled for the rest of my life. I should have named this chapter, 'hate', because that was all I had in me.

I couldn't get any food delivered as the minimum delivery was £40. I hated those days that I had to go out. I was exhausted as soon as I had tried to dress. Most of the time I went in my pyjamas, I didn't give a shit what I looked like.

When it came to work, I would start getting ready about five hours before so I could rest between each activity. I would then carry out the performance of my life, drive home and collapse into bed. It was never ending, this trudge through my existence.

The only thought that filled me with relief was the day I had planned to kill myself. I wouldn't leave a note, no one deserved to know why. They could all have the money from the house, what was left of it, I really didn't give a shit. The only thing I made a mental note to do was make sure that I left a note and some money for my babies, so that they were looked after following my death.

The fantasies of dying and meeting up with my dad and grandparents were sublime. The only time that I would smile would be from watching the babies or thinking of my existence after my suicide. To not be in any pain and be able to run and laugh again was too delicious to contemplate.

But then something happened. A very old friend, who I hadn't really had much recent contact with, turned up, and she has no clue about this, but she just might have put my suicidal plans on hold. The first Earth Angel since my accident had entered my life and intervened. That is also when the first miracle happened.

Chapter 8

P.S. I Love You

It was just after that last entry that a huge act of love happened.

I remember waking up with that normal sense of dread. When you have M.E., you spend a few minutes finding out what is wrong with your body that day. It can change from hour to hour. There are up to 200 symptoms of M.E. and fibromyalgia, so every time you wake up it's like a body bingo; you find out what numbers have come up for this session.

I had heart palpitations and felt that my lungs couldn't inflate properly so I was trying to slow my breathing down and breathe more deeply. My eye sockets were burning and every time I moved them I felt hot bolts of fire shooting through my head. I tried to sit up but my body was a leaden weight. I slumped back down again feeling shooting pains searing through my abdomen and ribs. My hips felt like they had been hit with a club hammer and the nerves in my legs were in spasm, giving me restless leg syndrome. When I tried to get up, I fell on the floor, so crawled to the bathroom crying my eyes out trying to get to the toilet. I didn't make it to the toilet most of the time. I ended up wrapping myself in towels and then discarding them when they were soaked.

The anger and grief of my situation blended with defeat and helplessness. I could see no future, I could see no life. I felt like a ghost just going through the motions of watching day turn into night.

They say you know who your true friends are so when there was a knock at the door I was surprised to see one of my oldest friends from the Police, Dawn, standing there with her partner, Jaime.

We had remained friends after I had left the police service

and shared many holidays scuba diving. My passion is to dive. It is the ultimate meditation, being in a safari of Mother Nature's riches that most humans do not experience unless they don scuba equipment and jump in to the blue! The silence of the ocean, the magnificence of its beauty never failed to take my breath away. It also took me from the material world, and so on reflection was my bit of heaven down here, which was precious.

She came in beaming and promptly announced that they were taking me away on holiday.

To begin with I refused as I said that I was too ill, but she wouldn't take no for an answer. She packed my suitcase, located my passport and said that we were going to Turkey in three weeks.

Dawn will never realise the true depth of this most thoughtful and loving act. I still look back, and can't believe what she and Jaime did for me. I truly felt far too ill to even contemplate going but they would have none of it.

Jaime picked me up on the day and I had wheelchair access all the way to the aeroplane. Strangely enough, when I got pushed into the airport I looked up at the time zone clocks. It was 11:11 UK time, so the whole board was full of elevens. This is an angel sign of spiritual awakening. I took a photo of it at the time. My God, how significant was that sign.

Before I knew it, I was in the shining hot sun amongst friends. The first couple of days I slept but then something magical happened: I felt happier and stronger. I started to get up and wander around managing my pain and trying to ignore the tiredness.

I felt a bit like my old self. Dawn and I in our police days were little minxes and got up to all types of naughtiness. So as the week progressed, I started to feel that old energy come back to me. One night I even got exceptionally drunk on a huge bowl of cocktails that I shared with Dawn and our other friend Jo. I hadn't laughed like that for a very long time. I felt a small surge of hope that everything was going to be alright. I could do this, I remember thinking, and I can get through all of this mess.

Fuelled by this holiday, I promptly booked another trip as Jo kindly said I could come back and stay with her in June.

June came around very swiftly. I counted down the days to the second holiday like a child waiting for Christmas. It was all I could focus on. I had no idea that on this holiday, I would experience one of the most amazing spirit visitations of my life.

One day we were floating in the pool by Jo's apartment and a local lady came up to us. She had heard that I was psychic and wanted to know if I wanted to trade readings with the local village seer. I felt a bit apprehensive as I was still quite weak and hadn't done a reading for months, but something inside me told me to go for it.

I walked into a cool shaded room and felt pretty intimidated as not only was the seer there but most of her family. No pressure there then!

The link to the spirit world was surprisingly easy apart from the interpreter delaying the messages! The lady's spirit husband and son came through telling me their names. They even took me through the whole process of a Muslim funeral which I had no idea about. They stated so many facts and foreign words that the smiles of delight and amazement from the family boosted me to deliver a first-class reading. They were all so happy and tearful. I think they thought I was just going to do a psychic reading, which is where you talk about life circumstances. So they not only got a psychic reading, but as a medium they got a direct call with their family members!

It was then my turn. In Turkey, the seers mainly do their readings by using the coffee syrup that they prepare in their coffee. I had to drink the strong, bitter coffee until the dregs of the syrup were left. I handed the cup to the lady who swirled it three times and then turned it upside down on to a saucer.

She then whispered something and lifted the cup up.

The first thing she described were my two little dogs, Teddy and Mia. She described them to a T, even down to their personalities and what they liked to eat. She showed me the pattern in the coffee syrup. I was amazed to see two little shapes of dogs. She stated how important they were to me and that they would save my life and my soul. I didn't really know what she meant at the time.

She then talked about my illness, and that I would have a very long path back to recovery. I wasn't too impressed with that comment as she was frowning and looking at me with such empathy in her eyes. She spoke of me moving house, and that I wouldn't be settled for a while. This is news I didn't want to hear. She spoke of a flood that would take place as well. To be honest I wasn't really enjoying the reading at this stage as it felt like all doom and gloom. However, everything she said was so accurate. I felt that familiar friend of fear rise up as she told me the 'not so good' stuff. She said I was one with the sea and that's where my journey would end. I didn't know what she meant with this, but I obviously adored the sea. She said that I walked with the Angels and the Dead, and that they would bring me back to a new life. I didn't have a clue what she meant by a new life, so I just smiled.

All in all I enjoyed the experience, but I wasn't so chuffed with the bad bits to be honest.

I walked out of the house and felt strangely overemotional. I asked Jo for the keys to the apartment as I needed some time out to let all that she had said sink in.

When I got into the apartment I sat on the balcony for a while but it was too hot. The apartment was slightly cooler but with the balcony doors open the heat was still making it slightly uncomfortable. It was 35 degrees outside.

I will never, ever forget what happened next. It will be engraved on my heart for eternity.

I was still feeling emotional, sitting on the sofa sipping a glass of water. I felt a shiver go down my spine and the hairs on the back of my neck went up. I then noticed the room freeze up like I had just walked in to a refrigerated food store. I could see mist coming from my mouth and couldn't believe what I was seeing. It was literally a scorching day in Turkey and I was shivering with mist on my breath.

I then heard as plain as day,

"Hello, darling."

I jumped, looked up and saw a human-sized form walk in front of me from my left-hand side.

I can only describe it as this.

Do you know the film *Predator*, where the alien is walking in a camouflaged state? You can make out its form but it's blurry and magnifies the landscape behind it? Or when you watch a sci-fi movie and they have a cloaking device but you can still see the shape of the aircraft? Sorry! That's the only way to describe it.

Well that's what I saw. The shape then stopped and my breath caught in my throat. The face on the body formed and it was my dad smiling at me as if he were alive and present in the room.

I remember staggering out the word, "Dad?" in between hysterical sobs.

He nodded and then sat down on the chair next to me.

I was so shocked. Normally you see spirit forms in a blink of an eye. The main way we see them is through clairvoyance where you see spirit people in your mind. To have your dead dad sit next to you in an armchair in normal time is unheard of. I could still see his face clearly but the rest of him was transparent with a white mist and light swirling around his body shape.

He was beaming at me and I was howling like a nutter! I just couldn't get over the fact that I was staring right into my dad's face and he wasn't disappearing.

He then stopped smiling and looked at me with such love and sadness.

"I haven't got long, Nick. You have got to listen to everything

I say, and you have to trust me."

I just nodded silently.

"You are going to go through the worst time of your life and I am so sorry about that." He looked like he was crying too.

"But trust me when I say you will get through this, and you will come out the other side working like you have never worked before. You will have a deeper spiritual understanding and a whole new life. You will have knowledge beyond anything you could ever imagine. You will work in a different way and you will have so much wisdom. Don't let men or people get in your way. They will ruin where you need to go. This is about you. You must do everything from now on for you. Do you understand?"

"Yes!" I sobbed. "Daddy, I'm so scared. Please help me. I miss you so much!"

I have never cried so hard in all of my life. Here was the man I had yearned to see since I was a nine-year-old child. This was the man who if he hadn't died, then I wouldn't have been abused and have a shattered family. The kaleidoscope of pain and sadness whirled through my whole being as I looked into his beautiful blue eyes.

I then saw him look up to a corner of the room. I sensed he was about to leave.

"Please don't leave me, Daddy!" I wailed. I felt like that scared nine-year-old again.

"Listen," he said sternly. "Look for this sign."

A picture then formed to the left of him. It was a weird triangle-shaped hill with the sun shining behind it, I then saw the name DAVE and MICHAEL written up.

"This is 2016; when you see this you must remember that this is nearly the end of your bad times. In 2018 your new life will begin. But you must hold on and trust us until then. You must also write."

I then saw a mountain symbol, which then turned into a triangle. I wondered if it was a publisher's logo even though I had never seen it before.

He then stood up.

I remember screaming,

"No, Daddy, don't go! Please don't go!"

He started to walk past me and then stopped.

"It will be OK, I love you."

I then watched his form disappear into the corner of the room.

I was in shock for a long time. I cried for what seemed an eternity.

I kept thinking about what he said repeating over and over in my mind. Archangel Gabriel had obviously granted him a visitation. I knew these were allowed when things were critical. I knew there was worse to come. But another five years until everything changed for the better? What the hell was I to go through that would warrant my dad visiting?

I shakily wrote in my soul journal every word he had said so that I wouldn't forget it. I then laid on the bed and that's when the recurring dream began.

I dreamt that I had walked from an unfamiliar house and passed some pine trees that opened up to a beach. I then found myself sat on a terrace laughing and watching children fly down on water tubes into a pool. The dream would then flick to a lake with large plastic swans floating on it. The swans had been in my dreams since I was a child but had somehow incorporated themselves into this new dream.

I had no idea why I would dream this same dream over and over again in the next few years.

But as they say, everything happens for a reason.

There are no words to thank Jaime and Dawn for what they did for me. No doubt, by my energy being raised by their kindness taking me on that first holiday, I would never have been in the right space to receive my dad's visitation on the second one.

I will be indebted to those beautiful people for eternity.

I would also like to add that on 3 June 2019, I was teaching at a spiritual retreat in Glastonbury. I had popped in to my friend's class and had a meditation. In the meditation I saw myself standing on top of a mountain which then turned into a large metal triangle. An hour after this meditation I received a contract offer for this book.

Chapter 9

Like Attracts Like

I came back from Turkey feeling refreshed and a little like my old self. I also felt confident as I had had Turkish men swooning around me the whole time so I felt like a million dollars. So rather than get on a spiritual path and start to work on my own healing, what did I do? Went on *Plenty of Fish*!

I didn't want to be alone. I didn't like myself. I wanted someone to fill the void that was ever growing in the pit of my stomach. It didn't take long to get a bite on my desperate fishing line, and before I knew it I was popping painkillers and using all of my energy on making myself up, dressing to the nines and visiting this man who we shall call Steve.

I presented myself as the old me, full of energy, fun, racy and up for anything. It turned out that he was a heavy drinker, so I got into the midst of drinking again which was great as it numbed my pain and senses. I had absolutely no boundaries, and was like an eager puppy trying to please him with every inch of life I had in me.

When I didn't see him I slept and slept trying to catch up on the overuse of my body and mind. I had no thought that this was totally wrong. I was abusing my body and had heeded not a word of what my dad had said. I reasoned with myself that my dad wouldn't want me to be alone. I then told myself that he told me to stay away from men and relationships as that's what a dad would say. I was like an addict trying to justify an addiction. I couldn't be alone, I couldn't love myself and had no respect for myself whatsoever.

So you won't be surprised to find out, as I did, that Steve had absolutely no respect for me whatsoever. He just took and took. He was nasty, controlling and had massive commitment issues. It is so true about how the Universe works. You do attract people around you that are a mirror of yourself. Look around you, you will see what I mean. It is the natural law that we are surrounded by the energy which we give out. The only opposing thing in these laws is if you are vulnerable you will attract a predator.

Everything I hated about myself oozed out of him like a sewer. But no matter how many times he belittled and criticised me, I came back for more. I figured at the time that at least I was with someone. I was sick of people on Facebook posting selfies with their boyfriends and husbands. I was sick of being single and alone and unloved.

So I took every bit of abuse that was thrown at me. I felt I didn't deserve any better, so I just waited for the moments when he was nice and paid me attention. As I write this I feel ashamed. It's as if I am writing about another poor girl, but no, this was me. I was doing this to myself.

For four months I experienced this tumultuous life living and breathing by his every word and action. I would buy him presents so he would like me. I would run baths for him, rub his feet, cook for him, buy his alcohol, in fact I did anything to get a morsel of his love.

He knew I was vulnerable so he preyed on my weaknesses. I was feeling my body dip into an oblivion of pain and exhaustion but I didn't care.

Everything I had achieved in Turkey had been decimated.

Eventually he tossed me away like a used newspaper as he had found another victim on *Plenty of Fish*.

I can't believe what I am about to write now, but I actually begged him not to get rid of me. I tried everything to win his affections, but eventually I had a huge M.E. crash and was back in my bed permanently.

The further kick in the teeth was that Dick had been found and arrested for my theft. He is the world's best conman so it was no surprise to me that he got away with absolutely everything. The CPS would not take it any further. With all the documentary evidence that I had given to the police I thought that he would be charged. Apparently though that was completely irrelevant. The injustice just added to my misery. I was also completely liable for the debt, as the banks stated that since he had been given an NFA (No Further Action) the debt still stayed with me.

Dick then proceeded to give false accounts of how I had lied and that he was the victim. He spread his explanation of 'innocence' to all of our joint friends and plastered every single defamatory thing you can think of on social media against me. He acted disgustingly. Friends, who I thought had my back, sided with him. It destroyed me.

If I had been well, I would have made a complaint to the police and appealed the decision. I didn't even have enough fight to get a jar top off, so taking on the police was pretty much impossible.

So sleep was my hero, galloping in to take me away from my efforts to try and get back with a complete narcissistic arsehole and get over another one!

When I was awake my demons came crawling in reminding me that nobody wanted me, that I was unlovable. The depression threw me into a deeper poor state. I didn't wash for weeks, I lived on biscuits, chocolate and tea as I had no energy to cook for myself or even get food in. I made sure the dogs were fed but that was about it. I ignored the phone whenever it rang. I wanted to have nothing to do with the world or the shitty people in it.

I would look into the mirror and have the most powerful hate for myself. I would literally voice all of my shortfalls and throw insults at my own reflection. Everything that was happening in my life I projected on to myself during those mirror sessions. I was tearing myself apart from the inside out. I had no way of stopping it and at the time did not realise the hurt I was causing myself.

It was such a surreal existence. You desperately want to have someone care for you and be there for you, but by the same token all you want to do is be alone and disappear.

Whilst I slept, the cogs of life continued to turn. As I slumbered the weeks away, the banks were about to wade in with their fat greedy hands rubbing together.

I had no idea or really couldn't comprehend the amount of trouble I was in. To be honest I really didn't care.

I also had no energy or fight left in me whatsoever. As the summer sun waned and the fresh rush of oranges and reds welcomed autumn, I was about to face the next loss in my life.

I had no option but to get out of my bed, as soon I would have nowhere to sleep.

Chapter 10

Time To Say Goodbye

What followed was like a surreal dream. It was a nightmare that no matter how hard I tried, I couldn't claw my way out of. I felt like I was screaming all of the time but there was no one there to hear it.

My neighbour Irene and friend Sophie helped me pack up the house, God bless their hearts. The day then came, the day that I had to say goodbye, yet another, with many more to come.

I sat in my car looking at the back of my house. The car was stacked solid with items I had managed to squeeze in, the rest in storage. I can't express the emotion at the time. I would go for 'numb'. It would be the last time that I looked at my house. It was gone, grasped by the hands of the fat cats.

You see, banks don't care if you have had a road accident that has stopped your life. They don't care if you had had tens of thousands of pounds stolen from you. They don't care that you have a chronic condition with no cure. The 'rest period' for paying my mortgage wasn't that at all. It was a loan apparently, six months of no mortgage payments and they wanted the lot with interest. I tried to argue the point with all and sundry but they just wouldn't have it. I insisted that I had been offered a mortgage holiday, not a loan. It was ridiculous, why would I have agreed to such a preposterous loan? They didn't care and had no time for me whatsoever. I panicked and arranged someone to rent the house to try and get some money together. The bank then sent me an official letter saying that I hadn't asked for permission to have a tenant, so I gave up. I was too weak, too broken to fight anymore. I just told them to do whatever the hell they wanted.

I was done.

It was surreal sitting on my back driveway. I thought of the first house I bought when I was 22. I was so proud. I had worked my way up on that property ladder and was so happy in this beautiful house. I remembered me getting the keys to this place and being so elated. It was a very large house situated in an enviable area in Hadleigh, Essex. I remembered walking across the road to the woods walking Meena and then Ted and Mia. I pictured me sitting at Hadleigh Castle looking over the estuary soaking in the view. I pictured the parties, the girls' nights in and all of the merriment that had taken place. Why does the mind do that? When you are faced with goodbyes it always fills you in with what you are going to miss and the rose-tinted views of the past. I felt sick to the stomach. It was not my fault that I could no longer live here, but no one cared.

I thought of all my belongings stashed in a cold room. I started to get hints of the past where I picked up my two bin bags at the end of my road all those years ago. I had achieved nothing. I was still that girl carrying bags of shit not knowing what to do next. The only anchor I had left was my holiday home in Devon. I shivered as a little voice asked how the hell I was going to keep that going as well. I hated my predicament and my existence. None of this was fair, none of it was just, none of it seemed real. I would end up staying with my mum, I reckoned, like a sad failure in her forties.

I came back into the real world, and ironically *Angels* by Robbie Williams was playing on the radio.

All I remember thinking was, "Where the fuck are they now?"

That little bit of sunshine that I had had both physically and metaphorically in Turkey had waned to nothing. I was dealing with bailiffs, credit companies and all manner of things including my deteriorating illness. The old fiery me would have fought tooth and nail to save what I had accomplished, but I was no longer that girl.

I cried all the way down to Devon. Everything was slipping

away and I had no way to stop it. How I drove down there I will never know. I was in agony, my body was shaking in defiance from the impromptu exercise, and my arms were burning from the exertion of holding the steering wheel.

Thank God I had the mobile home in Goodrington. I don't know what it is about Devon and why I love it so much. I had a previous life there so that may be why. My fondest childhood memories after my dad died were staying at my Aunt Rene's and Uncle Ron's in Cornwall. There is something about the South West of England that feels like home. I first visited Torbay through work back in 2009. I was doing a weekend at the Riviera Centre with Derek Acorah, Colin Fry and Stephen Holbrook. I had booked a couple of days' holiday after the weekend as a mini-break. I was enchanted by the little coves, the hidden beaches and Dartmoor.

So it was a no-brainer to get a holiday home there. It was right beside the sea. I adore the sea, so I felt a tiny glimmer of hope and excitement that I would be somewhere I loved. Perhaps things would change now I had moved down here. Surely I deserved a bit of luck? But then my dad did say, 2016 would start the change in my life. It was November 2013; I had another three years yet. I pushed the thought aside. He was wrong, I wasn't going to have any of it.

Despite being by the sea I spent most of it in bed in pain and sleeping. I realised this wasn't the best choice, as the caravan could be cold and us M.E. lot do not get on well with extreme heat or cold. Christmas went by. I didn't really take it in. I didn't even see New Year in, as I was fast asleep.

I realised that I was incredibly lonely. Everyone has their own life, so friends did pop in now and then, but most of the time I was by myself. I refused to ask for help. I didn't want to be a hindrance to anyone. I felt no one would want to help me anyway. The abandonment and self-hate demons made sure of that.

A few days after the New Year, I couldn't stand the loneliness anymore so I gobbled down a load of morphine and Red Bull, and drove in a daze to my mum's in Hayling Island, Hampshire. How I ever got there, God only knows.

Do you know that film *Sliding Doors*, where one split second decision leads to a certain outcome? I wonder what would have happened if I hadn't had gone to my mum's.

The big problem with people suffering with M.E. and fibro is that you have to try and make your friends and family understand how debilitating it is. My mum just didn't get it. I got all the same comments that, if I had a pound for every time I had heard them, I would be in a mansion being served delicacies by naked waiters!

"If you force yourself up in the morning, you will get a good night's sleep."

Or...

"You shouldn't sleep during the day or you won't sleep tonight."

"It's all about being positive, if you stop saying you are in pain, you won't be."

Or...

"You asleep again? You have just slept for twelve hours, it can't be good for you."

Or...

"If you start doing some exercise your body will get used to moving again."

The list is endless of these unhelpful observations. My mum came out with all of these comments and others which quite frankly did nothing but piss me off and make me feel worse. If you know someone with fibro or M.E., please research the condition before you stick your two pennies' worth in.

When we say we are exhausted, you could not comprehend the level of exhaustion we feel. You literally feel like you are dying. When we say we are in pain, we are talking teeth-clenching, wishing-for-death agony. Also bear in mind that we are permanently in pain, it's just the level of pain that changes. They are the two main symptoms but then you have digestive issues, ear and sight sensitivity, blurred vision, brain fog, loss of short-term memory, dizziness, lack of balance, nausea, IBS, sore throats, food intolerances, anxiety attacks. In fact I won't bore you with any more symptoms as I will bore myself!

Just know that this is an invisible disease. If we are smiling and joking along with you, don't forget that we are permanently in pain and exhausted. We just don't express it as it gets quite wearing for us and no doubt you. If we have the strength to do our hair one day, don't say things like, "Oh glad you are better." We are not better we are just having a reasonably good day where we want to smell like a normal human being! Just try to understand our condition, research it and know how to support us. The gift of you understanding our condition as loved ones is absolutely priceless.

Tuesday 21 January 2014
Time to get moving, Nick. Catherine showed me a pregnant belly in a dream I had. She said I was going to have a complete rebirth and that I have trodden the wrong path and have to clear everything to get back on track. All the mediums and messages I have had have been completely right but God has my faith been tested! I have to remain positive now, come what may, as I am so starting to see the wood for the trees. As I walked along the beach in Hayling today it all became clear. Complete new start in every way. So I will remain in the caravan until I see how everything pans out...

My mum and I didn't really have a closely-bonded relationship because of the past. I found it hard to explain to her how I was feeling. After a couple of weeks I gobbled down more painkillers and decided to go back home. I really did not want to go, as any company is good when you are so lonely, but I just needed my space and my own bed.

This was when the Turkish seer's first prediction came true.

Back in Devon, I stood in the pouring rain and seriously contemplated walking straight into the sea and never coming out again.

I remember swearing then and there that I must have been a serial killer in a previous life.

This cruel, sick turn of events was another punishment I felt that I obviously deserved.

I turned up to my mobile home, relieved that I would be in bed soon. It was a freezing day, Saturday, 8 February 2014. I felt nauseous. My joints and muscles had seized up and my back had gone into spasm. Looking back I remember that I was actually crying before I even went into the caravan.

As I turned the doorknob, the smell of damp hit me; my first step inside sank into a cold fluid. The splash that accompanied the first step made me look down. I was standing in a pool of water. I took a sharp intake of breath and realised that the kitchen and lounge were swimming in stagnant water. I couldn't believe what I was seeing.

Everything on the floor was saturated. The water had been absorbed by the furniture so it stank to high heaven. I waded through the hallway and could see all of the bedrooms and the bathroom were flooded. I followed the small rivulets of water and they led me to the end suite. Water was flowing from the bottom of the toilet. Despite the freezing cold and damp I sat on my bed staring around me and sobbed my heart out.

This was the only roof that I had over my head. I knew instinctively that this place could possibly be written off. Everything had been brand new in the caravan. It was all now sopping wet with mould already sprawling across it. The leak literally must have started as I left.

How could I lose my house and now this? What the hell was going on?

I eventually roused myself from my zombie state and stood up. I stared unblinkingly at my surroundings having absolutely no idea what to do. I walked outside to the car as the babies must have wondered where I was. Just to heighten the misery, Mother Nature decided to add to the atmosphere bringing driving freezing rain down on us. Ted and Mia stared at me from the back seat wondering why we weren't getting out.

Hope of this all being an illusion disintegrated as I watched the water pour out of the main door of the mobile home.

I pulled the doormat up to disturb the flow and promptly slammed the door. I locked it up in the pouring rain, snivelling like a child and got back in the car.

I sat in the car for about an hour. Where would I go now? Would the insurance cover this? Was I going to be homeless? I could feel the panic attack gripping my throat and chest. I had pictures of me sitting in a crappy hostel with just a bed, a chair and a single-ring gas cooker. I let the sick fantasy flow, watching me give my babies away as they weren't allowed in the hostel. I almost relished picturing my descent in my mind. I saw me lying dead on a single bed, pills and alcohol next to me. I then watched my own funeral with just my mum attending it. I refused to stop the endless projection of my own demise. I was self-destructing and did not want to stop for a minute.

After I had created every single catastrophe I could imagine, I realised that it was pretty stupid of me sitting in a car soaking wet in the rain. I drove to my friend at the time Janet's house. I stood on her doorstep soaking wet, holding two carrier bags with two shivering, soaked-through dogs.

I must have looked a sorry mess when she opened the door. I wept hysterically as I felt the last drop of strength and resolve drain from me.

I was homeless, completely homeless, and had never felt so vulnerable and scared in all of my life.

Chapter 11

The First Leg Up From Heaven

I spewed out a stream of hysterical babble as I tried to explain to Janet what had happened. The dogs were totally stressed and shaking as they watched their banshee mum let rip. She kindly said that I was welcome to stay as long as I wanted to, which calmed me down. She was a great help to me in the early days. I was losing the ability to cope and she had been put there to bridge the void that was opening up all around me.

After I had a hot bath and something to eat, I settled the babies in and went to bed. I waited patiently until Janet was asleep as I was about to let loose at that lot above that were supposed to be looking over me.

Like hell were they!

I was sobbing away and gritted my teeth, "What the hell have I done so wrong that you have punished me so badly?" I cried out.

"I have done everything I can to be your best ambassador and you leave me homeless, skint, ill and completely alone! I hate you all, you can all go and fuck yourself! You better turn this around as I am done!"

The dogs looked up at me as if I was some lunatic. They then sighed and went back to sleep. Oh to be a dog, what an easy uncomplicated life!

My mind kept turning, the self-pity oozing out of my skin. I felt hate, sadness, disbelief and anxiety in a frenzy of roller-coaster emotions. My throat and heart ached with the tragedy of my life. In between sobs, I kept picturing myself standing on the doorstep with just dustbin bags. That made me cry even more. I imagined my future yet again, living in a hostel with no job, no health and no partner. Who would want a skint, out-of-work forty-something inhabiting a 90-year-old body? No one, that's who. I then allowed my resentful thoughts to roll into self-hate and convinced myself that I was such a shit that I deserved everything that had happened to me.

I remember feeling my chest tighten with the pain of it all. I was rocking in a foetal position and saw nothing but black. A black present, a black future, there was no light to be seen. I was unable to bring myself comfort. I was at the end of my tether and just didn't want to engage anymore. I had had enough.

I kept saying in my mind, "Please help me!" as I drifted off to sleep in an exhausted state.

7am on Sunday, 9 February 2014 is a date and time that I will never forget. Janet had a habit of hoovering very early in the morning before going to work. I was awoken by the hoover banging the bedroom door. I was so annoyed as I had been brought from the most magnificent dream that I have ever had. I knew it was a psychic dream as it was so vibrant and real. I could feel every emotion and event that was taking place.

As I was awoken, I had just discovered I was an angel in my dream. I was flying over Iraq on a mission to help save the world.

I felt like my heart and soul had been torn from this dream as I awoke. I sighed and thought I might as well get up and have a coffee.

They had other plans.

"Go back to sleep!" boomed this voice in the room.

I was so shaken by the power of the voice that I put the quilt over my head. I was losing the plot, that was my first thought. I then started to see my wings spreading out and could feel my hair tussled by this dry warm wind, and before I knew it, I was back in my dreamy adventure.

I woke up at 12 midday and felt elated. I had tears streaming from my eyes as the dream had continued into the most amazing story I could have ever imagined.

As I lay there, the same voice then said, "You shall write what you have dreamt about."

I then saw the name 'Earth Walkers' come into my head.

I got my laptop out, and then and there wrote the first five chapters. It was like someone was telling me to write each word. I felt such joy in writing out the beginning of my dream. The words as they poured out of me made me feel relaxed. I found the writing to be very cathartic.

For the first time in ages I was not thinking of my predicament or the state of my life, I was reliving this amazing adventure that I had seen in my dreams.

Before I knew it, it was 4pm. I had written solidly for that time and knew exactly how the story was going to proceed and the ending. In fact in my mind three books had been mapped out covering the whole story.

I knew something magical had happened. I knew that I had to write these books. I had something that not only distracted me but gave birth to a passion I never really knew that I had.

That passion was writing.

I was so excited! I would bubble over with excitement to anyone who wanted to listen about my amazing dream and the story that it was conveying.

Without even thinking about it, the angel realms had given me my first leg up in my life and I didn't even realise it.

All I cared about was getting that story written. I found it hard on some days as my hands and fingers hurt.

Looking back, that is when my healing started to really begin.

The healing may have begun, but the hits kept coming. On the Monday I found out that the caravan site had sold me a really poor insurance policy. I had to argue out the fact that I had a claim, and realised that there were no contents covered. Everything I had spent on furnishing the place now laid in a soggy heap outside the caravan.

Again I thank God for my friends as they helped me get everything out of the caravan. The site managers were awful and did not help me at all.

I was in agonising pain, it was freezing cold and I was lugging all sorts of things out to take to the tip.

The caravan was assessed and was indeed a write-off. I was told that it would take months for the new caravan to be provided. So that was the beginning of my sofa-hopping days, staying on the next couch or spare bed that was available.

Sunday 16 February 2014
Well what a week! I came home to find my caravan stripped bare –
actually flooded from a cracked washer in the loo! So everything apart
from the lounge is flooded and ruined...

Then there's my colossal dream that will make an amazing
book. Earth Walkers: The Children of the Light. *I am, I believe,*
channelling the energy to write books, to bring fact into fiction, in this
case the angel hierarchy.

It's an amazing story with very impactive undertones. I know this
sounds odd but it could be my breakthrough.

This I pray will be one of the most important landmarks of my life.
Please, angels! Books channelled through dreams, priceless!

I just, if I'm truthful, really don't know what to do. Everything is
a whirl and I just have to take each day as it comes with no planning.
I'm just sick of juggling money. It's just so bloody sickening. I just
want a beautiful home with a view, a nice garden and some stability...

I may have had a bit of respite with this dream but I had no idea what was to follow. The healing phase had only just begun. I was about to enter the most enduring mind battle of my life. You see the dreams not only brought insight to keep me going, but they also brought horror and pain.

Sunday 16 February 2014
This morning, I woke up very upset. I had my 'police' dream again,
where I am waiting for my uniform to arrive and I meet up with my

old mates. I felt that I was back in the job again and I loved it. Lots of different faces from the past were all being briefed for various jobs. It was a lot more militant! I was looking out for any nice coppers! Lol. I also was sleeping on a bench settee which was taken over by a witness so I was going to admin to try and get a room and stay in the nick under the radar. As I write this I feel unstable obviously and familiarity of the job has been brought up in my consciousness. As I am pretty much homeless and out of control with my finances that is my last safety net, my stability. Perhaps I'm going through a grieving thing. I am crying again as I write this which started at 7.40 am. Oh, it's all so difficult now. I'm treading water trying to keep my head above it. It's getting sickening and tiring to be honest. I just want some good news. So I am going to immerse myself in writing Earth Walkers. *I desperately hope these dreams I am channelling are real and an intrinsic part of the future. I have pulled some angel cards.*

Stay resolute and driven.

Boundaries. Stay calm, wash away upset and keep going through life's storms.

Ring of life. Art and creativity are your future.

Wow. Pretty much bang on. We shall see...

I didn't realise at the time, but every single trauma and upset that I had had in my life was about to be relived in dream state. Some may call it healing, but I could only see it as a living hell.

When we are depressed, grieving or going through a crisis, our energy is very dense. The spirit world and the angel realms reside in a high frequency. They are so light that to blend with our dense energy especially when we are low is pretty impossible. It is like trying to mix water with oil. You will hear angels when they are near, you will get a high-pitched ringing in your ears. At the time I thought it was another M.E. symptom and completely ignored it. I remember going for ear tests because of it. It wasn't until later on that I learned that it was angel frequency.

As our energy is so dense during waking hours especially

with thoughts of sadness, fear, doubt and worry, they cannot influence us or help us. When we are in dream state, the alpha brain wave state, both the spirit world and the angel realms can enter into our consciousness and bring us what we need. It can be guidance, warnings, reassurance or even just a little message to say hello and that they are with us. The dreams will seem so real you normally wake up still feeling the emotion of the dream and remembering every single detail. These are normally psychic connections where the colour is vibrant, your feelings intensified and so real, it's unbelievable.

Dream state is the doorway for celestial entities. Take note of your dreams where you see spirit loved ones, make a note of what they say or show you in your dreams. You may have to research any symbols or google the definition of the dream on a dream analysing website to get the semantics of what the message is about. It is very common for spirit people to show you a quick vision that symbolises something as it takes less time and uses less of their energy.

They will also bring you signs and synchronicity during the day, but if you are anything like I was, I pretty much missed most of them. The trick is to know they are with you no matter what hell you are going through. You must have blind faith that everything is as it is meant to be and that your path and destiny will become clear.

For the record, I totally missed the trick.

I could see no reason on this earth why I would dream about every single trauma that I had endured in the past. To me it was punishment. To me, I felt they were just rubbing in the fact that I was a complete loony tune and had failed miserably in this particular lifetime. I had been forsaken as far as I was concerned, and this was going to be my penance for letting them down.

Chapter 12

Hello from the Other Side

Friday 28 March 2014

I feel like a ghost. Existing in a limbo time, having no reality or meaning. Every day drifts into the next. No goals, no home, no energy, no health, no special relationship, nothing to hold on to or have a foundation to spring from. Thank God for my friends who help. I am so desperately trying to be positive but it's so hard. I do hope I look back on this and reflect on how shit it was. Every reading I get and spirit connection from a medium sings of a bright future, a fantastic future. I have the book that I'm writing. That's something. I think that I am still grieving my old life. To be so tired and in pain all of the time thwarts any day when I'm feeling positive. Something will drag me down to a reality that I hate. The insurance are no further forward in getting my caravan sorted. The solicitors are dragging their heels for my accident. I have been living out of bin bags for two months and it's awful. I hope that this is spiritually led as I will be shocked to the core if this doesn't have a happy ending. I feel lonely. I still question my move here. The place is simply beautiful but everything has gone wrong since I moved, or is it all right? Have they been planning this? To change my path and to rest me for the new phase in my life? I get good days of hope but then they drop to hopeless days of despair. It is hard not to hate yourself when so much has crashed and burned around me. Is it my karma? The babies are being so good being dragged from pillar to post. Next I have to move out to Sue's in a week and a bit. Who knows what will happen, as I really don't anymore. I try my best to help myself but most days I just want to curl up and pretend that this isn't my life. I just don't seem to get it right. To have a holiday, to dive again, to not feel any pain or tiredness would be truly magical. I know that there are millions of people worse off than me, but we all have our own personal traumas. I just don't know which way to go anymore. Something has to give soon, surely, as I can't keep floating along. The days drift by, time is stealing my life away and I'm watching it go, helpless in trying to fill the time. I can only trust and hope that the Universe has it all in hand, because I certainly do not.

May God and the angels help me? Without this faith in what my dad said I have nothing, but I have to say it has never worn so thin in all of my life...

To be honest I was starting to hate the spirit world. I resented their 'lessons' that they were sending me. The more I fell into depression the less I meditated or even thought of connecting with them. As far as I was concerned they had a sick sense of humour.

They were trying though! They kept bringing me subtle signs and messages. I had a very brief euphoria, but within a day, I dropped back down to misery and futility. My happiness or will to fight was not sustainable; as soon as something happened no matter how minor I exploded into hysteria, stress and anxiety. I couldn't cope with anything. I couldn't pick up the phone or even read emails. I had relentless calls, messages and emails from people that wanted readings. I just ignored every single one of them. Telling them I was unable to work would have just made me feel I was sealing an interminable fate.

Tuesday 1 April 2014
Reached a corner I think and it coincided with the new moon on Sunday. Janet and I watched You Can Heal Your Life *by Louise Hay. It's changed my way of thinking so every time my mind stops, I fill it with positive affirmations. I certainly feel better already. It does work and now I will work it!*

I had a reading from Tracy yesterday at a spiritual meeting, I recorded it:

"It's so good to hear you laugh again as it has been so long. Your father is in spirit. He is so glad to hear you laugh at last. He looks very

much like you, same eyes, same smile. You have been in a maze and every time you think you have reached an exit you face a 60 foot wall. But that's coming to an end. You are coming out of it. You have been sad and very flat for a long time. You have been literally on the floor and have lost a lot. He is playing Pop Goes the Weasel. *Money has been a massive worry, and as soon as it has gone in, it has gone straight out. You need not worry for much longer. Sometimes you look like your mum, but when you smile it's your dad. He is worried about your mum. He is incredibly proud of you and has watched you go through a very difficult time. You are stronger than you think.*

There's the name Reg* that will be relevant to you. There's also a man who had really bad lungs [Granddad] and was on oxygen. He is also here. I can also see the 25th March. Keep on smiling, a massive weight will be lifted from your shoulders."

Pretty spot on reading for someone that didn't know me. I knew what Dad meant about my mum. She was declining in her health and I had a sense that she wouldn't be long for this world. The thing is, time to the spirit world runs a lot quicker than earth time! So when was this all going to end? I knew why she had brought up the 25th March. That was my sister's birthday. I had not heard from my brother or sister which only reinforced my self-hatred. Who wouldn't reach out when their sibling was in such a desperate state? I was obviously such an awful human being that they had no reason to want to reach out.

I then got another message from my friend Marie Hines, a lovely medium, the following week. I didn't realise it at the time, but her prophecies were going to come so true it still leaves me cold thinking about it.

Monday 28 April 2014
Sometimes I do truly want someone who is going to take me away from all of this. About six mediums keep telling me I am going to meet a tall dark haired man who is going to help me, where the fuck is he?

I got a message today from Marie. As usual I recorded it:

"You are going to move and the whole kitchen will be beige. There are two windows in the kitchen and they will have problems sticking. There's also problems with the pipe work in the kitchen. You will be spending out a lot of money soon. I can see the name Reg* (that name again!). You will also be meeting a new man, dark haired (him again!). You won't be staying in Devon (wtf?). There is also a man called Terry.* Definite energy around this Terry."

Well I need this man to come now lol or the dark haired one whichever is first!

At least I have some good news, my new caravan will be ready in July. Only a few more months of being homeless! I'm counting the days. I want my home, my bits around me. Living out of a bag is a fucking joke. Fucking nightmare! So money fairy, do your stuff already!!

It was then late March that I swear I heard the church bell of doom toll. I received an email reminding me that I was contracted to do a weekend residential retreat in Kent. It was sold out and I had no way of backing out without having to make major payouts. I also didn't want to let down the students who were coming.

How the hell was I going to get through it?

I had three months to prepare. By preparing I mean sleep and sleep and sleep in order to function for three days.

The stress of having to work overwhelmed me. I started to get more anxiety and suicidal thoughts. I was eating crap, basically. Whatever sweet morsel passed my lips I just reached out for more. I had put on two stone which helped my self-hate campaign to no end. I was going to have to pull off the biggest feat of my life. I would have to pretend to be this happy, strong spiritual person teaching eager students. What a joke! I felt a fraud.

Yet again, just as I started to spiral down, that lot from up above intervened to give me a firm kick up the arse.

I was forced to go and get some drum healing from my friend

Martine. I walked into Lupton full of resentment, and hated the world and everyone in it. I was exceptionally miserable as I was in pain and knew I would have to drive to Essex in a few days. My dreams were full of blackness, I was suffering with insomnia and each conversation I had to endure with people at Lupton was like medieval torture.

I went up to the treatment room, laid down and sighed, completely sure that it would do nothing at all to help me. As if it was going to help. This spiritual stuff was all a loads of bollocks...

Wednesday 11 June 2014

I have the three day course which I am totally dreading and have to go back up to Essex. But in true fashion right at the eleventh hour, that lot turn up to throw me a line. Yesterday Julianus visited me during the drum healing. It was lovely. He had his hood up, which means he means business. Just before he spoke I was told by a female voice that I was receiving the sacred feminine energy derived from the North. He leaned forward and gently touched my face. My face sizzled and popped from his touch.

He then said, "My child, do you honestly think that we would put you through all of this pain for no reason? It had to be done to clear you and get you ready for the next phase in your life and work."

As I felt his connection I then saw myself in a dark overgrown forest. I was far off of the path I should have been on. In order to get back to my path I had to battle through the overgrowth that I had wandered into, so I knew I had a long journey ahead of me. It's exactly what Catherine showed me a few weeks ago. They had stopped me in my tracks as I was in the wrong state of mind, surrounded by the wrong people and obviously I had a new way to represent them and everything had to be put back on track.

He then held my face with both hands and kissed both of my cheeks. I felt as if I had been kissed by fizzy, freezing water.

Julianus then showed me PSALM 56:22. It is one of his favourite things to do. He shows me quotes from his bible as a quick way to get a message across.

I made a mental note to google it later.

He then said, "The healing you are receiving is like lumps of fuel."
I then saw him holding lumps of what looked like coal.

"We are stacking them up within you, but you must not use them before you are completely sated and full. When it is time we shall light the fuel and allow it only to burn very slowly.

It will not be lit, Nichola, until it is properly full. You must cherish and preserve this fuel. April 2016 will be your turnaround, be patient. Stop worrying about small issues, people, and money. It is all on course."

He then backed away from me with the most loving smile I have ever seen. I felt sadness as I watched him disappear. I opened my eyes that were yet again welling with tears and smiled.

I googled the Psalm:

CAST THY BURDEN UPON THE LORD AND HE SHALL SUSTAIN THEE: HE SHALL NEVER SUFFER THE RIGHTEOUS TO BE MOVED.

How brilliant is that? He even raised my hand, which I didn't realise, to tell people in the room to shut up!

I feel so much better today. They are obviously trying to keep me in a protective spiritual bubble which can be frustrating at times but obviously necessary. I had such bad anxiety yesterday. I think it's mainly due to going back to the outside world, out of my healing zone. I hope to God it doesn't damage me too much.

I have rescued three bumblebees in the last four days, so I am thinking they must be an animal totem.

Google: All bees are productive, they stay focused on whatever they are doing and do not get side-tracked. We are being reminded to slow down, smell the flowers and taste the sweet nectar of life. If your energy is scattered the bumblebee can show you how to focus once more.

How apt was that message?

Animal totems or spirit animal totems are animals that visit you in real life, in dream state or meditation. Some of us have soul spirit animals that remain with us for our earth life. Their attributes reflect ours as they work as a kind of guide.

If you see an animal acting unnaturally or see the same animal repeatedly in a certain number of days, you have been sent a spirit animal and must research what they represent. I have had it so many times when an animal has rocked up in front of me. I google the animal and the message it brings is always totally correct. Some animals, however, can be sent from your loved ones as a message that they are with you. These can be robins, dragonflies, butterflies, ladybirds or their favourite animal. They have to make you notice them for an unusual reason. That is when you know you have been visited by a spirit animal totem.

I realised that they had given me a top-up to face my journey to Essex and then Kent.

Isn't it amazing how everything changes in a blink of an eye?

Yep, change was coming.

Chapter 13

You'll Meet a Tall Dark Haired Stranger

Having that intimate connection with Julianus and the bee visits really did perk me up. I found that I had a bit more energy and managed to get to Essex.

I stayed with one of my oldest, dearest friends Jo from the police service and her daughter Isla. It was great to be there and be able to talk to someone. Jo has always been an excellent listener. I had my doubts about the ensuing retreat weekend as I was losing my faith pretty swiftly, but then it was about teaching, not practising it for myself.

One night Jo and I were having a glass of wine. I was feeling quite happy, the weather had started to warm up and I was thrilled to be with Jo.

"Can you do me a favour?" Jo piped up out of the blue.

"Depends what it is!" I said dubiously.

"Well you are good at writing, can you write my profile for *Match.com*?"

So we laughed and giggled as I steered through her profile writing her up to be the best single female ever!

Jo popped upstairs so whilst I was waiting for her I decided to have a nose around. Don't even ask me why I did it as a man in my life was the last thing I needed at that point. But ego over divine whisperings of caution won out.

I was looking through profiles of men near Devon and a profile caught my eye.

The reason it did was because his profile name was *A333_keep smiling*.

This resonated with me straight away as A was for Alan, my dad's name. Three, three, three was the highest order of angel numbers and every time my dad communicated with a medium, he always ended the conversation by saying 'keep smiling'. I suppose I should mention at this juncture that my name is actually Nicky Morley. When I was involved in filming my first documentary, *Desolate Landscape*, the director suggested that I should have a stage name to disconnect me from my old police career. Of course I chose Alan, so I could work in memory of my beautiful dad.

So, back to *Match.com*! I immediately signed up on a temporary membership purely to message this man. I know, it was so impulsive and ridiculous; but it was his profile name that grabbed my attention.

We were on the phone within half an hour and spoke for hours. I think it was the first time for a couple of years that I had felt a bolt of excitement. This attention from this man, Jay, was exactly what I needed, or so I thought it was.

The little voices were cautioning me. I was in crisis, managing a severe chronic illness and yet there was I galloping along this fantasy path of romance and a 'happy ever after'. I didn't care. I was in with both feet and pushed all of my woes aside just waiting for the next ping of a text from Jay to stir my senses and my ego.

I then recalled my dad's visit. "Don't let men get in the way…"

I had an inward argument with myself. It was as plain as day; surely his profile name was a sign. Plus loads of mediums said I would meet this tall dark haired man. That's what that lot upstairs had always said to me, look for signs and synchronicity from the divine. That was my argument and I was sticking to it.

To be honest I was so lonely and bereft he could have been a knife-wielding, one-eyed, peg-legged maniac and I still would have dated him!

I didn't realise at the time but I hated my own company, probably because I didn't really like myself very much. I had codependency issues and always needed someone with me. It didn't matter if they weren't the right person. I just couldn't be alone.

On reflection, I was sticking my head in the sand. I wanted my fantasy being a reality, not the truth of what was happening to me. Sticking my head in the sand was fine by me. I was detaching myself from my inner voice and soul, and had no idea that I was doing it. Denial is a very powerful thing.

So with the promise of a new caravan and a possible new relationship on the horizon, I felt fully prepared to cope with a bunch of lovely students willing to learn from me.

The weekend was to be held at the Seekers Trust in Kent. Chaos hit within the first few hours. The organisers basically left me on my own with twenty-odd students with no help whatsoever. I was raging.

Thankfully as I watched the students arrive, I recognised a lot of them from previous workshops and seminars so I breathed a sigh of relief. I decided in the welcome meeting to explain to them that I was very ill and may have to rest more than usual. Well the angels were smiling that day. It turned out that a lot of the students also had M.E. and fibro so they understood. It is quite interesting how a lot of my psychic friends have gone down with this condition. Perhaps our spiritual souls can't take being in a heavy human cage.

As the hours progressed it turned out to be a blessing in disguise that I was the only tutor there. All of the girls were fabulous. We laughed, we cried, we bonded and most of all we learned a lot about the angel realms and the spirit world that weekend. They helped me out and didn't complain one bit. We all ganged together and had a blissful time. I was humbled as I drove back to Jo's that I could be surrounded by such wonderful girls. I cannot thank them enough for supporting me over that weekend.

I slept for three days after the weekend but the summer heat soon coaxed me out into the fresh air.

After staying at Jo's for a little while longer, I went to stay with my friend Sophie and yet again had fun and giggles. I needed to be near London as I had decided to record a new meditation CD, *Meeting Your Guides*. With this newfound confidence from recent events I agreed to do the project with my friend Mark. The name Mark has always been a positive influence on me. I met Mark when I was working with the late Colin Fry. He became my accountant but has turned out to be one of my ever-present rocks in life. I owe him so much.

I was convinced I was on the way up and that the CDs would sell like my first ones did. I spent a day in London in a recording studio and felt that I was on my way to getting back to work. I was gobbling morphine, tramadol and codeine like Smarties, normally washed down with wine. I was keeping the pretence up that I was normal, happy and still the old party girl that everyone loved.

I also stupidly arranged an evening of mediumship at my favourite spiritualist church, The Light on the Hill in Dartford, Kent. I adore Trevor and Patrick who run the place, so I thought whilst in Essex I would do an evening there. I also adored the audience that came to that place. I always felt a sense of joy whenever I served there.

See this is the other thing. When you are feeling a bit better and haven't had a horrendous day for a while you get into a false sense of security. You make plans that normally turn out to be cancelled or endured. I have learned never to make plans when I'm feeling good. Good days will never last, but I learned that the hard way.

I was so surprised. When I got to the church in Dartford it was heaving. There was a queue along the road for people trying to get in without a ticket. People were literally standing at the back in the entrance as there were no seats left. I felt so humbled. I also felt incredibly sad when I looked out on the audience as I knew I couldn't do what I adored full time anymore.

The evening was a blinder! The messages were outrageously

accurate. I enjoyed every single second. When I got back to Sophie's I fell into a coma-type sleep. The evening had taken every bit of my energy.

I was still in denial big time though. I avoided the bank and debt collectors' calls. I was having a fantasy life where my reality was pushed far away, out of sight, out of mind. I was pretending that I was back in my old life.

Eventually I returned to Devon as I couldn't wait to meet Jay. My friend was away on holiday so I said that I would house-sit, plus it gave me a roof over my head.

I remember Jay pulling up in his van looking so handsome. He had dark hair and was very tall, and I realised that this was the man the mediums had been predicting. I was thrilled, we hit it off straight away and had a lovely day in Brixham. When it came to the evening, the carefree Nicky told Jay that he should have a drink and stay with me at Nicky's. Oh the shame, but then again, I vowed to write the whole truth about my story, so there it is!

By 2 o'clock I became violently ill. Then by 4am so did Jay. We had eaten seafood earlier, so we deemed that the culprit. For three days we were very ill. We both swapped places at the toilet and laughed at this unusual start to our relationship.

I was on a high and refused to allow Jay to see the vulnerable, exceptionally ill side of me. When I didn't see him, I slept and let the pain have its way with me. I cared not for the consequences. I was in a false environment but I didn't care.

I drank wine to make the meds kick in and pushed myself to my limit. I was repeating the same behaviour as before, nothing was changing.

We went on weekends away and explored the Devon and Cornish coast together. Little did I know that I was standing on a time bomb.

I got my new caravan which was amazing, it even had a bath en suite. Everything was rosy in Nicky's rose-tinted garden. It wasn't a garden of lawns, flowerbeds and the odd ornament. My garden was full of unicorns, dragons, bubbles and magic. Totally unreal, but still, it painted a pretty picture in my kingdom of denial.

As I settled in to my new mobile home, the fat cats drew in. The owners of the caravan park refused to wait for the insurance money to cover the pitch fees whilst my new caravan was being made. They had agreed to this back in the spring but had now changed their minds.

They also, because they could raise the pitch fees whenever they wanted, decided to get greedy. Despite knowing my circumstances they increased my rent by an extra four hundred pounds a month. They stated it was because they had changed the rules, and as I had a drive and a sea view I should pay more.

I tried to argue. I tried to get a solicitor but couldn't afford one. I started to feel my coping mechanisms fail yet again. They had me in a tight clamp and wouldn't let go. The insurance people assured me that they would pay the pitch fees but the park management wouldn't listen.

They wouldn't allow me to sell the caravan, they wouldn't allow me to rent it out. They were disgusting in how they manipulated my position.

One night, I was sitting in the caravan, it was pouring with rain and just like that they cut off my electricity, water and gas.

Teddy and Mia started to cry as they sensed something was wrong.

The 'flatline' kicked in and I just sat there. I couldn't pay the fees, I couldn't pay the raised rent. I knew it was time to say goodbye to my home, yet again.

Like a robot I packed two dustbin bags, got the dogs in the car and drove to my friend's house. By the time she opened the door all three of us were soaked and I was crying hysterically. Yes, it was raining yet again! It was just a sick repeat of the last time.

They repossessed the caravan a week later.

It was October and I was homeless a second time. The caravan park also grabbed the insurance fees so yet again I had nowhere to live and no second option. In hindsight I should have taken the insurance write-off money and rented a place back in the spring, but I was far too busy living my fantasy life. The option had been there and I had not taken it. My ego overwhelmed my intuition. I knew I should have taken the money from the insurance and used it to rent somewhere, but no, I wanted the caravan by the sea. Standing on Janet's doorstep for a second time in the rain showed me I had moved no further forward. I had wasted eight months of my life because I didn't listen to what I should have done. It was a very strong lesson.

So again, it was just me and my two little dogs.

That is when the decline began.

I thought that I had been through the worst.

How stupid was I.

But there was one saving grace: Jay, the dark-haired stranger.

Chapter 14

The Downward Spiral

I was back at Janet's and jumped from panic to fear with every heartbeat. I was totally homeless now, and had no money and absolutely no idea what to do. Every penny was going to the debt collectors and banks from my police pension. I had no idea that they had no right to take money before my food, living and welfare costs. I was so scared of them, even though if I'd thought about it they had nothing else to take from me.

It was October and the nights were drawing in. As the darkness of the evening absorbed my room, the black reached through and grabbed my heart. I had palpitations as I lay in bed. I started to feel real terror. My ability to cope with stress was non-existent. I was flatlining.

It was 3am in the morning. I can remember trying to calm my breathing when I got a vision in my head. I saw my nan smiling, she then wrote on a white board, *Rightmove*. The vision then disappeared. I went straight on to *Rightmove* and the first place I saw looked wonderful. It was surrounded by trees and looked like an old Victorian cottage made out of old Devon stone that I adore.

I felt excitement. My gut told me I must go and view it. My head told me that I had no money and had no way to put a deposit down. I also had no credit rating anymore, so it was pretty impossible. It didn't matter though because as I repeatedly looked at the pictures of this cottage, I heard Julianus say, "Trust us."

The following morning I got Janet to drive me to the location, it was in Kingswear.

Now I need to take you back to 2009. This is when I first discovered Torbay and the surrounding areas. I adored

Dartmouth and would love to get on the ferry and visit the superb Blackpool Sands and Slapton Sands. Slapton holds a massive part of my soul. It was where they practised for the D-Day landings. I have a big affinity to the Second World War. I do believe I had a previous life during this era.

On your way to Slapton, you have to drive through Kingswear to get to the lower ferry that takes you across the river Dart. I would pass this stunning cottage that was on the grounds of Kingswear Cemetery.

I used to joke and say, "That will be my place one day," or "There's my cottage!" How funny would it be for a medium to live with the dead?

Well, as I was driving along with Janet to view this property, I found us going down the Brixham Road towards that cottage.

I couldn't believe my eyes when we pulled up on the drive.

It was the cemetery lodge cottage that I had joked about living in for years!

I didn't even go in. I phoned the estate agent and told them I wanted to rent it.

After they took my details I then realised that I didn't have a penny. What was I even thinking?

I then had an idea pop into my head. It was a cheeky one as I had only known him for a couple of months, but I somehow knew that he would help.

Jay.

I called him up; he didn't even hesitate. He loaned me the money to cover the deposit and four months of rent!

Don't even ask me how I got through the credit check, which in itself was a miracle as I was in debt up to my eyeballs and had stopped paying my mortgage on both places and paying my car loan. In real life this would have been impossible, but it was a little miracle, one of many to come.

I moved in on 7 November 2014. My friends, Darren and Rob, went and picked up my belongings that had been stashed in storage from my house in Essex. I was finally going to be reunited with all of my things and have a home!

It was exciting on the day as we unpacked everything. I also had to get all of the things from the caravan that were in storage as well.

I was pushing myself, but I didn't care.

I adored the fact that my lounge was two feet away from the first grave. I know, weird right?

I am not going to lie, I did sleep with the light on for the first few nights but found that the place wasn't haunted at all. Who wants to stay around a cemetery after they have passed?

The first couple of days I sat by the stream at the bottom of the cemetery listening to the water bubbling over the rocks. I wandered around the graves listening to the silence, finding a sense of peace. I would even talk to the people marked on the graves about their lives down here. I am sure if anyone saw me I would have been hastily taken to a secure compound! I lit massive fires in the lounge when I could get out of bed from the wood I had found in the nearby woodland. I remember sitting in front of the fire, cheeks burning, and thinking I was going to be OK.

I needed this place. It wasn't practical as it was in the middle of nowhere with no neighbours. Everywhere the eye could see there was nothing but trees and fields, oh and obviously graves! There was also a small chapel in the middle of the cemetery that I would go and sit in and send prayers up, desperately asking for help. It was like a spiritual retreat away from the chaotic world. I needed to withdraw and disappear, and this was the perfect place for it.

After a few days of moving in, I got out of bed and promptly collapsed on the floor. I couldn't get up. My body had given up. I had pushed it way too far during the move and it was now time to pay the price. The depression then started to kick in as I realised I was still desperately ill, and it was not going anywhere anytime soon. The pain was so overwhelming it hurt even to cry. Every breath made the muscles scream in my torso.

I managed to crawl back to bed, and slept on and off for days.

I remember one afternoon when I had been in bed for about five days. I hadn't washed, hadn't eaten and felt like death. The dogs started to bark at the window. I sat up instantly and saw a huge shadow start to darken the room. I wondered what the hell it was. I thought it might be a low-flying aeroplane, but there was no sound. I then saw through the landing the other rooms darken. I was terrified. I thought perhaps the house was haunted after all!

The hairs on the back of my neck went up and the room went cold. I could smell a strong floral scent, and then heard music as if women were chanting in a faraway place. I honestly thought that I was losing the plot!

I then heard Julianus, he was in my room.

"Ssh, don't worry, my love."

His velvet voice washed over me and I felt myself relax.

"The Seraphim are here. They are protecting your dwelling. This will now be your sanctuary. No one of detriment shall pass through your door. Your healing is now to begin."

Julianus then projected in my mind this huge angel in dark robes. Her black hair was cascading down over her shoulders. She looked like a warrior princess. I saw her cloaks cover every area of the cottage. I could hear her chanting. The dogs were going crazy. The darkness then lifted and everything went back to normal in a blink of an eye.

"What healing? How are you going to do it?" I asked out loud.

No one answered.

I laid back down and fell into a dreamless sleep. As I dozed off into the haven that took me from the pain, I registered that the dark cloaked woman was indeed a Seraphim. A warrior angel who travels on the frequency of song. They heal traumatised humans when they pass in the celestial garden's 'Fountain of life'.

They bring mass souls up during world disasters. They are the oldest hierarchy of angels and the most fearsome. "I am in good hands," I thought as I drifted off into the land of numbness.

Jay came down to visit the next weekend. I tried so hard to be happy and friendly but I was just too exhausted. We ended up laying on the sofa watching movies, which suited me fine. To be honest I wanted to be on my own. It's a curious condition: you want to be alone, but you want company. Ideally having someone in the house, but they aren't bothering you.

Jay said out of the blue,

"Your dad has sent me here to help you, that's what I am here for."

"Don't be silly!" I replied.

"No," he said more quietly. "That's not the reason I met you."

But I couldn't help feeling he was right. I was finding maintaining a relationship a living nightmare to be honest. I just couldn't be bothered. Did my dad send him then? Is that why his profile name was almost like a code from my dad? Had he been sent in just to help me and get a roof over my head? The following day pretty much nailed it for me as Jay had an Earth Angel message without even realising it.

The following day, Jay said, "There is something wrong with your claim. You need to get hold of your solicitor."

I said rather irritated, "It's fine, there's nothing wrong with it, it just takes time!" I then changed the subject.

The last thing I wanted to do was cope with talking to a solicitor. I was too exhausted mentally and emotionally. After Jay left to go home, his comment kept haunting me though. I decided to call the solicitors.

After the conversation, I put the phone down with sagging shoulders. I cried for hours. I was done, I wanted it all to end.

The solicitors had done absolutely nothing in three years to progress my claim. They had just left it in a drawer and ignored it. They tried to explain that it was a complex case. I put the phone down. Yet again I had been exposed to an injustice. It was going to be my answer to getting my own home, debt cleared and to pay for private treatment. What the hell was going on? A second set of solicitors had just done exactly the same as the first ones. They had done absolutely nothing. They made a veiled threat in response to me saying that I would put a complaint in. They said that the case would be frozen and I would miss the timeline for a claim. They also said it wouldn't reflect well after having them as a second set of solicitors after moving from the first company. They were making it sound like I didn't have a chance in hell in making a valid complaint. I was so sick of having arsehole corporates around me shaping my life and dictating my options. Bankers, debt collectors, doctors, caravan park management and now solicitors.

In three months' time it would be three years since the accident. I would not be able to raise any claim or court hearing after this. I knew from being a police officer that to get all of the medical evidence which I needed in before three months was impossible. This left me with an uncertain future. I thought of all the pathetic reasons that people sued each other for. I had had a life-changing accident that wasn't my fault and it looked like I was going to get absolutely no financial compensation whatsoever.

If I had had the energy I think I would have laughed hysterically at this surreal situation. It was just one punch in the face after another.

I felt absolutely gutted. Jay was right. Perhaps my dad did bring him into my life to look out for me and not for romance.

My mind went numb. No matter how I tried to find a solution to this new problem I just kept coming back with blanks. I looked online for local solicitors in Torbay. Most of them quoted in their services that they did not take cases on from other solicitors. I was ramming myself against a brick wall with no reprieve.

There was only one way to cope with this next crisis. It was the only way I knew how.

I took some painkillers, put the duvet over my head and disappeared into the oblivion of sleep.

Chapter 15

Me Myself and I

I continued to go downhill fast. I ignored the fact that I had no ongoing claim for my accident. I refused to talk to Jay and told him that I didn't want to see him. I felt guilty that the dogs weren't being exercised. I started to get insomnia every night. I was exhausted but my brain was wired, and rushed about like an out of control radio tuning into one random station after another. I refer to it now as 'tired and wired'.

At night I would wander around the cemetery, if I could walk, like some sort of phantom. The dogs could then have a good run around whilst I sat on a bench and listened to the sounds of the night. I would listen to the owls hooting and the foxes screeching, finding some comfort that I wasn't alone. I would listen to the brook bubbling away at the bottom of the meadow and pretend that I was sitting at some brilliant waterfall in some magical land away from all of this madness.

I slept through most of the day, and if I wasn't sleeping I was crying. I did try to stay awake during the day once for two days but still did not sleep at night. There is no logic to an M.E. brain. Sleep cycles are shot to pieces. You just have to grab it when you can. I learned very quickly that when you needed to sleep, you slept, it was as simple as that. To sleep during daylight hours and be awake during the darkness exacerbated the depression and the feelings of futility.

The sleep deprivation was taking its toll. I was on a long winding spiral down to depths of misery that no human should experience.

I would look out on the valley that led into Kingswear from my bed. The beauty of it was breathtaking. But then I would see figures rushing around in the distance getting on with their lives and I would draw the curtains. I was sick with jealousy and resentment of their 'normality'. I had reached my rock bottom and was quite happy to remain there.

I knew that I was heading for a mental breakdown. I did contemplate phoning up the local mental health unit and asking to be voluntarily sectioned. I then saw my babies at the end of the bed and wondered who would care for them, so that idea went out of the window. There was no support network. No one from the doctor's surgery gave me any leaflets or contacts for support. I was going through the biggest crisis of my life and had no professional backup.

The pain was ridiculous. It was a constant mind-shattering agony that would not dissipate. I found that I was too exhausted to go to the toilet so I would wet myself and place another towel under me. The room stank and so did I. I was a mess, physically, mentally and spiritually.

I saw no way out, apart from the suicide fantasies that became far more frequent and far more tempting again.

I wanted to go home. I wanted it all to end. I wanted to die.

I would look at my two babies though who sat staring at me, and no matter how much I wanted to kill myself, I just couldn't leave them laying by my dead body. That was the only thing that stopped me from taking an overdose. Perhaps this is what the Turkish seer meant, they were saving my life.

There was something that I noticed which was a bit weird. During this time I kept picking stuff out of the house move boxes that were the colour pale blue. Everything I could find in that colour I put around me in the bedroom. I had no idea why. I had never been drawn to that colour, but I was obsessed with it. I soon found out why and it was quite an epiphany.

It was 12 December. I stank of urine, was starving hungry and realised that I needed help. I had woken up and realised that my right eye had remained closed and wouldn't open. I was so scared. The muscles had obviously just given up and didn't want to open my eye. I took a photo of it as I was so appalled at how ill I looked.

I still hadn't learned to reach out and ask for help as I had always dealt with everything on my own, but I compromised and called the doctor. The GP who I had at the time was a disgrace. She refused to come out to me so I had to go to the surgery. I was in my pyjamas and just put a sweatshirt on over them and a pair of trainers.

I sat in front of her and cried hysterically spewing loads of jumbled words on my predicament and how ill that I was.

With most GPs as soon as you mention the word fibromyalgia or M.E. you see their faces go blank. They have no idea how to help you, they think it really isn't a condition and just throw one painkiller at you after another.

At one point she actually said to me, "It's not as if you have a broken arm or anything or that you are disabled. Pull yourself together and get back to work."

Yes, those words truly came from her lips, the stupid cow.

She made some referrals to services that frankly if I had known how useless they were I wouldn't have wasted my energy.

I just asked for my medication, limped out and went home.

You will find that at this point my diary entries are fewer. To even think about writing was beyond my capacity.

Sunday 14 December 2014
Two days ago I was put on Gabapentin. Feel bit better for it. Been referred to pain clinic, got physio on Tuesday, got M.E. clinic next week. I am a wreck! I so need to get my shit together. The only thing that I'm sure of is getting that bloody book finished! It's also frustrating with the house being packed still. It's getting there little by little.

I got struck off from physiotherapy because I couldn't do the Tai Chi that I was ordered to do. The physio made me feel like a failure. When I managed to make an appointment after cancelling twice before, he looked at me as if I had failed an exam on purpose for not getting up and doing the Tai Chi.

I asked if I could have hydrotherapy sessions as they might help ease the pain and assist in mobilising my limbs. Apparently the hydro pool was only used for people recovering from accidents and surgery.

Great.

I got struck off from the M.E. clinic because I was too ill to attend. I received a rather curt letter outlining the fact that I had failed to attend the last three sessions and was being discharged from the 'service'. Service, my arse, what the hell was the use of getting dressed only to sit in a group and moan about your condition? Then to go home and sleep for days because of the exertion of the session?

They also gave me this laughable chart that you had to fill in. You had to detail your activities to see if there was any pattern. How ridiculous! Sleep, toilet, sleep, pick the bones out of that one! They failed to see that the activities were totally irrelevant to how you felt. Pacing your activities was the right way forward, but asking for you to use your energy filling out a chart to look for patterns was about as useful as a trap door in a canoe!

At the anxiety and depression clinic I was told that I had a valid reason for my depression, and as it wasn't clinical, they couldn't help me.

I was offered six sessions of counselling through the GP but couldn't honour the appointments as they were in Totnes and I did not have the energy to travel there, do the session and then come home.

Ideally a home visiting psychotherapist would have been superb. If I had the money I would have had a cleaner and a carer.

I started being sick on the gabapentin, so that was useless.

Nothing and nobody from the medical profession were helping. I needed to find a new GP, but obviously that took a

Herculean effort, so I just went back to bed and rotted.

Basically if you were a millionaire this illness could be better managed. You could afford a permanent live-in carer, cleaner, chef, psychotherapist and physiotherapist. You could have holistic therapies daily, perhaps a pool to float in and a hot tub to soothe your body in. You could spend a fortune on the best supplements for the condition and have someone administer all of your meds and supplements, rather than you having to remember through brain fog. You could be whisked away on your private plane to a nice warm country where you could be cared for 24/7 in paradise without moving a muscle.

Well, unfortunately not many of us sufferers are millionaires, so we get the shit end of the stick!

Christmas went by in a haze. My friends brought a turkey around. I found on that day that alcohol made me feel physically sick. My body had decided then and there that it didn't like it. Looking back it was a blessing. From then on I didn't touch a drop for years.

By 3pm I was asleep and slept through Boxing Day and the days thereafter.

I tried to block out all of the fun parties people must have attended, all of the families happily joined around the Christmas tree opening their presents. I hated all of them with a vengeance. I stopped looking on Facebook. Watching people's lives made me feel sick to the core.

Thursday 1 January 2015
So another year is ahead of me. I pray with everything within me that this is a new year of hope, help, health and riddance to all of the pain and struggle. I sit alone, yet again. My book will be written, I hope it is the making of my next phase of life. This has been the worst crash of my life, but it has shown me my true friends.

My only priority is my health which I will strive in every way possible to get back to normality whatever it takes.

Archangel Michael, I call upon you for strength and movement.
Raphael, for healing.
Zadkiel, for the end of litigation.

I am on the edge so now time is of the essence. I have been tried and tested. Enough is enough, surely this is my year.

I have done things wrong in the past but surely my karma has dealt its final blow as we turn into the New Year. Every penny I get will be concentrated on me getting well. I cannot ever afford to crash like this again but now I have found security in my home finally the rest will flow, angels willing. So let us see what the New Year brings and let the positives flow with abundance. I pray that when I read this next New Year all of this madness and frustration is part of a dimming bad memory. I am important. I have to nurture and love this vessel. It is simple. So I ask the heavens to bring the right people to help me to get back to a permanent happy, healthy and serene reality.

HOPE HEALTH STRENGTH

See the thing is, if I was writing this now, I would know that everything would be honoured. But I was paying lip service. I had absolutely no faith at all and just wrote this down for the sake of it. There was no way I had invoked their help. You have to be in the right energy, you have to raise your vibration and help yourself as well. I also knew that I was going to do absolutely nothing to help myself. In the demon layer of my consciousness it was almost as if I was serving my sentence. I was imprisoned in this dark, dank existence, and to think about trying to help myself was futile. I was languishing in my own self-pity and struggle. There was no fight to survive; there was nothing holding my sanity together. The more I stank the more I could hate myself, which was my logic.

I had also developed night sweats where I was literally soaked every couple of hours. I started to get restless leg syndrome and repeated nightmares that I was still in the police but being ridiculed. They were horrendous.

I was still incontinent and couldn't wash myself. I was constipated because I was chucking tramadol, codeine and morphine down my throat every couple of hours. I had no food in the house and had no thought to ask for help.

It was just me, my bed and my onslaught of misery, pain and futility.

I was gritting my teeth so hard with the pain that I crumbled the top part of my canine off.

It was a relentless hell. Nausea also set in at this point and never dissipated. I had swords of pain rip through my head and body, and when I tried to walk, my limbs just trembled and gave way under me. The only thing I got up for was to feed the dogs and get water. I left the front door open for them to go in and out.

How I managed to hang on, God only knows.

Chapter 16

The Surrender

The days rolled on and I found that on top of everything else my skin broke out in painful blisters, sores and scabs. My hands, scalp, face and fingers were covered. I looked like a leper. I was also severely burned down below from the incontinence. It had now been over two months of being isolated and completely bed bound.

M.E. and fibromyalgia are like having the severest part of flu. All you want to do is dose yourself up, get your head under the duvet and sleep, blocking the world out. That's exactly what it was like. I craved sleep and escape.

The thoughts of ending it all were frequent. I realised that I had to change my faith. I realised that there was something up there that had been trying to help me. I was still a little sceptical, but what else could I hang on to? I couldn't reside in this darkness for much longer. It was truly killing me.

So, on the night of Wednesday, 7 January, I got up naked and put a robe on. I shuffled to the front door, walked into the middle of the cemetery and removed my robe. I sank down to my knees and looked up at the moon.

I knelt there naked as I wanted to depict my vulnerability, and almost recreate rebirth as I had entered the world, naked.

"I am now thinking of coming home every day. I know it isn't my path to come back early. I know I am here for a reason. I have blocked you out, I have forsaken you, and I now need you. My mind, body and spirit are dying and I don't want to die. I lay before you in my physical state and please ask you to come to my side, help me on my path.

I surrender, I surrender and hand myself over to your love and guidance. Please come to me, show me how I can get through this, bring me out to the other side, and show me how to win this ongoing battle. Please, I beg you!"

I then sank to the floor and gave in to the tears.

Wednesday 7 January 2015
It's 3 in the morning. I'm tired but my head is awake. Every evening I watch TV and then read to try and block out the reality of my life. I had a passing whim that perhaps these battles will lead to compensation that will keep me financially safe so it doesn't matter if I work or not. That I can do it for passion and love! If only!

I have handed my emails over to Janet as I can't handle the stress. I think that is what keeps me from recovering. The peace and silence of this place is so healing but also in brief moments can be lonely. I long for someone to cuddle me to sleep, stroking my hair. I just feel in my soul the need to wait and rest, nothing else apart from the need to write the book. But at the moment even that feels too much to handle. Every little thing is overwhelming. It's even hurting me to write this. I numb myself to reading, because it stops me thinking too much, of what I have lost, sleeping sometimes every day and waking up when it's dark already. The fact that I am 44 and my life seems to be dwindling away. I know other people are worse off than me but I have battled and fought for what feels like my entire life and now I just can't do it. I am letting go and come what may. I have to accept my situation as there is absolutely nothing I can do. I fear if I do something wrong, spiritually I will get more wrath.

I'm sick and tired of putting so much stress on myself. So the days can mould into weeks. I'm just pretty knackered. To survive is just to find some positives in each day, that's all I can really do.

I don't know what will be, but I don't have the strength to contemplate it. If it wasn't for my soul and a deep lying faith I would be in a hospital ward somewhere as I honestly feel that I finally, after all the pain, have had a breakdown. It's a surrender I suppose. Sometimes I feel driven and think I'm being lazy but all I have to do is stand up and feel the exhaustion or the pain or start contemplating my life and

I then realise that I am truly broken and just have to be kind to myself and if that means rotting away in bed, then so be it.

I sat in the moonlight in the cemetery tonight whilst the babies ran around. It was so amazing seeing how bright the moonlight shone across the graves which were all glistening with frost. I surrendered. It was bloody freezing! It is a truly beautiful place. I look forward to the summer! My hand is totally killing me now. I will end up sleeping to stupid o'clock. The insomnia can be such a bitch...

In the morning for the first time ever, Teddy was standing on my chest doing this sort of sniff thing to wake me up. As I opened my eyes, I can only describe it as a shift within me. There was the tiniest bubble of happiness. Teddy kept whining and wouldn't shut up until I got up. I thought he wanted a wee, so I went downstairs and opened the front door.

There on the step to my amazement was a hamper, laden with food, toiletries and snacks. I couldn't believe what I was seeing. Someone had cared enough to leave it on my doorstep.

Was it coincidence that I had surrendered the night before or was it something else?

I found out that it was my friend Leigh-Anne who had a thought completely out of the blue to deliver me the hamper that morning. How magical is that. For the first time in a long time, I cried happy tears.

From that day on, at ten in the morning on the dot, Teddy started to wake me up. Even though I still had the insomnia I forced myself up, so at least I was laying on the sofa. I was near the toilet so the layers of urine-soaked towels stopped. At around 2pm he would do the same thing, jump on my chest and snort until I woke up. He would then do it around 6pm. It became a regular thing every day. I now realise he was monitoring me and waking me so that I could move about and function, albeit for a very limited time.

Funnily enough he still does it now when I am bed bound. He

is a beautiful Earth Angel, that one. If I don't get up he will cry until I physically get out of bed.

I will make a cup of tea and I will then find him lying in my bed space as if to say, "You are not getting back in here, Mum. Stay up for a while and move about!"

When we are out walking, he will run ahead and every few minutes will run back, stop and look at me as if to say, "Are you OK?"

I then say, "I'm OK, Teddy, good boy!" He will then sniff and run ahead again. My amazing little boy!

During this time I started to get random thoughts of what I was grateful for that weren't my own. I started to write out every morning three things I was grateful for. They could be the smallest things, but they set me up with some form of positivity for the day.

On 11 January, I had another amazing dream that again was so lucid and clear. I knew it was another book that they wanted me to write. I was being pushed and pushed to write, I just knew it.

On Thursday, 22 January I was woken up by Ted as usual and the first thought that came to me was I must phone a solicitor. It was like a powerful need to make the call then and there.

I googled local solicitors. There was one that caught my eye. The reason it caught my eye was because one of the solicitors at the firm was called Mark. As you know the name Mark has always been positive for me, so I dialled the number before I lost my courage.

I ended up talking to Mark and also ended up pretty hysterical.

He was lovely. He said that even though it wasn't the usual practice to take a case over, he was so appalled by how I had been treated and by my story that he agreed to take the claim on. I couldn't believe it.

So the following day I went to his offices, looking like an extra from *The Walking Dead*, and gave him all the documents that I had. He told me not to worry about the claim ending in two months and that he would apply for an immediate extension. He also warned me though that I would get nowhere near what I was due as a lot of the medical evidence had been lost. I didn't care, anything would help me get back on my feet.

Friday 23 January 2015
Truly mixed times. I have a new solicitor Mark, it seems the Universe has prevailed and this case has another lease of life. I hope this all comes to an end soon. I'm so weak and exceptionally poorly. Day after day I am getting lost in the Lost *box set! All the days continue to roll into one. I have a hell of a fight coming but I have no option and I'm on the floor anyway. I think the emotion of visiting the solicitors has wiped me out. I'm in the hands of the angels. I'm doing absolutely no work whatsoever. It's all about me now. I have seen so many synchronicity numbers since I surrendered, so I know everything is as it should be. I hope that I have a long life as at the moment it feels like precious time is being wasted. It's exhausting just talking to people, I am still isolating a bit. I just need to.*

Saturday 24 January 2015
I didn't realise that yesterday marked exactly three years since my road accident! Jesus what a ride that has been. I sat in the sun today on a bench at the bottom of the cemetery garden. It was beautiful and nice to get a bit of sun. Last night at 3.33 am Zeus, who I am dog sitting for, got up and growled, as soon as he did there were three large bangs, I shit myself! They were so loud I honestly thought that someone was trying to break in! I was going to grab the phone but then looked at the clock. I realised that perhaps it was more spiritual. There were no other sounds so I presume that it was them, not sure but what an adrenaline rush! I hope that they are telling me it's all OK and they are with me as I drew some random cards online and they said about synchronicity was all around me and the other cards were about having a really bad time in the recent past and this was the new dawn and brilliant things

to come! Let us hope, dear God let us hope.

Teddy continued to wake me up every morning. I started a small routine. At the time I didn't realise it, but as soon as the moon episode had taken place, there was a definite shift occurring very slowly. Teddy would force me out of bed, I would make a cup of tea and then shuffle in my pyjamas down to the end of the cemetery. The cemetery and the cottage are literally surrounded by forest. The Brixham Road runs parallel to the land. That is the only sound of life, the cars driving into Kingswear. Apart from that there is nothing but sounds of nature and wildlife. It truly was a healing sanctuary.

Wednesday 4 February 2015
So I am laying here as usual and have had a pretty positive day. Sat at the bench at the end of the cemetery in the sun with the babies. Looked like a nutty banshee in PJs and boots whilst two men turned up to remove a headstone. Cleared the dressing room out, did the rubbish and cooked a stir fry! That's more than I have done in three months! But by evening the mood swings kicked in to feeling depressed again and pretty shitty.

So I put Kevin Kendle on and decided to write it out which is pretty tough when my hands are fucking killing me when I write. I've been thinking a lot about the future. The tax people, creditors, bank, bailiffs, mortgage and council tax are all on my back. None of these people give a fuck, they just want money, and it sickens me. So as I'm mostly bed and housebound you get to thinking a lot. I don't know if this condition will ever leave me. At the moment, which may change, who knows? Should I just retire? Fuck off to Spain? Perhaps I have been fired from my spirit work. Just like everything else I work towards and it's blown up in my face. I'm so fucking sick of money and debt. I'm sick of my life. At the moment I don't even know that I am happy in Devon. Would I be happy anywhere? Is it that I have a severe mental illness developed from all of this shit? The spirit world and angels show their synchronicity but why have I had to endure so much trauma? Something at the moment I don't know if I will ever recover from.

I can't even cope mentally with the smallest tasks. I feel broken. I resent everything and then I get scared that I am sending the wrong energy out to the Universe, but fucking hell it can't be any worse. I think I have got around £200 for the month. That's for food, electric, bills, everything. I have yet again cancelled the dentist, dogs need grooming, windows need cleaning, and house needs cleaning. I am just so fucked off with, oh you got to be positive, heal yourself, blah fucking blah! Tonight I don't feel like that at all.

I don't know what triggered it. Not got a clue but I feel miserable, tearful, negative and yeah fuck it, sorry for myself. I'm horrible and that's why this has all happened. Groundhog Day that's what this is and it's not over yet. I'm going to be ripped to pieces by the other side's solicitors. My whole world I worked my bollocks off to create smashed and they are going to go for the jugular. There's so much injustice that has happened over the last three years. No one cares if you've had an accident. No one cares if you can't buy food, no one gives a fuck.

I have no emotional energy to even think about carrying on writing a book. The way it's going it will be a complete failure anyway. The CD is a joke. It's not even fucking selling. I have just had enough of everything. Perhaps I do need to just fuck off in the sun for a few months when I can actually walk without having to sleep for 24 hours the next day. I fucking hate my life. I hate everything to do with it.

No doubt there will be some sign telling me to trust but FUCK OFF!

I just want a cuddle. I want someone to stroke my hair and tell me they love me and it's going to be OK. I am so lonely. I'm having suicidal thoughts again. The physical and emotional pain is relentless every day. Take loads of tablets! But my poor babies and some people I would leave behind. The pain would be bad for them. But to me I fantasise about the transition. Being in heaven away from all this human shit and human rules. My own family don't even want to help when I'm on my knees.

Day after day I sit watching Lost *and* Downton *so I can lose myself in non-reality. Eating shit because I can't get out to get it and can't afford to buy good food anyway. Put on two stone. I feel like a fat, ugly, old piece of shit.*

I have so had enough. I'm fucking sick. Sick of it all. I'm so sick of fighting. I so desperately want to give up, I have nothing left. I'm just so tired of it all. I'm so fucking tired. God help me.

As you can tell, those angels, guides and spirit people had a hell of a battle on their hands in trying to help me!

One thing I have learned from all of this, never limit what the celestial world is capable of...

Chapter 17

Raguel Has Just Entered the Building

The biggest part on reading over my Soul Journals was the battle of the mind. Looking back and reading my thoughts and emotions makes me realise that anyone suffering from mental illness or chronic illness can win their war if they just engage in mindfulness. Any thought leads to emotion and then to a subsequent behaviour. It's the first thought that we must change in order for the emotion and behaviour to have a different, more positive outcome.

The angels and the spirit world were slowly working their magic but I was in such despair, I couldn't see it. The roller coaster that was my thought process continued to rise and fall at any given moment.

Friday 13 February 2015
So I'm still sitting in my prison rotting away. It's weird, I only started writing this because I have just been down for a wee, came upstairs and the TV had changed channel by itself whilst I was downstairs to Vintage TV, Sultans of Swing. The channel number was still visible as well which it shouldn't be. It was Channel 369 – angel numbers. I was crying earlier so perhaps they are showing synchronicity. Also the night before when I was sending thoughts up I had this weird name, RAGUEL, come into my head. I have never heard of it. I assumed he was an angel so invoked him to come and help me. I Googled it afterwards and couldn't believe it, he exists! He is the Archangel of harmony, justice and miracles!

He brings end to injustice and people and relationships in the past! How weird is that? Each day is like a roller coaster. Some days I can cope, others I just want to die as I don't see the future. I'm in pain and totally exhausted. I really can't do much at all without my body moaning, it's a fucking joke. Mum's cancer remission has been revoked because of nodules found on her lung and ear.

I wish I had enough oomph to write my book but I can't even do that. I keep making spelling mistakes just writing this!

Anyway, I Google 369.

Angel number 369 is a message from your angels to continue forth upon your life purpose and soul mission safe in the knowledge that your material wants and needs will be met as needed. Your light working duties to serve and help humanity are important and you are being encouraged to put extra focus on your spiritual path and purpose. Devote yourself to your soul mission without delay.

Angel number 369 indicates that your prayers and positive affirmations about your spiritual path and purpose have been heard and are being responded to by the angels and those in the higher realms. Listen to your intuition and take action as guided.

Give any fears or worries about monetary issues to the angels and get on with pursuing your purpose. The angels, Archangels and ascended masters fully support you and will ensure that your material wants and needs are met as you carry on your light work.

Research, study, schooling, education and learning will enhance your life purpose and personal growth and development at this time.

The angels will guide you with all that you need to learn and grow.

Holy shit!

Weird as the thing about books/study came up in an angel card the other day. I wonder if this means about the book? I find it very hard to do anything at the moment but perhaps I need to try harder.

What's also weird is the year on Vintage TV was 1979, the last year dad was alive. Who knows? But what I do know is, the mysterious changing over of the channel has given me a much needed lift as I am seriously struggling. Hopefully I will feel strong enough to get back on the book tomorrow! It's not as if I have anything else to do!

Light can only shine through a broken vessel.

Bear Grylls

I have to get the book done. This is my time to write, I have the thought every day. It must be what this is all about.

I checked when I had returned to the bedroom to see if one of the dogs had sat on the remote. The remote was on the side cabinet far away from the dogs. It was also unexplainable how the Vintage channel number was still displayed, as if an invisible hand was still pressing the button. They had made their presence known, they were walking my daunting path with me. It gave me a huge lift especially Archangel Raguel making himself known.

OMFG! I just realised why I have all this bloody pale blue stuff around me in the bedroom! Earlier today I found in one of my drawers a necklace I didn't even recognise.

It's a pale blue crystal angel with a darker blue crystal as a halo. It hung on a pale blue satin ribbon. You never guess what colour Raguel works on? Pale Blue!

Just had to write this, I have just woken up and the time is 1.11am. Spiritual awakening angel numbers! How exciting is this? I'm smiling and have decided that when I wake up I am going to change my bed clothes because the night sweats and temperature problems are saturating the bed! I'm going to put a wash load on and have a bath! Hopefully I can manage that.

Something shifted yet again after Raguel entered my life. I started thinking every morning of three tiny goals to achieve for the day. I was also mindful not to beat myself up if I didn't manage them.

There was one thing that started to haunt me though. Since Raguel had made his presence known, my dreams changed. Every night I had the recurring dream of something horrific from my past. My sexual assault as a child came back with a vengeance. Every night the ending would change, but I still had to sit as a tiny little child and watch this monster do unspeakable things to me. What the hell was this? Was I revisiting it to heal the memory, or was I suffering even more with mental illness?

Saturday 14 March 2015
Jay has been staying, it's been lovely having the company. It is clear that we are just friends now which is good. It was really great as I went out for the first time in months! He drove me to Shaldon where I managed to walk along the beach for a short distance, it killed me but I didn't care. We then had a picnic at Labrador Bay and Jay had brought his angel cards. I couldn't believe what I picked!

The first card was about temporary setbacks and to watch others' motives.

The second was Archangel Gabriel, the messenger and then... Archangel Raguel! Justice, better finance and paying off all debts! How he is going to pull that off Christ only knows!

Get in! It also said there was a new career change. It's just got to be the writing, I'd be so surprised if it isn't!

Those little signs that I got kept me going for a while. But I soon would have another dip as dealing with this condition is absolutely devastating to your mind and body. I remember I used to sneer at the people with M.E., the 'Yuppie flu', and just thought they were lazy hypochondriacs. My God, I regret that judgement now!

What I have noticed whilst writing this is at the time I had inadvertently started to write more and more in my soul journals. It was excellent therapy and I didn't even know it. I had made a decision though to ask for help, so my friend Darren would come in once a week to do any jobs that I needed doing, which took a lot of stress off.

Saturday 21 March 2015
It's very hard to know what's right, what's wrong and what to do, where to go, make any plans at all. When you have this condition you

try and find a hard place. Anything to take you from the dark abyss that you gestate in day after day, night after night. I keep fantasising about being in Spain, buying a house by the sea, being in love, blah blah. Perhaps the simple thing is to make myself happy here. Make the best of the roof I have over me here. It doesn't feel like home as I spend nearly every day in bed. I may as well be in a hospital room really. It's hard to know what will make you happy because you can't make plans. I don't know what I'm doing, what's going to happen. It appears that the other side are delving into everything even as far back as the assault at King George's. How incredible. So now I have to yet again go through every demon and no doubt every trauma for them to pick at and fault. Will my trials ever end? Am I really that disgusting of a human that this all happens to me deservedly? Will there be a happy ending? The cards and the spiritual side seem to think so. I think what they underestimate is if you are going to make it to the end of the rainbow. How much can a human take? There's only so much you can entertain yourself with when your body and mind feel dead every single day.

It makes me feel sick that my honesty and illness is to be dissected and I will no doubt be humiliated during this accident litigation. The synchronicity from Raguel has been positive for me. This last week I have isolated as I just don't want to talk to anyone. I had to go to Lupton to get paperwork done for the solicitor. Everyone asked if I was better. 'NO' you don't get better with this! It doesn't work like the flu for Christ sake! It's obviously going to be a very slow process. Its soul destroying and eats away at you like a cancer every minute that you are awake. Jay has been here. Sometimes I think it's good, other times I think it is a nightmare. One day is completely different from another. I hope I read this in a year's time and think thank Christ I'm on my way to a new life. I am totally comfort eating. I crave chocolate and sweet things like I have never done in my life. I am getting fatter every week. So I feel bloated, ugly and useless which doesn't help the process, but I simply don't give a flying fuck.

The only thing that jolts my heart, whom I have to make sure are safe and happy, is Teddy and Mia. Yet again my life force. Taking the job over from Meena. This life makes me feel like I am being punished. So self-hate dangles on a string enticingly before me. Karma works, the Universe reflects, so I must be bad, right?

I'm so tired of keeping myself in check spiritually or I will receive even more Karma. I feel guilty of every selfish thought as it may come back on me a hundredfold. I resent the good in other people's lives and how they are moving on, not good but I'm honest. I never know what's right. I never know what advice to take. I don't know what's good for me and what isn't. I thought I would be getting lots of treatments done now but the fact is I don't know if I will be wasting my money or if it's a long expensive process. The truth of the matter is, I really don't know anymore, I really don't. No matter what I do I end up paying for it physically. Going out, you end up in bed for days. I just need to 'be' at the moment as there is a small silent voice saying, rest, wait. But I don't know if it's right or wrong.

I will continue with my book when I feel well enough, who knows I may be a successful author!

Jesus I have an awful tummy, I am writing this on the loo! Darren put the stone pic up for me and the cabinet as a surprise. It looks so much better. Perhaps once everything is unpacked I will settle in. Half of my mind wanders to moving and not to unpack. It's all so confusing and unsure. I just don't know how to feel or what to do. I really don't. Tough times.

On writing out these last excerpts I can clearly see the natural stages of grieving working their way out. The denial of my situation, the anger and the guilt that I was expressing is so clear to see now. I may have felt it was dire at the time, but all along I was on my way to healing, who knew.

Isn't hindsight a fabulous thing?

Chapter 18

Akashic Wake Up

I think Julianus and all the people who were looking after me up there were getting pretty sick of my misery! So the next phase of my journey was to start hitting me right in the soul.

Dreams of my sexual attack as a child stopped abruptly after a few weeks of having the same dream every night. I was then having more pleasant dreams of me writing by the sea, surrounded by countryside and being happy.

The dream of me walking through the pine trees on to a beach kept repeating itself as well. The big plastic swans on a lake flashed and these huge water slides were ever present. I had no idea what they meant but it was respite from the sexual attacks I had to relive every night.

The dreams were so lucid they might as well have been real life. It was extraordinary.

The dreams, however, in a funny sort of way made me realise that I have had an extreme amount of trauma in my life. I started to look at myself as a little child, and I actually started to feel a little affection for that child and a sense of wanting to protect her.

It also gave me the strength to call the local care people as I knew I needed some help at home.

I went to Lupton on a good day on Friday, 17 April 2015. I felt good enough to actually get dressed and do the five-minute drive. When I got there I saw a flash of Julianus' face in my mind and so I decided to find a quiet space and meditate. As I went to sit down I spied a crystal ball in the corner of the room. I laughed at myself as I automatically went over and picked it up. Typical fortune teller's bit of kit! I sat for a while and then was shocked to see images starting to form from a swirling white mist.

My granddad used to scry through a black Victorian mirror which I now have, so it didn't surprise me to realise after the initial shock that I could see visions through a similar portal.

The word AKASHIC started to bubble into form. I knew what I was being told, to meditate in the layer of Akashic knowledge.

What is Akashic you ask? Exactly, I didn't have a clue years ago either! It was during many meditations, however, that I discovered what the Akashic records were.

In 2003, I kept getting the same meditation over and over. I didn't realise at the time that it was showing me the stage of where my soul was at. It was also trying to tell me that our souls are logged and monitored. I would walk along a rock path with jagged rocks to both sides. Khan, one of my guides, would walk along with me, let me go and I would sway off and fall into the sea.

Time and time again I had it during the first stages of my development in circle. I just didn't get it. I kept having the same meditation for about a year. It was doing my head in. Then, finally, I managed to stay on this path and got to some steps. Julianus was there smiling and so was my paternal granddad, Fred. He stepped forward and said,

"Well done! You've made it!"

I didn't have a clue what he was talking about. He then pointed to a set of big heavy dark wooden doors, and as I looked at them they opened. I walked up the three steps and entered on my own into a big marble hallway. The tiles were all chequered. As I walked along I saw metal plaques with names on. I walked closer to read a name as I wanted to prove to myself later that this was real. As I read the plaque it said, 'Harold Truman'. I didn't know who he was. Sorry, I know, history is so not my forte!

I then carried on walking, the hallway reminded me of the impressive halls that you walk through at the Old Bailey courthouse. The ceiling was exceptionally high with beautifully carved plinths on the walls. I could hear my soft footsteps as I walked past a very impressive statue; it was pure white stone and I had no clue who the figures were. (I have since discovered they were the first humans that had a soul placed within their bodies, most would refer to them as Adam and Eve.)

I continued to walk past the plaques until I saw another set of double doors. As I approached them, they swung open. I then saw a white-haired man, with half-moon glasses hanging on the end of his nose. He was writing with a quill and didn't look up initially. (I have subsequently discovered that he was Archangel Metatron, the scribe of God.) I hesitantly walked towards him and finally he looked up with firstly a stern expression which then led to a whisper of a smile.

"Please take a seat."

He motioned towards the chair I was standing next to. I sat opposite him with a huge marble desk separating us. The room was huge and spacious with nothing but crystal type shapes, stone and marble.

He then reached across the table to grab a huge book that was brown in colour, possibly leather. It had the most beautiful gold leafing around the spine, the front cover and around the title which read, 'AKASHIC' something (couldn't see the rest). As he hauled the massive book towards him I could see that all the pages were edged with gold also.

He then turned the book around and opened it up to face me. I could see entries in the book, but I couldn't understand the writing.

He then said,

"Congratulations, you are now able to sign this and enter into its agreement."

He then handed me the quill pen.

"Oh my God," I thought. "This is the blinking devil, I'm signing my soul away!" I hesitated for a second and he looked at me with the most loving and pure smile.

"Go ahead," he encouraged.

I then took the pen and started to sign the entry. I had no clue what I was writing as it came out in weird symbols and writing I could not understand, like Arabic or something.

Having signed this book he then snapped it shut and said nothing but, "Welcome!"

I then sensed I had to get up. He took my hand and I then turned back towards the door.

I walked back out through the hall and out through the doors to the arms of my granddad who gave me a big hug. He then said,

"Now you have signed, you can come to this place and use this!"

He led me to a large fountain that was throwing out the most beautiful green, silver and blue iridescent coloured water. He bent over and started to swirl his finger into the pool at the bottom of the fountain. The water started to twist and turn creating a whirlpool. I then saw one of my best friends' form in the pool.

"You can ask whatever you wish and see whatever you need to see."

I asked about her future as I swirled my finger in the water. I then saw her standing the other side of a rainbow from me, by her family. It felt that she would no longer be in my life, which felt ludicrous as I adored her.

The image then vanished. My granddad then said,

"Use it only when you need to, Nichola, if it serves you or the person for the greater good."

I was then taken by my granddad and Julianus along the rock path and they waved goodbye to me as I walked away. I then came around and was back in the room.

I had absolutely no clue what any of what I had seen meant, not a clue.

It wasn't until seven months down the line that I found out

what the meditation was all about. I met up with a dear friend Ian. He is the most inspirational, knowledgeable, pure soul that I have ever had the privilege to meet. When I explained to him if he could understand my meditation his jaw dropped open.

He had stated that he knew exactly what it meant. That I had been given permission to consult the Akashic record, the Book of Life, and only higher beings have that opportunity. The plaque names were most probably humans who had also been noted as Akashic consultants, and he believed that I was most probably signing the book in Aramaic. He then went on to describe the fountain as being the fountain of life, and that I have the ability and apparent permission to tap into anyone's path or life existence. Blimey heavy stuff, it was particularly gobsmacking as he had read and studied everything I had seen in my meditation and I didn't have a clue.

And for the record, I googled Harold Truman, an ex-president of America!

The other spooky thing was that the vision I saw about my best friend came true years later. She did and said such malicious things, and hurt me to the core over a family member of hers. The pool had been 100 per cent correct.

So when I saw the word form in the crystal ball, I knew that Julianus wanted me to start meditating at the pool and monitor my soul.

Then the most incredible thing happened. After my meditation, I walked down to the main office where some of my friends were. I was still feeling the effects of Julianus' guidance when I suddenly blurted out, "When I write that story that I dreamt about, I know I am not writing all of it. It's like an invisible force is telling me what to write. I write words I don't even know the meaning of! I am going to channel Julianus, have a chat with him."

Now I had not done any channelling at all since I had been ill. It was the last thing on my mind to channel guides or spirit beings. But there I was breathing deeply preparing myself to channel Julianus.

The first thing I remember was seeing hundreds of beautiful golden, blue, green and silver lights floating around me. I then saw Julianus.

"Don't worry," he smiled. "You are just seeing all of the elementals that are in the ether."

Elementals are spirits of the land. They can either be fairies, sprites, imps, animal entities; and some are good, some are not so great. I didn't believe in them, but I have seen far too many now to say they don't exist.

I remember relaxing and going even deeper into trance knowing I was surrounded by lovely elementals.

The next thing I knew I woke up and the girls were excitedly telling me that a lady called Elizabeth Bowen, who was a writer, was helping me with my writing and that she had picked me to work with.

Straight away I was hitting that Google button!

I was gobsmacked.

Elizabeth Bowen was a Victorian novelist. Among her works she used to write fantasy and supernatural fiction.

Wow, that really gave me a boost that day.

Julianus knows I have to prove everything that he shows me, so to see this woman's face come up on Wikipedia was incredible.

Thank you, Elizabeth, for helping me transition into realising my passion which is writing.

Thursday 23 April 2015
Well it's Akashic week! I did a bit of a meditation last Friday into the big crystal at Lupton as went there for an hour for coffee.

I saw a big tower with a crystal on top and in my mind heard "meditate with the Akashic records" and the name "Peter".

I then got locked out of my house on Wednesday and Donna turns up with a book, the Akashic record in her hand. She then says to me that I need to speak to a man that was written on the card, his name is PETER!

Still don't know if I should see Peter but defo need to meditate in Akashic energy!

Dreams have been quite prominent. Have been really positive, Monday, Tuesday. But I have overdone it again and am beyond exhausted. It's an emotional roller coaster with the most severe high and lows ever.

Can't remember my first dream but yesterday I dreamt of people being stabbed and blood everywhere!

It signifies an emotional cry for help!

NO SHIT!

Had a lovely man phone, Derek, today that runs a voluntary service so I think help is coming. I can't wait to get my front garden done as I will have a place to sit out. I'm trying to focus on positive stuff at the mo but finding it hard today. I hope that I wake up feeling better tomorrow. My hand and arm are hurting me so much writing this. I am so scared I'm going to be like this forever. I've got pain management help as well so who knows.

I didn't go to see Peter in the end. Looking back I know he could have helped me move quicker along my healing journey, but with free will if you don't take the opportunity up it leads to a longer struggle. I chose the longer route.

I also didn't initially delve into the Akashic records, but one day I sensed a presence in the doorway of my bedroom. It was Julianus. He had his hood up so I knew he meant business.

"Why are you disregarding everything I am trying to show you?" he asked.

"I'm not, you just don't get it, I'm too tired!" I complained.

"Nichola, you are not too tired to close your eyes and send intent to the Akashic layer. Do it!"

He then disappeared.

So I did what he asked. All I did was close my eyes and

focus on the word Akashic. I then would be taken on the most amazing journeys where the beauty of my surroundings would be an understatement. I started to see my soul as broken and I could see all of the celestial beings working hard to fix it. I felt responsible then that I must make an effort as they were. Every time I came round from a meditation, I felt inspired to do something which was extremely productive.

On one occasion during meditation, I saw steps, and as I trod on them I saw money signs flash. Archangel Raguel then stood before me and said, "Take action."

So I googled (God bless Google!) steps and money, and came up with StepChange. They were voluntary debt counsellors. They were a Godsend, well angel-sent if truth be told!

I realised that all of my money didn't have to go to these debt collectors in place of money for food and bills.

Before I knew it, I had money to get food deliveries. The credit people weren't taking my money any longer because StepChange were representing me. I didn't know as I had never been in debt before that creditors are not allowed to take money if it dips into your food and living allowances. I was giving them every penny!

So to have some financial freedom was amazing.

I could also afford a cleaner as I needed help. She made me cups of tea, changed my bedding and it was a bit of company as well. I also had a pain management counsellor turn up at my home every week. She was so helpful. She arranged an inflatable bath seat in the bath. The first time I got in that bath was heavenly. I hadn't bathed for months.

In one meditation, I saw the healing sign of the snake and called the doctors straight away afterwards and demanded a different GP.

I went to see my new GP in Galmpton and he was totally proactive on M.E. and fibromyalgia. He was also another heaven-sent human. I was being shown on no uncertain terms that if I meditated and went to their territory in the skies, they would tell

me exactly what I needed. It was incredible to experience.
Things were on the up.
But how long would that last?

Chapter 19

That's The Spirit!

The shift that was taking place was amazing. I had support around me and I started to attract even more help from my friends without even asking. Darling Leigh-Anne would still leave food bundles, and would come in and help heal me with laser light therapy. I would get taken on drives out so that I was not confined to the house so much. I started to like people being around me a bit more. One night during this time, I woke up at 4.44 as my computer had turned itself on and was playing angel music. I immediately googled 444:

I found that angel number 4 represented passion and ambition. It also reflects the four elements, earth, fire, water and air. With all the fours it means that all of the element energies and influences are heightened. It represents stability and forming solid foundations. Hard work and determination to reach my goals were needed. It also encourages you to work harmoniously and with intent to reach your goals and turn dreams into reality.

They were giving me a pep talk: "Keep on going, keep on fighting," was all I could interpret from this wake-up call.

I was still in terrible pain and had many symptoms, but I felt a bit more at peace with myself. I started to notice birdsong and the beauty of nature. I started to appreciate the simplest things in life that in the past I had taken for granted. I still had bad days and exceptional bouts of depression. The insomnia was also horrendous. Months and months without proper sleep at night can really mess with you.

I needed to be careful though with my nightly walks in the cemetery! I was walking up to the chapel one night where I would sit in the silence and pray. The chapel sits in the middle of the cemetery. I had my hooded white fleece on and took a hurricane lamp with me as it was pitch black. Someone must have seen me as they drove by as I heard a skid when they nearly hit the trees! I realised that they must have thought they had seen a ghost! I couldn't stop laughing about that!

I was getting more and more signs that I was on the right path. Dragonflies and butterflies would land on me having flown into the bedroom. I would get things moved in the house or objects go missing and then miraculously reappear. I was surrounded by synchronicity and signs all day and every day.

My next dream boot camp wasn't too pleasant though. My dreams each night were of the abuse that I had received off of my mum's husband.

Each night I would endure the punches all over again, the sneering comments of inadequacy would reverberate through my mind and body. The unwanted sexual advances would make me wake up feeling physically sick. I embraced them though. Somewhere deep inside I knew that I was being purged of all of my pain.

Tuesday 19 May 2015

Its early hours and I wonder if it's to allow me to think on things or insomnia! I believe that despite the severe downs of this condition, I have never been such a calm person, in touch with myself, a nicer, purer person. Julianus spent six months in a cave. I believe the time I am having now is the conditioning process which will be colossal. It certainly wouldn't have happened beforehand. I don't drink, I am starting to seriously look at what I eat. I feel comfortable in my own space and have so much time for introspection. Despite the physical, the spiritual is recovering, growing, shaping and preparing.

I'm completely in touch with the Universe. It is unbelievable how I am reminded in oh so many ways. I just did a card reading from a website. The thing I asked about was justice! It was so spot on even down to my illness. I keep getting the Emperor card, putting my trust in a man? Or would it purely be Julianus?

I had a housefly just sit on the bed next to me. I twice tried to shove it away but it refused to move. The next time I looked it had gone but I couldn't see it fly anywhere. I just went to look it up and inserted on the page was:

"Nothing can stop you now! You have the persistence and ingenuity to see things through."

It's reminding me to be persistent in reaching my goals which will bear fruit sooner or later and to act quickly to changing conditions whether favourable or not. Exponential source of abundance is available to me right now.

It's all going as it should. The court case is stressy but it will be, I trust the process completely.

I broke down the other day and said out loud, "Dad, I just want to know you are here, I'm finding it so hard."

Straight away my iPhone started playing Bridge over Troubled Water *and was then followed by* Somewhere Over the Rainbow, *then stopped, amazing.*

Synchronicity and signs from the spirit world come in all different forms, but one of the most common ways for them to communicate is through music.

My dad's favourite song was *Bridge over Troubled Water*, so he always plays that or arranges for me to be exposed to it so that I know he is around.

The Rainbow is my sign from Meena my first dog. So the song means that she is also present with me.

The iPhone played these two songs and then switched off. Totally unexplainable, totally paranormal.

Don't get me wrong. I had definitely shifted on my healing journey, but there was still an exceptionally long way to go.

I did feel the presence of my spirit family and angels, however, more and more. They were gently easing me into getting my faith restored.

What I also noticed was that I started to get cravings for certain foods and drinks. Out of curiosity I would google their properties and amazingly they were all beneficial for people with M.E. My body was telling me what I needed through these cravings. I started to feel an awakening. It was very subtle and exceptionally slow, but after my surrender under the moonlight and the shove by Julianus to go to the Akashic layer of heaven, I was, without realising it, finally steering myself in the right direction. The blackness was slowly starting to shift to a charcoal grey.

I had switched off from doing readings for well over a year. I had not been connected with any visiting spirit people as I had lost my confidence and needed time to heal. I was also scared that I had lost my ability, and I still had a fundamental belief system that I had been banished from the spirit world as one of their ambassadors.

They must have heard my fears!

I had been sitting out by my front door and the men who cut the grass in the cemetery had turned up. I went down to chat to them as I was starting to feel a little more confident in talking to people. I was getting used to meeting people with no make-up on, hair not brushed and wearing pyjamas. I didn't realise at the time that this was yet another shift in my self-esteem. I was prepared for people to see me at my rawest, no make-up, and no fake smiles. I was showing my transparency, the real me.

As I was chatting with one of the men, Dave, I couldn't believe what started to happen. To his right-hand side a spirit lady started to manifest right by him.

She was an older lady with light grey hair and quite rotund. She reminded me of my nan. I was so excited as I hadn't seen a spirit person for ages!

She started telling me that she had massive mobility problems before she passed, and walked with a heavily-burdened gait. She then did a little dance to show how pleased she was that she could move about again so freely! She was a very homely, friendly lady, and she made me pay attention to what she was wearing. It was a very smart beige two-piece suit. She kept telling me how important it was that I tell Dave what she was wearing. I'm sure she was his mum or mother-in-law. She kept trying to say a name beginning with J. I couldn't focus enough to see if she was saying Jane or Jo. I just wasn't strong enough to blend in with her to get the proper name.

I said all this to Dave, and he just looked at me with a blank face and said he didn't know what I was talking about. I felt crestfallen. The sceptical demon jumped on my back.

"See it's a load of crap. You are just making this up, he hasn't got a clue," was all I could hear in my mind.

I said goodbye and walked back to the cottage. I was crap, I wasn't a medium. That's what I kept telling myself, and to be honest it put me on a bit of a downer. Then something magnificent happened the following day.

I desperately need to get some paperwork done for Mark. I'm still reeling from my failed attempt at doing a reading yesterday. The computer wouldn't power up, so I am getting the double hump. I wasn't going to go out at all but I decided to go up to the computer shop. The battery had died even though it's fairly new. I wasn't too impressed as it was the first time I had used it since it was repaired. I got the new battery and thought randomly that I would pop into Lupton for a coffee.

When I was there a lady came up called Sharon. It was her first day out for three months as her mum had just passed. Turns out she is Dave's wife!

It also turns out that the lady I saw was her mum. She said that was her description and that she was so frustrated with her lack of mobility before she died. The Jo was Jody who missed her passing, her granddaughter. She said she didn't want Jody to see her pass and it was OK. FAB!

Sharon couldn't believe it and told me I had changed her life! She said that the suit that I had seen her mum wearing was a wedding suit. They buried her in that beige suit as it was what she wore to Sharon's wedding! She said that she hadn't slept since her mum's passing but truly felt that she would that night. How bloody wonderful...

What is even more amazing is when I got back home, the computer fired up as if there was nothing wrong! Someone, perhaps Sharon's mum, had drained the energy from the battery to make me get up and get a new one! I would never have left my bed otherwise.

I had forgotten the golden rule of mediumship. NEVER listen to your recipient, always trust the spirit person that is communicating. Sharon couldn't believe that Dave didn't recognise his own mother-in-law. What are the odds of meeting her husband in the cemetery then me randomly needing to go to Lupton at the exact time that Sharon went?

I was starting to feel the old jitter of excitement that I always felt when the spirit world spun out their miracles. It was a very important day for me. It was a day to show me that I had not been forsaken. I was a spirit ambassador. I was just being taken out from the world to heal my broken spirit and grieving heart.

Incredibly, when I got home I got an email from my friend Brett. He was offering to walk my dogs for me. So three times a week the dogs expectantly waited for their fun couple of hours out with Brett. The guilt of them being stuck in the garden had been lifted.

I was heightening my vibration, and with that you attract abundance and help from all quarters.

But nothing prepared me for my next spirit visitation.

I still can't believe now what happened.

My dead nan turned up, and yet again my life took on a whole new meaning.

Chapter 20

Go On That Facebook Thingy

Despite the recent positive events, there is always a comedown with this condition. The struggle to keep on going when you are in permanent pain and experiencing pure exhaustion is hard enough without all the other stresses of life. I had been given every single painkiller and absolutely nothing worked. I even tried cannabis but it just made me puke. I had also developed the worst heartburn ever, and was pretty low to be honest.

I even tried to come off of most of my medication to see if that would help. The doctors normally prescribe you with duloxetine, an antidepressant which is used for nerve pain. Trying to get off of that I would assume is akin to coming off heroin. It was nightmarish so I had to concede and stay on it, which I really didn't like.

I prayed every night for something medicinally to help me cope with the pain and other symptoms. The insomnia which had been running into years was also a major problem. My head was continually fuzzy and I was unable to deal with anything. I was also suffering every day with a bad stomach and had no idea why.

A small miracle happened in an innocent comment on a Facebook forum for chronic illness. A lovely lady from America suggested I start taking freshly chopped ginger in a glass of juice twice a day. My friend went and got me some. I couldn't believe it. Within hours the heartburn disappeared. I thanked the lady, we got chatting and she introduced me into a little group called the Barmy Sisters.

It was a private group of chronic illness sufferers from all around the world.

That group of angels will never know how much of an impact

they had on my well-being. We didn't all sit there moaning; we supported each other and had a laugh.

We have got so close that we send each other presents, cards and gifts. You must connect with people who know how you are feeling. No one else will ever understand it, trust me.

To this day we all stand united over the Internet, there for each other.

The abuse dreams stopped as quickly as they had begun. The last few dreams I was actually sitting there looking at the animal who had made me and my family's life a living hell. I was sitting there looking at him feeling sorry for him.

The healing for that phase of my life had obviously been completed.

I also had to surrender and accept that whenever I went out, which was rare, I would have to be in a wheelchair.

That is an experience in its own right! People treat you differently. They look at you like you are some sort of idiot. They also speak over you like you won't understand a word they are saying. Think on, people, when you next see someone in a wheelchair!

Tuesday 23 June 2015

Its 5 am in the morning and yet again I am awake and yet again it will fuck me up for the day. I knew that I would suffer though. I went out for the day Saturday on a major shop to warehouse and Trago. It was a long day out but I was wheeled around so I thought I would be OK. I'm still fucked and in pain three days later and of course I have no body clock whatsoever. The insomnia makes everything worse. I was going to write a lot but it's really hurting my hand. I'm feeling sorry for myself and lonely. Think I miss a cuddle and a kiss, I think that's what I miss. I'm eating shit loads of sugar like there's no tomorrow. I have been positive for a long time but the bust after the boom has brought me down. I can't be arsed to do the Tai Chi, write the book, just haven't got it in me at the moment. The fact I got no social life is getting to me a bit and the fact I can't get out with no repercussions is hitting me a bit.

I have been enjoying nature, naughty squirrel on the bird feed! But I suppose I have to honour this short dip. I am absolutely loving how the house is taking shape. Gonna try and write tomorrow. It's all about ISIS at the mo and nearly at the end of book one!

Bought a Ninja bullet so gonna do some smoothies. Sometimes I wish I was married and had an understanding soulmate who could give me a cuddle. But that isn't going to happen anytime soon. Just feeling a little sad. Just feel that I haven't got anyone really close. I just want to be a bit stronger, a bit more self-sufficient, so I can get out and about. I'm certainly improving but it is a long, slow recovery.

As I wrote this, I could see that I still had codependent issues. I wanted to be carried away on a white steed rather than face my life and have the strength and self-love to do it all myself.

Monday 29 June 2015

Struggling a lot this week. I'm paying for Trago but I am also concerned I need the Pregabalin which I have stopped. Had a very vivid dream about being on stage in a play.

The dream book says:

ACTOR – We may be using artificial personality or not taking charge of our own destiny. We are being given the opportunity to create a new personality. We need to take responsibility for our actions and the act of living.

STAGE – Making oneself visible. Representation of our own life play. Able to observe and be objective about what's going on. By externalising the 'play' into a framework we can manipulate our lives.

THEATRE – Life being highlighted. Need to be noticed.

All totally relevant.

Think I saw a mouse in the kitchen!

I bloody love living here. I might as well be living in the woods but naughty Cyril the squirrel has chewed through the bloody bird feeder little bugger!

I desperately try so hard but when I'm completely knackered and in pain it's bloody hard.

Keep Going!

I started to find that my dreams were constant messages from the Universe. They were either sending me symbolic guidance or healing my past traumas. They were so clear and easy to understand.

I then had the most amazing thing happen.

My prayers had been answered.

It was the evening of Monday, 27 July 2015. My mum had come down to stay with me. Her friends had driven her down. It was such a joy to have her there. She rarely left her house, so I knew how much effort this had taken her.

On the second night, I was in bed and the bedroom door was open. Everyone had gone to sleep. In fact my mum was snoring right next to me!

I saw flashes of silver light streaming across the hall. Ted woke up and sat motionless watching the lights. They were like slivers of light; like little tadpoles flying around. There was a glow to the left of the door which looked like someone had turned a small lamp on. The glow then started to exude a silver haze. It grew and grew until the whole of the landing was lit up. I then started to see a hand in the left-hand side of the door, followed by an arm and a body. I recognised it as my nan, my mum's mum, Eva. She was walking side on and stopped in the doorway. Her beautiful face then turned to me.

All she said was, "Go on that Facebook thingy."

That was it! She carried on walking and disappeared through the wall.

I could not believe what I had just seen. To be honest I was a little disappointed! She had come all this way to tell me to go on Facebook? What the hell? Obviously it was important so I immediately logged on.

The first thing on the feed was a lady crying her eyes out with happiness.

She was telling the story of how she had been in bed with M.E. for ten years. She then had discovered a drug called LDN (Low Dose Naltrexone) and within days was in the park with her grandchildren playing.

Now ordinarily I would have thought that this was a load of rubbish. However, my dead nan had just told me to go on Facebook and the first thing I saw was about M.E. There had to be something in it. I put to use my insomnia that night and researched the drug to death. (Pardon the pun!)

As the person who had created LDN didn't want it to be an expensive drug, he refused to sell it to pharmaceutical companies and therefore it hadn't gone through the FDA. It is described as a red label drug. It is a lottery apparently as to whether your doctor will prescribe it or not.

Its full-strength version is the HIV drug that was introduced to HIV patients so that they could lead a normal life. It also is used for drug and alcohol addiction. However, in small doses it helps M.E., fibromyalgia, MS, arthritis, Hashimoto's, dementia, cancer and any chronic illness or pain sufferers. I was so angry that it wasn't offered by GPs. You literally, like I did, find out about it and then push your GPs to prescribe it.

I called my lovely GP the following day. He didn't hesitate in prescribing it, bless his beautiful heart. I couldn't believe it.

LDN, if it isn't compounded from the main place, a chemist in Glasgow, comes in tablet form and you have to dissolve it in distilled water.

You then have to find your 'happy spot' by experimenting with how many milligrams your body can take dissolved in the water. I have to say after a few days, I started to sleep! I had had insomnia for two years, it was absolute bliss to fall asleep. There were teething problems initially finding the right dose but my God it changed my life.

It ended the restless leg syndrome. I did not need any other painkillers; the teeth-gritting agony had finally abated. It reduced my anxiety and panic attacks to near enough zero. It cleared my mind a lot more and started to make me feel that my body could actually make it through this life.

If you are suffering from any of the diseases I have mentioned, please consider this wonder drug. It may not be the cure but it will help. I will add though that there are thousands of people leading completely normal lives using this drug.

This is another crime against humanity: the drug not being readably available because it is a non-profit drug.

If you have to get it privately, however, it is not a problem. My new GP would not prescribe it and has never heard of it. So I pay £20 a month for it to be compounded at Dickson Chemist in Glasgow. This includes it being couriered to my door every month and the prescription fee. It's worth every bloody penny.

I once thought I would come off it as it has no side effects and you don't have to wean yourself off. The pain I experienced after day three of not being on it made me realise how incredible it really is.

I don't care if I have to be on it for the rest of my life. I would say that it improved my condition by about 60 per cent. But I would have that 60 per cent every day of the week, thank you very much!

Amazingly, I also got a call from Jay. He had just been diagnosed with M.E. It appears we had met each other to hold each other up. He helped me and I would go on to help him come to terms with his new life as an M.E. sufferer. What are the odds?

With this new drug in my system I finally started to feel hope. Thanks, Nan x.

Chapter 21

Here's To My Ex!

Despite me having definite signs of improvement from taking the LDN, I continued having this awful skin condition. The blotches also started appearing on my face and this resulted in me getting the most horrific cold sores that lined all of my lips. I would look in the mirror and sob as I looked like a freak. It was a weird sensation though as I didn't hate myself for looking so awful. I had empathy for myself, which was a very new feeling.

There seemed to be no end to my symptoms. As soon as something else popped up, I would google it, and sure enough it was yet another symptom of this relentless condition.

To see the physical blemishes appear on such a pale withdrawn face helped me to descend into bouts of depression that I had to claw my way out of with every single inch of strength that I could muster.

On top of this, those divine beings upstairs had decided that my next dream healing sessions would be about all of my relationships with men that had impacted me emotionally.

This turned out to be one of the most emotional healing phases yet.

I have had two long-term relationships. I adored both of those men. The first main relationship started when I was 20. As the years drew on, I realised that I was very young, and as we got older I started to feel the sense of drawing away from him. It was my decision to part. It was heartbreaking but I knew that he deserved someone who was 100 per cent committed to him and I knew that I wasn't. In hindsight he was the healthiest relationship that I had ever had. I walked from that. That said a lot for my sense of self and my reflection on relationships. He was good for me. I perhaps couldn't relate to that at the time as all I had ever known was abusive relationships when it came to men.

I was with him for nine years.

I ended up buying a house in Thundersley, Essex. Once I was in there for a while I started to regress back to what my self-esteem depicted that I deserved, unhealthy relationships. At the time I was on CID at Basildon. I would be a party girl, drink a lot and make sure I was the entertainment for all and sundry. I also started to enter into ridiculously one-sided relationships. They were either married or really didn't want me, but as I was so eager to please, these men could treat me however they wanted and I let it happen.

I feel so ashamed to write that I saw married men, but it was who I was at the time. Psychologically I can see now that I had no self-value at all. My previous partner had provided that confidence in me. He had provided the love that I obviously didn't have for myself.

Now, back on my own, I had regressed back into the abusive years where I was made to feel in no uncertain terms that I wasn't worth anything. Who in their right mind would want me? So with this energy pulsing through my soul, I went through one disastrous liaison after another. I would then sit crying after being treated like a bit of dirt, wondering why no one wanted me.

In a tragic way, I can see now that I was more comfortable being treated this way and abandoned because it was familiar to me.

I adored my dad, he died. I adored my mum, she chose a monster over me. I loved my brother and sister, but all they saw was a matriarch figure and not a sister.

That's all I could see in respect of my close family members and that stuck in my psyche.

I would not allow myself to be in a healthy committed relationship as I was convinced that they would eventually abandon me and with that I couldn't cope. So I would be used for sex or whatever these men required, and when I was tossed aside I could experience that same feeling of rejection again. It was ongoing self-punishment and I had nothing in my itinerary to stop it.

After a few years of this self-abuse, I then met my next main partner. I was 30 at the time.

I wanted to be with this man more than anything. But again I put myself in a chase to get him. He had baggage with three children and a very aggressive and difficult ex-wife. He also had a drinking problem. The issues surrounding our relationship attracted me because again it was full of drama and endless challenges.

I was with him for eight years. I ended up loving his children very much. I would say that he was the love of my life at that time. The drinking still was an issue and caused lots of problems.

I had during this relationship been retired from the police service and had entered into a long amount of therapy, so I did start to see the unhealthy way our relationship was chugging along at.

I finally found the strength to walk away from him. It was the hardest thing that I ever had to do as I was also saying goodbye to the children. Not a day goes by that I don't think of him. I can honestly say, if drink wasn't his first love, I would still be with him now.

My career as a medium was soaring when I had left him, so I sank all of my energy into it.

Being on a spiritual mission to help the world was all that I had on my mind, so thankfully I stayed away from men.

Then on my fortieth birthday, the loneliness and desperation monster of being alone reared its ugly head and I entered into a catastrophic relationship. I wanted to be like everyone else and have a person that loved me. I don't think I ever felt love for him but I pretended and went along with it because of my codependent issues.

I knew that he was wrong for me, I didn't trust him. None of my friends really liked him and my family certainly didn't. I didn't care though. I skipped over the reality of the situation and created an illusion of a perfect relationship.

So when he disappeared off of the face of the earth with all of my money, yet again I could play out my, "There you go again, Nicky, you are worthless and this has happened to you because that's all you deserve," number.

As I write this, it still amazes me what state my personal life and thought processes were in. In the spiritual arena as Nicky Alan I was the most self-assured, confident and happy person when doing my work. The real Nicky, the stripped back version, was a very insecure, vulnerable, scared little girl with many issues. I hated myself and was in permanent fear of people finding out about the real Nicky under the veneer of the smiling, bubbling energy of Nicky Alan.

So it came as no surprise that the spirit world were going to put me through the paces on my relationship issues!

There was one particular married man who stole my heart. We all have one, the one that got away. We still think about them and wonder what they are doing now. We still wonder what would have happened if it had continued. We all still think what would happen if they did indeed come back into our life.

Well he took up a whole week of dreams! It started on 27 July 2015. Every night there were different scenarios where we would be together. I would wake up most nights crying and sobbing as it felt like I was with him physically then and there.

Halfway through the week, though, the dreams started to take a different turn. They started to show how selfish he was, and his complacency in having an affair knowing his wife and children were at home. I was starting to be shown the reality of who he was and how I was being mistreated.

The end dream was surreal. I was smiling at him and telling him how sorry I was for him that he was in a marriage where he felt so weak that he had to seek other women to make him happy. I walked away from him whilst he was sitting on a bench. I was walking through a flower-filled meadow, and I remember as clear as day turning back and smiling. I said to him, "I am so sorry for your unhappiness and I am so sorry for allowing myself to be part of it."

I woke up feeling a shift of energy.

They hadn't finished with me though. All different relationships came popping up night after night. Some were sad, some were tragic and some were victorious. It was a very odd few weeks. During the day I would almost feel that I was back in that particular relationship. It felt like I had broken up with them the day before. It was painful but also strengthening as I honoured one messed-up relationship dream after another.

Monday 27 July 2015

Spiritually I am pretty pants at meditation, well visually. I tried last night and all I got was "LOOK AND LISTEN!" then I lost my focus and saw random crap.

My meditation is sitting watching the birds on the bird feeder. I am realising that meditation isn't just sitting with wafty music on and trying to concentrate. I sit in the cemetery and I am in my silence.

In fact I am learning so much about myself I'm actually very content to be just in nature. I love creativity and writing my book. I love the truth of simplicity. I love improving my darling home. I adore my cottage and cannot wait to get out and about in Kingswear and Dartmouth! So want to make the Regatta! I love the silence and the thrill of every chapter I write in Earth Walkers. *I know I will be writing more.*

It's been hell, there is no denying that but I just know there is a fairy tale ending, I just know it.

Every week I randomly sell something, so I am so being looked after financially and that was such a nightmare for me last year.

So apart from the M.E., my life is bloody lovely and this time no bloody man is going to fuck it up.

I think I'm starting to have a clearing as last night I dreamt of Dan.* I explained it to my friend this morning so perhaps it was another thing to get rid of, men! So I am going to draw the sea gaff of my dreams now! I hope that this positive energy remains.

Choose misery or happiness. Your choice!

The ex-partner dreams lasted for about a month. I want to say a huge thank you to all of the men I have been involved with. I no longer see them as mistakes. I see them as a valuable lesson to who I was and who I am now.

During this entry in my soul journal I had decided to draw a house of my dreams, a place I wanted to stay in abroad. The idea came completely out of the blue. Don't even ask me why I decided to do this!

Little did I know that this whim was in fact the first lesson from the spirit world on how to cosmic order and get the Universe to deliver your desires.

It has a massive impact on me later. It completely changed my every waking thought and intention.

I drew the house by a big lake in the Caribbean. It had a jetty at the end of the garden. As you walked up the jetty on to a stone path there was a sloping garden. To the right of the garden as you looked up at the house there was a swimming pool. The house had a lovely balcony looking out over the sea and the pool. I planned each bedroom, the kitchen, the lounge and even placed articles of furniture in it and where the TV would be.

There was a vast cellar area underneath where you could live or have a lower seating area. At the front of the house there were large metal gates that led on to a sloping drive with beautiful gardens. I even intricately drew the curled iron around the rods on that gate. The gardens were filled with all of the exotic plants that the Caribbean provides.

The entrance door to the house led into a vast open-planned area with marble flooring. The hallway gave way to the dining space with an open-plan kitchen and lounge. The back wall was nothing but glass affording the most magnificent view of the bay.

As I drew the front and the back of the house, I pictured in my mind every detail and me actually being in the kitchen making a cup of tea. I had even pictured in my mind where the appliances would be and exactly where I would stand to make the cup of tea.

I envisioned me being in my bedroom hearing the night frogs sing their chorus, and the gentle whisper of the sea lapping against the jetty.

I put myself completely in the zone of that house energy.

I envisioned sitting on the balcony looking out to all the beautiful foliage and the sparkling gems created on the crest of every wave.

I was there as I drew my house.

I thought that I was just embarking on a fantasy to cheer me up as I drew every last detail.

You will not believe what happens later. I enter into a whole new ball game understanding my relationship with the Universe.

Chapter 22

Meet My Crew!

It has occurred to me that I have mentioned Julianus, Khan and Catherine, and you must be thinking, well who the bloody hell are they?

As you have most probably figured out by now, I am not a fluffy psychic that wears cobweb dresses and thinks everything is spiritual. So when I introduce you to my guides, I can tell you now that they proved their existence in more ways than one!

So here goes:

Let us start with my dear Julianus. He is my main soul guide and is basically there whenever I need him.

I first became aware of him in my early 20s. I had no clue who he was. I used to meditate and go to this little shack on a remote island. There I would see all of my spirit family sitting around a fire in the middle of the building. This grey-haired, heavily-stubbled man would be sitting in the corner wearing what appeared to be a brown sackcloth habit with a rope around his waist. He reminded me a little of the TV character *Steptoe*!

Honestly, he had a very scruffy appearance. I chose to ignore him and would just say hello to my nan and dad!

How awful, Nicky! You naughty girl! But he said nothing, he would just smile and stare at me. I couldn't for the life of me imagine why he was always there for years not saying anything.

I now realise that I was in the police then and obviously wasn't ready to meet him and walk my path alongside him. After being retired from the police it didn't take long for him to introduce himself!

I was sunbathing in my back garden, it was a glorious summer's day in 2003. My mind was at rest listening to the birdsong in the garden. I was totally relaxed and feeling completely calm. I decided to do a little meditation.

I suddenly felt exceptionally cold and realised I was in a cave. I could smell the damp moist soil on the cave floor and hear the incessant tap-tapping of a water source somewhere nearby, dripping on to the rocks. I started to try and open my eyes, but realised that this was an important meditation as I heard a voice say,

"It is time that I introduced myself. I am Julianus. I will show you how we met and that I have been responsible for you ever since."

Now when I say, 'heard a voice,' it's a bit different from human hearing. Sometimes they are discarnate, in the ether, like a proper human voice. The majority for me are in my head. It's like a loud insistent thought that you know is not your own; I can sense the tone and accent easily. A bit like when I channel through spirit people during readings, or the angel realms. They all have a different energy and power. The angel realm voice is like a startling command, it's quite amazing.

Well this voice was melodic and velvety with a slight Italian accent. I fell in love with the energy of this stranger's voice immediately. I was intoxicated with each word.

The rocks at the entrance of the cave then started to drag open. I walked out and found myself in a very hot climate looking out at a beautiful landscape lined with Cypress trees.

I asked, "Where are we?"

He replied, "Trastevere, Rome."

"What is the year?" I asked.

"1452."

"Why am I here?"

"This is where we shared a life together, your name was Mary."

I then felt a massive whoosh as if I was lifted into the air, and found myself outside a stunning church with white pillars fronting the entrance. I looked up and saw the name of the church, ST CECILIA'S.

This man that I then recognised as the man who had been sitting in my shack for years took my hand and said,

"You were welcomed here in the House of Mary Magdalena in this year."

I looked into his bright blue eyes and wanted to cry; the care and love that exuded from them was indescribable.

He then took me through to a courtyard and led me through an archway to the left. He pointed to the arch and said,

"Here I write the word of the Lord. My prophecies will remain here intact forever." We then came out through the arch and were standing by a tomb, St Cecilia's tomb.

"This was your home, Mary."

In the sun I looked to the crypt and saw the outline of my habit in silhouette form. It had a square shape.

He then said,

"I have someone for you to meet."

A man approached me with the most beautiful thick wavy hair. His face just represented total serenity and love. He took my hands and said,

"Mary, I am Nicholas, I preside over you and the men in this space. I am here to protect you." I saw the letter V in my head.

He placed a kiss on my forehead. I could feel the emotion spread through me like an unknown heat. His love was infinite.

He looked up to the sky and said, "Come, we must make haste, Ava Mary is upon us!"

He gently led me towards the church where I heard the most stunning chanting.

I was then 'back in the room' as they say. I was wide awake and crying my eyes out. It was one of the most beautiful things that I had ever experienced in my life.

Once I had blown my nose the next thing, as all ex-detectives would have done, was hit the Google button! It was a weird experience because every time I tried to google St Cecilia's I would get to a link but then the computer would go down or the Internet was lost. I sensed that perhaps it wasn't the right time. To be honest I was a little scared that my miracle introduction was just my imagination. I didn't want to discover that it didn't exist. Silly me!

From then on Julianus was a regular visitor. He was quite a sombre man in those days. In trance he came across as very foreboding and took no nonsense. He even used medieval Italian and sometimes Polish words that were recorded and translated into lucid messages. It was simply amazing.

But there came a time when I realised being a spiritual ambassador wouldn't just work on my word only. I needed proof that he and I existed, so that I could challenge the sceptics with my evidence. I decided to get a ticket to Rome.

In Rome, I got to the hotel, dumped my suitcase and went outside to hail a taxi. I cannot tell you the fear that smashed through me as I got into the taxi and asked the driver, "Can you take me to St Cecilia's church, Trastevere?"

He just said, "Si."

My heart was beating out of my mouth as he drove straight into a square and stopped.

I looked up and let out a gasp mixed with a sob. I was in St Cecilia's Square and was looking up to the familiar church frontage with the white pillars and 'Santa Cecilia' written as bold as anything across the rendering.

I walked through the courtyard in a daze looking at everything I had seen years before in my meditation.

I could see the gated area to my left that I knew led to St Cecilia's crypt, and the archway that had Julianus' writing etched into it. I was exceptionally frustrated as the gate was locked.

I then walked into the church and saw a bust of a monk. It was a Franciscan monk, which I later discovered did a sabbatical in a cave prior to serving God. That explained the cave then! I went on to discover that Julianus was here in 1452, and did write words of prophecy in the arch that lead to the house of Mary Magdalena. Nuns were welcomed into the church here in 1452 where they were allowed to reside with the monks.

It was simply staggering. I was standing in a place that I knew so well, 500 years later!

To say it was overwhelming was an understatement. Now I knew why I was always completely at peace in churches despite not being religious. I had to have incense burning all of the time as well. I just couldn't stop crying. I also learned that 'Ava Mary' was what they called the Ave Maria prayer in that time which was chanted at sunset, hence why Nicholas looked up to the sky.

"Nicholas," I thought, "I now need to find Nicholas."

Reluctantly I left the church and headed straight for the Vatican.

If you have ever been to the Vatican you will know it's like a house for giants. It is colossal with thousands of people wandering around everywhere. Well I knew it like the back of my hand even though I had never been to it in this life. I went straight over to a guide and asked quite impatiently,

"Where is Pope Nicholas V's crypt from 1452, please?"

The guide looked into his guidebook.

"No, he is not here, Signorina."

"Yes he is! Look again," I said, frustration lacing my words.

"No, Signorina, there is nothing here."

"Oh don't worry!" I said abruptly, which was quite out of character for me.

I then turned around like a woman possessed, and walked towards this concrete opening with complete confidence and bounced down the stairs frantically.

The second crypt on the right, I threw my body over and sobbed like a baby. I had nuns coming up to me asking if I was OK! I then looked down to the plaque and saw, 'Pope Nicholas V'. From his details I saw that he did cover the Trastevere diocese during 1452.

I was so amazed and humbled at the same time. Previous incarnations, soul guides and everything I had ever seen since a child was real; this was never a figment of my imagination. I had proved it to myself.

After what seemed a lifetime I reluctantly pulled myself away from his crypt and went back up to the main hallways.

Amazingly the same guide came running towards me.

"Signorina," he smiled. "My apologies. How did you know of his crypt? It is in no guidebook, but I asked one of the oldest guides here and he told me it was indeed down below in the crypt room!"

I had no words to answer him, I just smiled.

"You are a special lady, come with me!"

The next thing, he was guiding me towards this small shop in the Vatican.

"Go buy two phials."

Without questioning him I went into the shop and picked two small bottles. At the till the lady gave me my change. I looked at the coins and said,

"This is unusual, you have given me a gold coin in my change!"

"It should not be here, it is the Vatican's currency." She frowned looking confused.

She was obviously in two minds as to whether it should be given to a member of public.

She hesitated but then made her decision, "Well it was obviously meant for you, take it!"

I thanked her enthusiastically. Wow, one of the Pope's special gold coins!

I then gave the two phials to the guide, and he spoke in Italian on his radio.

An armed man with an earpiece then arrived and spoke to the guide, and then they both looked at me.

He smiled at me and then took the two phials.

I had no idea what was going on. A little later he returned with the two phials filled with water.

"This is from the Pope's private font. Take it with you and use it wisely," the guide smiled.

I couldn't believe it! I took the phials, and thanked him and the armed guard with so much zest they must have thought that I was a nutter! How lucky was I?

I have asked sceptics, very well-known ones in fact, about my story. They have said that they can't explain it, but it's not supernatural (?) or I fell asleep in front of a history programme! What nonsense!

Khan is my healing guide; he is always there when my health dips or I have a crisis.

He is very tall, a Native American Navajo and is exceptionally handsome. He has long dark wavy hair with the most stunning green eyes and a headband that sports a white feather with a red tip. His tribal name is Hammer Hawk, which is explainable as he always carries one in his right hand. He told me that he was my father in Arizona in the 1800s, and lost me when the white men had taken our lands. He referred to them as the Buffalo (I assume soldiers). He said that we lived on the plains and walked many miles during our life. He introduced himself when I was in my first development circle in 2004.

Straight after the meditation, the circle leader said, "You have a new guide, his name is Hammer Hawk."

This was affirmed a second time when I was at the Arthur Findlay College a few months later. The Arthur Findlay College is a centre for spiritual development in Stansted, Essex. A psychic artist drew Khan with hammer hawk in hand sporting his white feather with a red tip. She then wrote 'Hammer Hawk' at the bottom of the page. He calls me Ankalla (or a word like that). I was told by a Native American that this means daughter. Everything from my funeral, to where we lived and what we lived in was corroborated on research. I have yet to go to Arizona to find my old tribe.

Catherine came to me also in 2004, when I found myself exceptionally frustrated by not being able to pick up on people psychically. I could see spirit people around them but could not blend with the person in front of me at all. I ended up running out (to my shame) of a psychic class as I could not for the life of me read a person. The following day, Catherine introduced herself. She was standing on a cliff in Cornwall wearing a black hooded cloak. She has pagan origins as well as Celtic. She reminds me of Catherine Zeta-Jones. She had rune stones in her hand, and as she blew on to them they turned into doves and flew away.

She then said to me, "You now have the art of prophecy."

The following week in my own teaching circle, four students came out of their meditation describing Catherine and naming her. Since her appearing, I have been able to see people's life path, their soul, their futures, their past, internal ailments and illnesses. She sometimes appears as a hag in a hut in a forest. This is when she needs to bring me medicine for the soul or teach me something important. She was a healer but escaped the witch inquisitions in the 1600s. She also tells me what crystals to wear when major events are coming up. I adore her, she is my rock. She showed me a previous life in Devon, which I have discovered and proved but that is for a different book! This is why I feel I have a massive pull to Devon and Cornwall.

So there they are, my crew, they must be one of the hardest-working bunch for looking after me! I now know from their evidence that reincarnation and guides definitely exist.

Now let me get back to my story...

Chapter 23

Hello from the Other Side (2)

DC 3098 Nicky Morley. It is still bittersweet when I see my old police title in black and white. When I see a police car go by, I get a pang of wanting. Being retired from my job was the hardest thing that I ever had to endure. I found out who my true police friends were. A lot faded and some stayed in touch. The institution of the police service and the 'family' you find yourself in leaves you bereft when you are out of it.

I felt alone, lost and very isolated. I learned to steer away from any past colleagues on Facebook. I didn't want and couldn't handle contact with people who I had laughed, cried and worked hard with during some of the best years of my life.

I found if I watched anything police orientated on TV, I would have nightmares about being in the police but not belonging there. It was a haunting that resumed year after year.

It was no surprise that my following healing period was to seriously nip this pain in the bud. My next phase of dreaming was being in the police every single night.

It would range from being in the Major Investigation office wearing a tracksuit and trying desperately to order a police uniform as I was no longer a detective, to back in the early days patrolling in the police car in uniform. There were a lot of injustices towards the end of my service, and the exit from my precious career was akin to being discarded like an old rag. People who had been in the wrong were especially highlighted in my dreams.

The dreams were so real that I felt myself physically in that time and space reliving the pain or joy of whatever dream was brought to me. During the first few weeks I had nothing but anger and sadness ripping through my soul when I was awake. I would look over old photos of when I was in the cadets and pictures of when I was at social evenings. There was one particular photo of me when I was night cover on CID. Someone took an instant Kodak picture of me with one of the night shift officers. I cried a thousand tears as I looked at this photo regularly. The pain was so intense it was remarkable.

I didn't realise how much trauma leaving the police had marked my heart and soul. The dreams went on and on week after week.

I felt like I was perhaps entering into another breakdown. My friend Leigh-Anne who is psychic then called me one day. She evidenced and described my family members. She described my paternal granddad Fred and nan Doris. She even brought through my old pony Bimbo! My dad came in, our old neighbour Pam, and even one of my oldest friends Jean came and said hello. All of their messages were different but held the same fundamental tone.

"Hang on in there, we have your back."

Friday 14 August 2015

Been a dark couple of days. Been up and down with the LDN, so now on 1 mg as .5 did nothing. Dissolving it into distilled water. Feel like shit. Feel very depressed and have aggressive mood swings. Feel disconnected again. The dreams of being in the job and hated have come back every night. I don't know how to release it. I have been made aware of a thing called the Dark Night of the Soul, I have to read about it, I think that I am going through it. I hope I am as it means I will come out the other side. I'm so bored and sick of being stuck in my home. I tried to meditate but fell asleep after about five minutes! I have no motivation again which kills me mentally. It's so fucking hard having no life, no family. I have decided to go to my mum's for Christmas. Christ knows how I'm going to get there!

I got an inflatable cushion for the bath so I can have a sit-down shower which is lovely! I also sat on Thursday and had a look at the meteorite shower which was nice, listening to the crickets and watching the shooting stars. It's beautiful here. The garden is coming on, so frustrating that I can't tend to it. I have to ride this through and desperately hope that it gets better. Come on, LDN!

Looking back at this, even though I was suffering, I was finding ways to try and get positivity and mindfulness into my life. I had no idea I was doing it, but seeking solace in nature and appreciating simple things was automatically happening now. I was being taught perfect ways to improve mental health and happiness, and didn't even realise I was in a spiritual series of lessons in an invisible classroom.

I also found out about the dark night of the soul. It is a spiritual episode that takes you through your own personal darkness in order to heal you. Give it a look online and see if it resonates with you.

Readings from my friends were very important to me. They were my stabiliser and proof that I was being looked after by invisible forces.

I had a destiny card reading. The destiny book delivers your reading through numerology and astrology. It gives you details of your destiny reading from your last birthday to your next one.

I can tell you now everything that was written in that reading came to fruition. It was scarily accurate. Just to demonstrate how amazing us light workers are and how the divine works, here is the reading:

7 CLUBS DISPLACEMENT CARD
Underlying all the different events and experiences of this year will be a subtle personal challenge that you will be facing and working on.

This will likely be that of your learning to adopt a more positive attitude and a more positive expression of your ideas and feelings.

The 7 Clubs represents a higher spiritual mind. In its highest state, this card brings profound realisations about the true meanings of life along with a sense of unencumbered freedom from all life's worries and fears.

You might say that this is one of your goals this year, to achieve more of the high side of this card. In doing so, you may face negative patterns of thought and communications that are holding you back in an old habitually negative response to life. If you are interested in spiritual philosophy and concepts, this will be the year that you have to put these into solid practice.

This may seem a difficult year in some respects, but it has a very good purpose as seen from a higher perspective.

You are being prepared for a rebirth into a newer much higher life than you have been living lately.

After all, you are in the middle of one of the most significant circles of your life, one which peaks next year as you reach the pinnacle position.

This year of mental housecleaning will be just the right kind of preparation you need to fully experience the wonderful changes that are coming.

2 CLUBS LONG RANGE CARD

The 2 Clubs tells us that a partnership involved in some Mercury ruled activity will play a major role for you this year. Mercury rules the WRITTEN and spoken word and all kinds of mental activities.

Studying, teaching, writing, publishing and advertising all fall under this jurisdiction.

This also indicates that meetings or discussions and arguments could be the major theme this year as well.

You will be wanting to share your thoughts and ideas with others and this will probably attract a lot of other people into your life this year. The 2 Clubs can even represent your being somewhat afraid of being alone, but this might just be what you need to motivate you into seeking others to be with.

Just how you communicate with others will be brought to your

157

attention this year in a big way.

You will most likely find yourself in one or more situations that require you to develop harmonious lines of communication with others, there may be one special person with whom you share many ideas and thoughts who becomes the focus of this year for you.

In any event, your ability to share what you know with those around you without arousing their opposition will be in focus.

As you continue on my journey with me you will see how these cards were amazingly accurate.

My dad's birthday is on the 27th August. I was somewhat dismayed that I hadn't got any signs from him; but in true form, by late evening I got a random message sent to me from my medium friend Carol who had just been visited by my dad! I hadn't really stayed in touch with her through my illness so it was a surprise to hear from her.

He said the following:

"On the 5th of the month, you will be signing contracts and papers to do with a house move. The change in your medication will help you. After Christmas there are new beginnings and happy times."

She didn't know that my dad's name was Alan.

Carol – "He mentions the name Alan but also said Michael will be massively significant in the New Year."

As I read this I remember thinking, a house move? Is he having a laugh? I have no money and am going nowhere from this cottage! I also could not envisage happy times ahead or new beginnings. I had no idea who Michael was, but my God the significance in my future was colossal. My dad had also mentioned Michael all that time ago in Turkey.

Incredibly I then got another message a day later from another medium friend of mine, Julia, who needed to give me a reading! Again I had not heard from her for a while and she had no idea of my circumstances.

She wrote:

"Fear at the moment – this feels related to things not working out as planned and also I feel there is an element here about people around you – like who you can truly trust.

All you want to do is rebuild and lay down those foundations for your future which yes does involve money and the materialistic side of life.

I do feel we need to keep going with writing a book as I see success coming, we just need to kerb that feeling of being trapped.

Saying that everything happens for a reason and I feel this quiet time, when you feel well and able, is to finish the book.

10 cups and 6 wands are screaming yes, the book will be successful and with your final card, the magician you just need to keep going as there are opportunities around the corner.

Even though you feel disconnected you need to learn to gain trust in your own intuition more.

The Brian Card is a fab one, I love it when a plan comes together – SUCCESS – pat yourself on the back as all that hard work and effort will pay off.

I am seeing you moving in April, but you really are going to weigh it up, should I stay or should I go?"

Yet again I got another reading talking about me moving and about my writing. I really, in the pit of my stomach, felt that the writing was an escape and not a future career option. I also couldn't understand about staying or going.

Incredibly a couple of weeks later I got a message from Carol again saying that she needed to talk to me. My lot up there were really working hard to get the message across. They could obviously sense that I was losing faith and needed assurance.

This is what Carol said on 29th September 2015:

"Your dad is saying that the medication is working. You also need to start using natural remedies and foods. You will connect with a TV producer in the year. Your health will be better after Christmas but you are still in the process of deeper healing. They are still cranking up your engine to get it working properly. Are you moving? You also need to bring yourself back into society and around people. You are going away at Christmas. You have to be positively thinking with the spirit world. You have lost your confidence, stop worrying they will be there when you are ready."

She then described my mum as being unwell and my friend Jean came through again.

"Watch caffeine! Drink only herbal stuff. Flush out all of your toxins. Everything is coming back to you. When feeling negative be mindful of not going really down.

You will decide to move January, February time. The time is right.

It is like you are going through a repair at the body shop. They are putting all the bits together ready for the road. 22, 27th is significant. There will be positive links to America. Don't give up hope. There will be magazine work starting up again. The publishing will bring you a boost. Everything coming back even better than before. New people coming in, new work. Let go of the negative people that used you and abused you. The black mist is leaving your body. Next year is so much better. The LDN is excellent and will change you slowly. Carry on writing."

My friend Jean then popped in again.

"Jean is going to help you. At the hospital be empowered. Say how it is. Don't feel intimidated, there will be a solicitor involved with this as well."

All of the moving thing and the new life seemed a million miles away. Yet again writing seemed to be an important direction for me, but I just couldn't see how I was going to get writing jobs when I had been out of the loop for so long. Needing a solicitor around a hospital environment, what was all that about?

Little did I know that everything that you have just read may have just been the end chapter of this book.

Spirit people, guides and angels know the path we have planned. They know what is to come. When you are down on your knees they will jump in and send you messages to keep you on your path of faith. By the end of the year I did indeed meet a TV producer, Annie, who I am still in contact with now.

I also found out why I would be involved in a disgraceful situation with a doctor and a solicitor. My solicitor Mark was trying to get rushed medical evidence in for my accident claim. He arranged for me to see a pain specialist in London. My friend Lin offered to take me, bless her. The journey up on the train was horrific. I was sitting in my wheelchair in agony. The pain and the exhaustion led to nausea, severe anxiety and dizziness. By the time we were sitting in the hotel in London, I was broken physically and mentally. The following day Lin helped me dress and she pushed me to Harley Street. I was exhausted, emotional and in pain. I really had no clue where I was or what day it was. By the time this doctor called me in I was shaking, in tears and beyond able to cope following such a harrowing journey. He looked at me as if I was a hypochondriac. He filmed me and got impatient when he tried to move my limbs as I was screaming out begging him not to move me. Everyone with this condition knows even to touch your skin is like feeling molten lava hit you. The pain is excruciating. The doctor kept tutting and was so clearly disbelieving my pain and exhaustion. That trip took me four weeks to get over.

The doctor sent a report to my solicitor basically saying that I was a malingerer and there was no evidence to suggest why I was in so much pain. He basically made me sound like I was over exaggerating. This ignorant 'specialist' had sealed my fate. I was in no way going to receive anywhere near to what I had lost. I felt humiliated and angry. Yet again I had been forsaken by the medical profession. No matter how much I argued, the doctor's report was all the defence had to go on, so I pretty much had lost before I even started.

Despite this knock-back, what was to come was truly mind blowing.

Chapter 24

There Might Just Be a Future

The LDN was starting to help me improve. I made it a goal every morning after Ted woke me up to lay on the settee in the lounge rather than in my bed. I also started to take very small walks every day along the cemetery path. They say that graded exercise (GET) works for people with M.E. That's absolute rubbish. You must never force yourself to exercise as your body literally cannot take more than just keeping you alive.

The beauty of this condition, I started to learn, was that you have never been so conscious in your life of what your mind and body need.

I could feel the need and ability to try the walks, so I did.

I also made three goals to achieve every day.

It didn't matter if I failed to achieve them. They could be putting some washing on, making sure I cleaned my teeth and actually making something to eat. They were things that any other healthy human being would take for granted, but for us chronic illness sufferers these tasks are an immense victory.

My police dreams had ended after weeks of them being relentless. The last ones were pleasant dreams where I was at my most happiest, in uniform at Epping police station. Amazingly just after they stopped one of my oldest friends from the police, Lindsey, asked if she could come and stay completely out of the blue. I hadn't seen her for many years. I of course said yes and found the visit a pleasant one! We laughed so much at the antics we got up to in the police. It was cathartic. I also knew that it was a final conclusion to my pain of that particular loss in my life. We are now the closest of friends after all these years.

That month I remember watching a programme about a veteran who had been blown up in conflict. He was so badly damaged that his family were given a dire prognosis, and it was recommended that he be switched off whilst in a coma, his body broken. They said if he did regain consciousness he would be in a vegetative state.

The programme followed the journey of this amazing man who through sheer grit and determination learned to talk and walk despite missing limbs.

He then trained himself to go on a huge canoeing venture with fellow injured vets in Canada. He succeeded in freezing conditions, where even the healthy volunteers struggled.

I figured if he can do that I can get on a holiday. My friend Wendy was living in Grenada and had kept asking me to go out there. I knew that I was not going to even make it to the airport so I always politely declined.

But something in me kept pushing the notion of going out there, on a daily basis. In the end I gave in and booked the flights for May the following year. I couldn't believe that I had taken the first step to having a future goal to aspire to!

I was also getting encouragement in the strangest ways:

Wednesday 21 October 2015
Yesterday I was sitting in the garden feeling quite tired and had just thought about whether I should walk the dogs. I decided that I wouldn't but in that split second a robin flew up and skimmed the whole of my leg, landed in the spirit tree and just looked at me. It made me smile and I just knew it was a 'get up off your arse' moment, so I did and ended up walking right to the end of the path where I could see the estuary in Dartmouth. It was a beautiful sunny day and it felt great to see the sun glittering off of the water. I can't wait to be well enough to go to Dartmouth and mooch around the shops!

I was a bit achy when I got back in the hips and lower back but nothing outrageous. I did a lot today, again a bit achy but not agonising. The balance is shifting! I'm getting more good days than bad. The new beginning is starting next year. I'm going to make up

for everything I missed out on. I'm going to holiday and dive like it's
going out of fashion.
     My God I think I'm going to make it!

Two things that I want to mention here. My spirit tree was a
small tree that I had fixed Tibetan ribbons to. I had also added
fairies and angels in the branches. I had fixed dragonfly fairy
lights around its boughs so that whenever I wanted to sit and
relax and think of the spirit world, the tree would give me a
reminder.

I also want to talk about the robin. Remember when I described
animal totems before? I started to get the oddest things happen
by wildlife right in front of me, and various animals would turn
up in my dreams. When I googled what they represented, it
made total sense what they were trying to say to me.

As an aside, the most peculiar spirit animal that I ever got
involved with was when a lady in Essex phoned me up scared
out of her wits. She kept finding a blackbird in her lounge every
morning.

I agreed to go round fully believing that they were coming
in through the chimney or something. My interest piqued when
I realised that her chimney had been capped and there were no
holes or places that the bird could get into, in any part of the
house.

I asked her to monitor it and three days later she was still
finding a blackbird in her lounge.

I went round and linked up to the spirit world to see if it was
anything paranormal. Straight away the lady's mum blended
with me. She was a very formidable lady with a sharp wit and
strong personality. After her proving her identity with names
and dates she then went on to laugh.

She said, "Tell my daughter she has a very bad memory. I
said before I died that I would come back and haunt her as a
blackbird because she hates the things!"

When I told the lady, she changed to a curious shade of grey. She then laughed and cried as the memory came flooding back.

After that day the bird never returned again. I am sure that the phenomena of what had happened to her will resound in any dinner party for the rest of her life!

So as I said before, if you have any creature that acts oddly in front of you, see if that creature connects to anyone in the spirit world. If not, google the animal under animal totems and I can bet you anything that the message that animal brings will ring true to your current situation.

2 November 2015

Something amazing happened today. I have had a serious dip and been in bed since Thursday, today is Monday. Leigh-Anne and her mum Lin turned up with a veg juice that she was inspired to make for me. I drank it. She then said that I needed to purge. We went upstairs. Lin placed her hands on me which were on fire. We lit my amethyst candleholder and Leigh said that she needed to shake something. Enter the healing rattle. She then burnt sage and before I know it I'm releasing groans, sobbing and crying my whole heart out!

It was amazing and through the whole time Teddy was laying on the back of my knees almost grounding me.

I then came down to write this listening to Krishna Das. I pulled an angel card:

ARCHANGEL MICHAEL

The angels have sent you this card because of the positive changes coming into your life.

Expect and enjoy beneficial new opportunities as they present themselves. This is an optimal time to make big and small changes.

Take the leap with the knowledge that everything will work well for you.

Old blocks are lifting and everything now moves forward quickly. If recent events shook your faith, you'll now see how they were actually positive for you.

Rapid advancement is likely now!

I was so happy to read this but surely it wasn't going to all be hearts and roses? Should I buy a house if I got a payout? Should I move? Should I stay renting? How could I when I was up to my neck in debt? How was I going to be strong enough to move or start changing my life? How was rapid advancement even possible?

Little did I know that Archangel Michael was going to take over my life in such a huge way. I still can't believe it when I look back.

I also had a massive epiphany when Leigh and Lin did their healing session.

I knew that I had to change what was going into my body.

I started to drink vegetable juice smoothies. I started to end drinking caffeine as it had been mentioned in a recent reading anyway. I also started to limit sugary foods.

I allowed Leigh and Lin to help me more. When I was feeling bad, I would have the courage to phone and ask for help. I would stay at Lin's and be looked after. It took a lot for me to ask for help, but I was so glad that I did it. Just to hear the energy of a family moving around the house whilst I was in bed felt comforting and less lonely.

I will never forget their kindness, compassion and unlimited love when I needed it the most.

I decided to be with my mum for Christmas. I saved my energy for the drive and managed to get there. I spent most of Christmas in my pyjamas but at least I was with family.

Wednesday 30 December 2015
So I am here at Mum's drowning out the bloody telly! Listening to a chakra clearing meditation. It's been a mostly stagnant year. I have an exceptionally slow recovery but have to honour that. I have started to make a really lovely home with roots being planted. I hope I can get out

more and meet people in the New Year. I have felt despair, loneliness, sadness, defeat but I have also conquered this through strength, courage, determination, peace, calm, self-love and self-discovery.

I have no clue where I will end up but I suppose that's the mystery of life and the future. I have finally got the courage to go to Grenada! A month in the sun may help me to decide where I end up living.

This year I will travel. I will get these books finished and also find my place.

When I am at home I look forward to going to my mum's but after a couple of days I want to go home and miss it.

I pray to Archangel Raphael that I have healing, just enough to get out and about and continue my recovery.

I need to push and get out there. Lots of holidays!

Most readings have proved promised future abundance, success and prosperity.

I hope that I make more friends and have more of a social life next year as I cannot carry on as it has been. I'm still so unsure about living where I am. I get days where I absolutely love it then days when I question if I am far too isolated.

Time will tell and synchronicity will as well. The nature and the nurture of the place is second to one. I am sure that when I am out and about more, it will not feel so isolated.

As I think of it now, it is indeed my slice of heaven! It's just the security of owning a home, but I don't think for one second that I would ever have to move out. I desperately want to be able to dive this year so fingers crossed I have the strength to do so.

Grenada here I come!

I have just read my entries for this time last year. The energy was a bit more depleted in me then. I feel calmer, stronger, more in tune with myself.

I have found me. I have found I like painting furniture, designing rooms and being creative.

I love my own company.

I have let go so much of the past.

I love adventure, action and war stories.

I adore nature and reading.

I belong with the sea.

I do not judge and criticise people for who they are, I am far more accepting and have no anger.

I am being rested and prepared for very high Universal work which I know is being part of the book being done.

I love myself and am happy with who I am.

I am very proud of how I have maintained my faith and strength.

I have been bed bound pretty much all year but I accept that.

I definitely am improving.

I am more spiritual.

I am no longer a people pleaser craving for their acceptance.

I am dealing with the debt. I will have that concluded in the next couple of months.

I have improved my diet and think a lot more seriously about holistic approaches and what's good for me.

I tried a couple of tipples in my coffee over Christmas but my body truly hates it! So I will be having virgin rum punches in Grenada!

I see people for who they are. I will never let anyone take my power from me ever again.

I am the mermaid. I am free to swim in the abundant ocean of life. To be surrounded by nature and God's creatures. Embracing the tranquillity and flowing of the universal source, water, the sea, the ocean. This year will be interesting. Many conclusions have been drawn. The accident. The loss. Now all I have to do is focus on the positive and draw positivity towards me en masse.

I truly hope that I read this next year and smile at everything that I achieved and finally have a positive direction.

But if I don't.

That's OK.

A few days after this entry I had a mermaid tattooed on my arm to signify my transition and my freedom. I have a fibromyalgia/

M.E. ribbon on her arm and a dive flag as her bikini. It marked my journey so far and my aspirations for the future.

Nicky had fallen in love with herself and discovered for the first time ever what she truly loved.

Nicky didn't need a man or anyone else to feed her love? Who knew?

Chapter 25

The Miracles That Angels Bring

I don't care if you are a sceptic, don't believe in angels or have no faith. The next few months were so angel led, there is no other way to explain what happened. See what you think.

Straight after Christmas there was a huge flood in my kitchen. Yet again another flood! When things go wrong and it isn't your home you are at the mercy of the landlords. Things got done, but not in your time which could be a tad frustrating. A few days later I then found the most curious thing in the spare room. I can only describe it as a thick treacle-type substance oozing down the walls. I then discovered it was starting to come down on my bedroom wall. It turned out to be some sort of damp that came through the old timbers.

M.E. and damp do not mix, so I was starting to get concerned.

Then just to add to the mix an army of mice decided to descend on the place. They were everywhere, in the walls, the ceilings and in all of my drawers. There was mice poo everywhere. They had started to eat through my clothes in the wardrobe and one even had the cheek to come out every night by my bed and look for food. I am not going to lie though, I called her Minnie and subjected her to all sorts of conversations!

I started to get the sense that it was my time to move on. The damp was apparently quite a serious problem, so there was going to be a lot of renovation and repair. But how was I to move on with no money, debt and a weakened body?

My mind, however, was totally made up on Thursday, 11 February 2016. It was no coincidence that it was the eleventh, a number that depicts new beginnings.

I woke up in the morning and I was truly emotional. I had been having the most amazing dream where I was sitting before

Archangel Raguel. He was stroking my hair and telling me that in order to create the right balance I must deal with my debt.

On waking, I was so pumped up that I wanted to start phoning around all of the banks, but after a cup of tea, I started to lose my nerve.

I pulled an angel card and gasped as it was Archangel Raguel. I knew that I had to deal with this now. How was I going to address this? I was £65,000 in debt.

I stopped myself from analysing the situation and promptly got all of the numbers and started my calls.

I had learned by this stage that honesty and transparency were the only way forward.

I spoke to each and every bank explaining my condition, the fact that there was no cure and did they want to be getting £20 a month from a disabled person that had no real prospect of ever working again. I asked them were they comfortable with taking that from me for the rest of my life which wouldn't even cover the interest that I owed.

Words cannot even go into how I felt by the end of the day. That beautiful angel had prompted me to do the thing that I feared the most.

By the end of the day, I had cleared £65,000 of debt. If anyone had told me a couple of years before that an angel was going to prompt me to phone banks and my debt would be cleared in a day, I would have laughed at them in their face!

Within a week I then to my amazement got an out of court settlement for the court case! I had money awarded for my accident. I just couldn't believe how much my life had changed in only one week!

My mind was made up, it was time to move. I had no idea how I was going to be physically able to do it, but I had made the decision. I trusted that the rest would follow.

I started to look at houses in Devon, but every property either fell through, was too expensive or just didn't feel right.

Because of the mice and damp I started to go and stay with Jay in Somerset.

I found myself drawn to Glastonbury, so I suggested that we went to the White Spring. The White Spring is a sacred space in Glastonbury. It has pools of water that run directly from the Tor and are believed to be guarded by the Goddess Brigid and the King of the Fairy realm. The waters have been documented for thousands of years as having healing qualities. One spring provides white calcium-rich water, the other red iron-enriched water from the Chalice gardens.

I had never been there before, but I knew that I had to go there. On Thursday, 24 March 2016, as I walked through the sacred doorway of the spring, I had no idea that this innocent visit would completely change my life.

You enter into a dark cavern where the water runs in waterfalls into the pools and along trenches in the floor. It is full of candles, crystals and gifts to the King and Goddess. I found it to be mesmerising. I was somewhat surprised when I saw many naked bodies immersed in the pools, embracing the healing waters! I felt like I was coming home as I sat on a bench before the main water source.

I decided to try and meditate.

Within seconds I felt a wave of energy hit my body. It almost felt as if I had had an anaesthetic as I dropped into a deep state of consciousness. I was aware of the distant flow of water but apart from that I sat there numb waiting in an almost expectant state.

There before me stood Archangel Michael. I felt the hum of his energy standing before me. Every single cell of my body tingled, the hairs on my arms stood up.

I could see him so clearly in my mind's eye looking down at me. The strength of emotion in my heart felt like it was going to burst. I felt sadness for my plight, happiness for my future and humbleness for being in the presence of the main Archangel, the warrior Michael.

He said absolutely nothing, he just stood there smiling at me. He had long waves of blond curls framing the most beautiful face that I had ever seen. His azure blue eyes pierced through my soul. He had long royal blue robes on, and every now and then I saw a picture of a sword. That is how I identified this angel as Michael.

I then said in my mind, "Michael, I am lost. I do not know how to go forward. I need to find my home. I need stability to help me heal. I need your guidance."

He replied, "You sit on the line that is mine. You shall go from this place and where my name is signed, there you shall be. I am with you. I will show you the way. You will continue to heal in this place of light."

I then opened my eyes and found tears rolling down my face. I dipped my crystals into the pool and placed them in my pockets.

I turned to Jay and said, "We have to go for a drive now."

As we walked out the man who is the gatekeeper of the spring smiled at me.

He then said, "Are you OK?"

I said, "Yes, I just had a really big experience. I just saw Archangel Michael."

He replied, "That makes sense, this spring lays on the line of Archangel Michael. It's like his ley line."

I had no clue what to say to this. Michael had just said that I was sat on his line!

I nodded to the man unable to say anything as we left the spring.

Jay drove us out through country lanes. I didn't realise how beautiful Somerset was. It has an enormous sense of space with the levels sprawling out for hundreds of miles.

We had just started to drive through a village called Othery when my heart started to thump in my chest. I felt breathless and sat up in the seat. I looked at every single cottage but there was nothing for sale.

Jay then turned off and we ended up in a back lane by a huge church. It was simply beautiful. I then caught a breath as I saw the name of the church.

It was called the church of St Michael.

We continued on and came out back on the main road in Othery.

As we drove along I saw a long white cottage. It was the very last cottage as you left the village. It had a 'For Sale' sign on it.

I just knew I was supposed to have it.

An estate agent was unbelievably nearby and was able to let us in for a viewing. It was in disrepair and looked unloved.

I put the most ridiculous offer in, as that was all I could afford. The estate agent stated that it really was not going to be accepted but put it in anyway. I had put an offer in for sixty thousand under the marked price.

I didn't care. I knew it was my next house.

Three days later the offer was accepted.

I later went on to find out that the cottage sat directly on the Archangel Michael ley line. From the Burrow Mump where Archangel Michael's church sat further down the road, the line ran through my cottage directly to Glastonbury Tor.

I was in for another shock. When I finally visited Burrow Mump, the sun was just sitting behind the curious small hill of the Mump. The Mump is basically a smaller version of Glastonbury Tor.

Looking at it, it looks like a giant has scooped up the earth in a triangular pile and popped a church on it!

As I looked up, my memory took me back to when my dad had visited me in Turkey. He had drawn a small triangular hill with the sun behind it. He had mentioned the name DAVID and MICHAEL. He had also said that 2016 would be the beginning of my rebirth. Michael, did he mean Archangel Michael?

The next time I visited the house, a man called David

introduced himself. He used to look after the lady that lived there. He and his wife Maggie turned out to be amazing friends. Whatever I needed they were there like a shot. Yet again my dad had nailed it.

I remember going back to Jay's house and taking in everything that had happened. Purely on the word of Archangel Michael and my dead dad, I bought a house in a place I had no connections with and knew no one except for Jay.

What was I thinking?

The shift in my life did bring back tiny demons though. I was aware that my condition would come back with a vengeance at any sign of stress. I was petrified that I had made the wrong decision coming away from Devon. I did, however, remember Marie Hines' prediction, "You are moving away from Devon..."

Tuesday 19 April 2016

I'm scared shitless about this move as every move I have made since the accident has been a very bad decision. The house is adorable, I adore the surrounding area and Somerset but there's so much to be done, planned and organised. Healthy, it would be exciting but a day like today, I feel deflated and pensive. Just when I think I am improving again, I slam back down. Fucking condition, I hate it with a vengeance. It makes me so down and unable to see the light. I'm in an enviable situation materially but that's all well and good if you are healthy. But I'm stuck here stuck in bed completely annihilated for having a bath. I'm trying to not eat bad things either as my body is becoming floppy and fat. I'm losing my self-esteem again and am feeling exceptionally unattractive. Jesus I hope this cloud lifts as I feel totally shit, weak and miserable.

I keep asking the angels for help and better health. I'm sure when the move comes I will find the energy from somewhere. I just don't want to crash like I did last time. My dreams, on analysing them, reflect the need for stability, vulnerability and feelings of lack of control.

Hey ho.

Things can only get better.

I was about to make a huge change in my life. I was still not mentally or physically healthy, but my growing trust in the flow of the Universe and the angel messages overwhelmed my human worries.

Shit or bust, is the expression I think!

Chapter 26

A Home To Call My Own

They say moving is stressful but try doing it on your own with severe chronic illness!

I managed to get into my new cottage before I had to get out of the lodge in Kingswear so that took the pressure off. Looking back now I still don't know how I found the energy to do what I did. I slept on a little camp bed and paced myself with tiny little jobs each day.

I got all of the stuff out that was left dumped there and started to clean as best I could.

I also, with Jay's help, started to paint some of the walls.

The cottage was magnificent. I had always dreamed of living in an old cottage. There were exposed beams everywhere, stunning inglenook fires upstairs and downstairs with original medieval blessing bricks and an original bread oven and stove. The lounge was reversed and was upstairs. There was a sunroom that looked over the moors and you could see Glastonbury Tor in the distance. Right next to my window was a large field that was full of cows. They startled me to begin with when they all started mooing at me, but when we got used to each other it was magical. I would sit under a blanket in that room and stare at them for hours.

They even started coming up and poking their head through the window and I used to rub their noses!

I had found yet another peaceful sanctuary to continue my journey of healing and happiness.

Friday 6 May 2016
Well I am sitting in my new home in the kitchen with one granny chair to sit on! The weather is glorious. Maggie and Dave have been

magnificent. I have totally landed on my feet. I have cleaned, painted and have hardly stopped. I'm very proud of myself, how I have managed to keep going. Some days have been fucking horrendous. But there is no doubt this place was left for me. I'm going to be exceptionally happy here, it is truly beautiful and the surrounding area is magnificent. I walked the babies over the Levels the other day, it was like walking in Spain. I was a bit wary of walking past the cattle but they were OK! The small canals and rivers are stunning, just magnificent. The locals have been so friendly and the postman Rob is very helpful. Just had my first cooked dinner here!

I'm not going to lie though, I did leave the bedroom light on for the first couple of nights as this place is pitch black, no street lighting. But it's calm and has a lovely vibe here.

When I look at any room in the cottage, I know it's worth it without a doubt.

I'm not looking forward to going back to Devon and finishing all the crap off there. The move is going to be exhausting, but I will just have to push through.

I had to muster every bit of strength that I had to get through the next couple of months. I kept driving back to Devon and packing boxes up, then driving back to the cottage. I didn't put any entries in my soul journal as I was literally sleeping or trying to get things sorted. I was shattered.

Two days before the removal men were due to move my stuff from Devon to Somerset I was in the lounge of the lodge trying to sweep up all of the dust and dirt. My back went into spasm so severely that I dropped to the floor in a heap. The pain was so excruciating I kept holding my breath gritting my teeth.

I started to cry as I knew I had no choice but to push on, but my body was having none of it.

"Please, whoever is up there, I need help, I just can't do this on my own."

I remember lying in a foetal position on the floor rocking

back and forth. I was at the end of my tether.

My phone then dinged, and someone wanted to buy the settee I had up for sale on Facebook. They wanted to come round straight away and have a look.

That man was called Mark. Now, as you know, the name Mark has always been a solid name for me. Every Mark I have known has helped me in some beautiful way.

This was no exception.

Mark turned up about half an hour later. I was still sitting on the floor as he walked in. I was quite distressed. I could instantly sense that he was a kind man. He helped me up on to the sofa where I spewed out my desperation and my worries of how to cope.

That man was simply amazing. He turned up the following day and packed up, cleaned and cleared everything in the house for me and refused to be paid. I couldn't believe his kindness. A stranger who had only turned up to buy a settee was there for my time of need. Coincidence, or had the angels heard my plea?

Either way, he turned up the following day and oversaw the removal men as they packed everything up.

He was and still is my hero.

After that I never heard from him again!

Thank goodness, the removal men were brilliant. I explained my condition (so they didn't think I was lazy!) and they took care of everything.

That night laying in my bed, in my new home, was undeniably momentous.

I had achieved the move. I had trusted the process and gone with the flow. My bedroom had patio doors that led out on to one of the side gardens. Every morning I would wake up to the chorus of the hedgerow birds in their hundreds singing me awake. I was entranced by the place.

I would stay in bed most of the day and then unpack a box at my own pace. I started to get workmen in to redo the electrics and treat the damp.

Very slowly I was finally making a home for myself, something that I hadn't had for years.

I started to feel safe again. The weather that summer was glorious. I would spend as much time as I could in the sun to keep my vitamin D levels up, and took everything very easy.

The next momentous achievement was my trip to Grenada.

I had vowed that I would do a dive.

The journey to Grenada was very easy. I had a taxi pick me up from my mum's house and was met by an assistant the other side who pushed me around the shops and got me to my plane. I felt happy to accept my disability as I would never have made it through security without collapsing in exhaustion. Plus being pushed around the shops was a total bonus!

I felt a sense of victory when the tropical air hit my pale face as I was carried down the steps from the plane. I was welling up every few minutes, I was so proud of myself! When I saw Wendy waiting for me I felt a surge of happiness and love. I was going to have a blast!

My friend Wendy knew the local dive owner, Yvonne. I explained that I needed a little assistance to get in the sea and she helped me to no end.

I remember it so clearly. The emerald gems sparkled in the tropical heat as the dive boat shot across the Caribbean Sea.

My friend Wendy looked at me and said, "You did it, Nicky, you are going to dive!"

I started to cry. The tears were with pride for myself and the fact that I had yearned for this moment since my illness began. It was the only vision that I kept in my head when I was really down. I looked down triumphantly at my mermaid tattoo. I had achieved one of my main goals.

It was finally time. I was so lucky as it was just me and the dive guide so we didn't have to rush. As I descended into the crystalline blue of the sea, I let out the longest sigh. There I was looking at a Caribbean reef full of sea life and I could hear nothing but the bubbles coming from my regulator.

I started to float over the reef feeling happier than I had felt in years. I had to make no effort at all, so there was no stress on my body. I just let the soft swell of the sea carry me along. I then spotted a nurse shark sleeping under a coral shelf. It's an absolute 'no, no' to touch any sea life but I knew that I had to. I gently skimmed along the seabed and got level with the shark. I stretched a furtive hand out, the shark didn't move one bit.

I started to stroke its back and its tail. I stayed there for ages just feasting on the beauty of what I was doing, here in nature connecting with a wild sea animal. After this I then laid flat on the seabed and just trickled the sand through my fingers.

I was in absolute bliss.

When I came up from that dive, the shift in my energy was amazing. I was beyond happy and so very proud. I was helped the whole time with my equipment so I found that I only got a bit achy and tired later on. I was so relieved that I wasn't in major pain.

I then met one of Wendy's friends Rolanda. She was house-hunting and wanted us to go and see a house that she was buying.

We drove out to the house, and as we got to the wrought iron gates, the hairs on the back of my neck went up. My heart started to thump as I saw the familiar twists of the iron in the gates. I then saw the roof of the house and stood stock-still completely shocked.

There in front of me was the house I had drawn on the 27th July 2015.

Inside, the furniture was exactly as I had drawn it. I knew where I was going and recognised every single room. Outside the pool was exactly where I had drawn it. I saw the quay at the end of the garden running into the lagoon.

I showed Rolanda my drawing and she couldn't believe it.

I had innocently drawn a house where I wanted to be and

there it was standing right in front of me.

I became brilliant friends with Rolanda and even stayed at her house on another visit!

It was then that I was made aware of the true power of cosmic ordering. All you had to do was concentrate on what you wanted, see it as a reality and trust the Universe to do the rest.

It worked, and from that day on, I started to work it at any chance I got.

For the rest of the holiday, I swam, walked and even had a couple of rum punches! I managed another two dives, which to me was an incredible feat.

I was worried, however, that this burst of energy wasn't going to last. I did rest a lot during the activities but one day I was in so much pain I started to panic. We had been to the mud springs, and when we got back on the yacht I was suffering from the bumpy drive there and back.

"Wendy, am I ever going to get well?" I asked her anxiously.

My friend Wendy is very psychic. She sat me down and said to me,

"You are not there yet, Nicky. Couple more years and you will be well. Trust me, this isn't going to be forever."

I hoped with all my heart that she was right.

The Zika virus was being carried by the mosquitoes in Grenada at that time in a massive way. Two days before I was due to go home, I started to feel very ill. I couldn't believe it.

When I got home I was confirmed as one of only four people in the UK to have the Zika virus and Dengue.

Our autoimmune systems are shot as M.E. sufferers, so I went downhill horrendously. My body couldn't fight the two viruses, so I found myself bedridden yet again as soon as I was home.

Wednesday 24 August 2016

Well I did it! I dived, I danced, I snorkelled, I swam, I walked, I did everything I set out to do. I felt invincible, so proud of myself. When

I did my first dive and had a little tickle on a Nurse shark's tail it was amazing! I don't know if it was the fact I was with people or the sun, the sea, but it worked. I had a few dodgy days but I'm not surprised.

I felt so happy.

Since being back it's been pretty shit.

I came back with the Zika virus and am still ill. It seems all the magic has been taken away by reality. Feeling slightly low, feeling I'm back on my own and fearing that I will be crap again. My fingers are killing me writing this because of the stupid virus. Mind you, shocking how I drew Rolanda's villa that she bought when I was out there!

Books have to be done. Cottage needs to be straight. Driving me nuts, shit everywhere.

So I had an amazing holiday and it's like I never went. Who knows what is to come?

Who knows, cos I certainly don't?

What I do know now that I didn't know then was that my next challenge was about to take place.

Chapter 27

Life Is a Roller Coaster

It was four days before my birthday and I knew that I would be spending it yet again alone and in bed. The Dengue and Zika virus had catastrophically affected my body. Yet again I was plunged into the darkness that is M.E.

Tuesday 13 September 2016
My life is a roller coaster of emotions. One day I wake up and feel positive about achieving the simplest of things, other days I just want to keep my head under the duvet and lose myself to the land of dreams where the reality of my existence disappears without a trace.

I feel abandoned in my darker times.

I am so 'half full' or 'half empty'. There's nothing in between, like a contented balance.

But I'm always running. Wanting and striving for something. I now have a mortgage-free home. It's beautiful countryside, made some lovely new friends but then I go to Goodrington and start telling myself I should never have left Devon. I can only put it down to my health or is it a mental thing now? I had pain and exhaustion in Grenada but generally felt alive. But then again it's a false situation.

Every day I drag myself up feeling knackered or achy and as soon as you feel that, the day looks less pleasant.

Is the book the way forward, or a fantasy to hang on to? The spiritual side says it's no fantasy, the human side fears that when they are finished, there's a fear of them going nowhere.

My fucking hand is killing me already, writing this.

Perhaps I have to give this place a chance. Reach out to the people I have met and strive to get out more. I am my own worst enemy, I cry because I'm alone but then don't have the energy to have friends around or make arrangements. My only pure joy are my babies and actually when I'm writing I feel that pure buzz. There must be something in it as I wouldn't have had the dream and been told of Elizabeth.

I see people moan about their family but they have no idea how it feels to be almost alone. Rejected by your siblings. Cousins, aunts and uncles who only meet up at weddings and funerals and a mum who gave up when her husband died. It pains me to see all her ailments but she still continues to do nothing to help herself. Perhaps it's in our genes!

The dragonfly on my cushion staring up at me representing the illusion of life. In the book Billy Fingers *he talks of human lives as being tiny specks of no importance compared to the enormity of the spirit world and the Universe. I totally get that but it's so hard when you are encased in a human body caged by human emotion and impulse. It's a bloody nightmare. Yes I could be a whole lot worse off, but we all have our sadness, regrets and hang-ups.*

I just need to pick, sow and reap the benefits of a positive seed, for the harvest surely brings evidence of that hard work. So I must continue to strive and see what comes.

I have dips and troughs every day. Since coming back from Grenada this stupid Zika virus has given me permanent headaches. I'm popping Paracetamol like smarties! So that hasn't helped.

I'm back up to 60 mg Duloxetine because coming down to 40 mg was hell and I don't think I'm ready to start the bitch of weaning off them yet.

God I was scuba diving a couple of weeks ago! Now look at me. Crying my eyes out and writing this at 3am. What the fuck?

The answers are there, within, but when you start the day with an achy sigh of exhaustion, it's bloody hard. No routine, no reason to get up. Escaping in box sets and hoping for a new future. It's bloody hard and I don't know how to change it.

Perhaps I should live somewhere like Brixham, in a fisherman's cottage where I can just walk to the sea, shops and pubs. Perhaps the three year plan of me getting back there is doable. Who knows?

The only sure thing I can hang on to is the book whether it is a false hope or not. Trying to do things in the garden. Taking the babies out. Making an effort with new friends. Going away as much as possible. Doing the odd reading. Slowly getting there. There's part of me that reminds me to be very kind to myself as I have been through every painful human experience imaginable.

Dad said I mustn't allow myself to be distracted by men so I should heed that. But human conditioning of wanting to be loved makes that exceptionally difficult.

If I had a genie, my dream would be to be a successful author of spiritual stuff, it's manageable as I can write in bed. I enjoy it and it could send a message to the masses that I could never achieve through all of the dems and readings I did over the years.

It seems to come to me, so I pray that the writing is my future. I can write from anywhere and it does seem to flow.

Very therapeutic this writing, it clears the mind and hopefully will fill me with peace so that I can sleep.

Everyone should keep a soul journal.

No doubt I will read this back and the answers are between every line. Sitting silently on every page, waiting patiently to come to their blatant conclusion!

Tomorrow I shall write.

Tomorrow I shall read a couple of sections of my mindfulness course.

But then tomorrow is another day. Who knows what will transpire between sleep and waking. But I hope I can fulfil my intentions!

HANG ON IN THERE!

On the 23rd September I had a dream.

I was laying in the lap of Archangel Gabriel. He was telling me that I must start to reach people spiritually again through readings. Part of his mission for us is as a messenger to humankind. The dream was magnificent. Not surprisingly I did not want to wake up and face my harsh reality.

In true fashion in my waking hours, I let the dream burn

away into my subconscious. I had neither the energy nor the inclination to start doing telephone readings again. I had also lost my confidence and felt that I could not be the medium that I once was.

However, the following day, as I was sitting in the sunroom watching the cows, I jumped as I heard a voice say,

"Do it, now!"

Sunday 25 September 2016
Yesterday I decided to go public on telephone readings. It just came upon me, "Do it now!"

I have booked three this week to ease me in. I want to have a sense of purpose, feel more connected so I can switch back on to the spirit world. It will on a human level help me pay to get everything done. I need to earn some money so I can get this place as cosy as possible for winter anyway and get Grenada tokens!

I am a bit apprehensive with the readings but TR trust! I have to watch that I don't burn myself out though. Two days ago I started placing some of the Pope's holy water on my head and asked Archangel Raphael to help. I hope it helps. It certainly got rid of Meena's tumour.

I feel more content now that I am partly working. At last count it was 111 emails! Pretty interesting number.

I truly hope that this gives me the incentive to move forward and to get the book written. I want to dedicate a couple of hours of it tomorrow. The only problem is, how the hell am I going to get it out there? I have no columns, I have been out of the loop for years, and I have lost a lot of my following. It will take a miracle for anyone to bother reading it as I am now someone who spends her time in bed all day, not doing shows and moving my career forward!

ROUTINE. DISCIPLINE. SELF-WORTH. FORTHRIGHTNESS. CONTROL.

Spiritual life has never let me down, so I know that I have to switch back into it. Personal life is not great so why not!

I adore the meditation time that I have with the babies by the

canal. It's a precious sanctuary where there is 360 degrees of complete countryside spreading out for miles.

I think I am slowly bonding here. The sea, however, still calls to me, but who knows what will take place in the future?

HERE'S TO MY FIRST WEEK BACK WORKING!

So I just asked for guidance about my health and whether it was right to start working again.

So what did I get?

CHAMUEL – Self-love and allowing love to flow to others.

RAPHAEL – Who I asked to draw near using the holy water.

BEGINNINGS – New phase of life with fresh ideas.

OMG!

The affirmations are:

I welcome and nurture the new in my life.

I am happy, healthy and abundant.

My heart is filled with the flame of love.

You just couldn't make it up!

As always I needn't have worried about my readings. The first one was with a lovely girl called Kesley. I knew that her dog was very poorly. I knew that the dog was not going to see Christmas. Sounds like a bad reading but I gave her everything I could to prepare her and her family for the loss.

Monday 10 October 2016

Been a pretty shite week health wise, I am still ill from the virus. The headaches are killing me.

Mind you, had a lovely text from Kesley. Her dog has been confirmed as having cancer as I thought and it's too late to be caught. I gave her the low-down on the Rainbow Bridge and where spirit animals go. Her text made me smile and realise a very important thing. She came down the stairs today, having said nothing to the children about the reading and bugger me, her little daughter was drawing a rainbow!

How amazing is that?

Sometimes it's not about all the info I strive to get on a spirit person. This gem has given her the faith to cope with Kaya's passing when it comes.
PRICELESS!

Monday 7 November 2016
Sometimes I don't even know why I write this. Depression has crept its way back and I feel like death again. Could be the winter months. Wrist hurting, can't write.

I purged into a week of complete darkness. I cancelled the readings I had booked. I ate nothing and stayed in bed not washing, and feeling like I wanted to die. I could not push myself out of this blackened fog. The pain was excruciating and my head was banging from the virus that my body still couldn't get rid of. The doctors were useless and just wanted to put me on more drugs. So yet again I felt alone, useless, weak and not worthy of anything.

A bright shining star came, however, in the form of Claire. I looked forward to her visits twice a week with relish. She cleaned my home for me, made me breakfast, changed my bed and was a fantastic ear when I needed to talk. Her beautiful energy and shining optimism helped me to no end on the bad days. God Bless her kind heart.

The following Sunday, the 6th November, I was sitting in my bed wailing like a child. I was hearing all the fireworks over the weekend and seeing excited children walking along hand in hand with their parents going to their happy little bonfire nights and it made me want to be sick. With every firework, there came a sharp pang of loneliness and futility firing through me.

I thought of all the things that normally helped me feel positive, but as every suggestion of positivity came flashing into my mind, I promptly shot each one down in flames. My babies, they would die soon. My house, it was freezing and needed too much work. Somerset, it was lonely. Friends, I had no true friends. Health, I was never going to get better. Writing, what was the point? It was not going to go anywhere.

I remember shouting at the ceiling saying that I couldn't do it anymore. I had nothing to live for and nothing to aspire to.

"Why can't you just give me a break? Why can't you just do something to help me? For fuck sake, just do something!"

I yelled as I wiped the snot from my face and rocked in a foetal position.

But always remember, life is a roller coaster, up and down.

What happened in 48 hours' time was pretty much a miracle.

Chapter 28

The Birth of a Writer

Just when I couldn't take any more, in true fashion the powers that be made me look ungrateful and pretty much stupid in my despair-ridden pleas and rantings.

On the Tuesday after my Sunday foetal rocking nightmare, I hobbled to the kitchen and made a cup of tea. I then walked back into my bedroom and with a resigned sigh checked my emails.

One caught my eye.

I thought that I was seeing things.

This never happens. You do not get offers like this out of the blue. You have to work very hard and stay in the limelight, so how in God's name had this happened?

Tuesday 8 November 2016

My good God! Just when you get in a huge dip. When you cry your eyes out for hours just as I did Sunday, when you think that you are working your arse off on a book that's not going to go anywhere, BOOM!

I get an email from Carina at Fate and Fortune *magazine. They have offered me a column as the Psychic Detective! YES! Can you believe it? Last week the smallest, silent voice in my head thought 'I need a column' as I remember most agents need that. Well fuck me they delivered in style! So hopefully this will be a leg up for the books.*

They obviously want them out there so it will be. I have worked on them nearly every day when I am fit enough.

OMG this will help me as an author. This is such good news! The first column will go out May next year! I got a feeling 2017 is going to be the Phoenix year! OMG! BRING IT ON!

Nicky Alan… Psychic Detective…

Just one email had changed my perspective on life. I had something to work towards now. It would also give me an opportunity to raise my profile. The ashes of my life were starting to smoulder again and I could feel excitement that I hadn't felt for ages.

Christmas due to my weakened body was a non-event. I went to my mum's but spent most of the day in bed exhausted. New Year's Eve I managed half a glass of wine whilst watching the Robbie Williams' New Year concert on the television. He is my favourite artist so I enjoyed that evening. Little did I know that later on, that evening would be so significant in a lot of ways, as I sat with my mum dreaming of a better and healthier New Year.

I booked to go to Grenada again. I was thinking about how well I was the last time. I then started to think if I should move over there. There was a serious decision to be made. If I was better in the heat, why not go and live somewhere that would help me? I would make my decision when I was back out there. I had booked six weeks out there to see if it would be the right move.

Friday 27 January 2017
Started my column early so it's out for April, weird one, the Marfa lights will be my first contribution. Hope it reads well.

I can't believe that Grenada is only four weeks away! Thank God I will be in the heat as I am just suffering so much in the cold at the moment that it is a joke. I'm just hibernating.

Thursday 2 February 2017
Three days until my dad's passing anniversary, it never leaves you, the loss. What do I do? I'm so scared to move abroad but what if it's the only place my symptoms can be eased? A very huge journey to do alone. Besides I love my cottage and want to see it grow. Perhaps I should spend as much time as possible in the sun and await for fate to deliver its verdict on my writing. I just had to do the second column for

Fate and Fortune. *It's on the mystery of Jerome in Sandy Bay in Nova Scotia. It appears that the editor and Carina are totally chuffed with my first column so I'm really pleased I am doing OK. On positive days I see myself as a best-seller with all my prayers answered and delivered. On bad days I see myself forever with this illness, rotting year after year realising that I have nobody but the good will of my friends who have their own lives. Am I going to be the poor old cow who is found dead with no next of kin like you see on the police documentaries? I realise that I treated people badly in the past but I have changed. Or is it because I am on my own everyday with no one to hurt? These are my demons that come and greet me with relish on bad days. The main one being self-hate. I hate having to rely on people who I hardly even know living here. It's a very terrifying and lonely existence I have. Without the writing I don't know what I would do. It keeps me alive. Sometimes I feel like I would rather be dead but on good days the old survival instinct kicks back in. Battles of good and bad, despair and faith.*

It took me two months to pack my suitcase as unlike normal people you can't just rush around and do it in a couple of hours. I would pack a couple of things then be too exhausted to do anymore. You find when you have chronic illness that you cannot operate like normal people. Everything has to be planned or worked towards over a series of weeks or months before so that you adequately pace yourself.

I had full disabled access at the airport so I wasted no energy as I was wheeled round. This time I found that it was horrible being pushed around in a wheelchair. Children stare at you, shop assistants talk to you over kindly with a pitied look upon their face and others just ignore you as if you are not important in the world. These are the ones I love to shove in the ankles with my wheelchair if they fail to move out of the way. I look up at them with sorrowful eyes as they clutch their ankles. They can't be angry at me, which gives me a sick pleasure and instant gratification!

M.E. and fibro are weird conditions. They are not like any other disability. That is why we get such a hard time claiming for disability. The questions asked in the paperwork are ridiculous. We can be walking one day and then bedridden for months. So the standard requirement for disability in our society is fraught with issues when it comes to our unique condition.

Questions like, "How far can you walk?" Well on a good day a few metres, on a bad day none at all. "Can you cook for yourself?" Yes and no. "That's not an answer." Well, yes, it is.

On a bad day I can do nothing, on a good day I can cook a meal.

The questions basically all have the same pattern. They relate to people with permanent disability, not this stupid up and down condition that can change every hour.

Many of my friends have had to go to Tribunals to prove that they are disabled and can't work. The stress of doing this makes them worse which the authorities fail to recognise. We are struggling to be acknowledged in the medical profession and with our local authorities. It's hurtful, it's damaging and there are limited people in our corner fighting for our rights. Very slowly MPs are starting to give us a voice in Parliament, but I am sure it is going to take years before we are recognised.

It is incredible that M.E. and fibro is becoming one of the fastest growing pandemics in the Western hemisphere with the least support or help from society. Go figure. As I've previously said, you will find on social media that we are known as the 'millions missing' forced to live our lives confined to our beds and homes. We are missing from everyday life, unable to work, socialise or integrate in society. All I can do is just pray that one day our millions of voices will unite and the world will hear.

Anyway, as usual I digress! I landed in Grenada, but this time I had to get a taxi to the apartment. I felt hopeful as I lay shattered on the bed that in a few days I would be swimming and running around like a gazelle.

It's funny really, when you question your next move, mine being shall I move abroad, the angel realms will slam the yes or no answer so far down your throat that you can do nothing but say, "OK, I get it."

Sunday 5 March 2017
This is terrible! I have slept for the first three days. I feel lonely and shit! I feel homesick. I have not been able to get up and get water or food. I got stung three times last night by this tropical wasp and that has just about finished me. I tried to write but I just can't concentrate. My skin is burning, my body will not drop its temperature and I feel like I have had the shit kicked out of me, and I just want to go home. I hope I improve or all this organisation and money has been a complete waste of time. Fucking gutted.

Monday 6 March 2017
Meditation – An angel was wrapping up an endless load of white stuff. After wrapping one up it was placed and sealed into a ball. It was then tagged January 19th. Christ what is going to happen next January? Then another, October 2004. That was my breakdown after losing my career. I then saw an elephant which represents self-nourishment. Blah fucking blah.

I am stuck in a room exhausted and in pain that is amplified with every fucking sound. If it isn't the fucking dogs barking, it's the cars zooming past beeping and playing their stupid fucking music or some loudmouth or the chickens or Christ knows what else. I'm sad, lonely, bored to fuck and just want to go home. This has been the most stupid idea to think that there is some magic here. I'm fucking fed up. Sick of this illness, sick of being on my own and sick to death of my fucking existence. I have had enough of all of it. Everything just fucks up all the time. What the fuck is the POINT! FUCK OFF!

My body temperature would not drop at all. I would lay on the bed sweating profusely with heart palpitations. My wrists and ankles were badly swollen, it was agony to walk. I could not get to the shops for food or water so kept finding myself dehydrated and hungry. I had a permanently bad tummy and my stomach was bloated like a pregnant elephant! Wendy was busy working, so I found myself alone, uncomfortable in the heat and severely depressed.

Needless to say I came home early! The only flight available was first class. I couldn't sit up anyway so wasted all of my air miles on that flight home.

I felt disillusioned but I also had an answer to the thing that had been burning on my mind and conscience for a while. Heat does not help this condition in any way whatsoever. There was no way I was going to move abroad. They had answered my question. It was certainly a harsh lesson, but valid all the same.

So when I got home, I started concentrating on doing my house up. One day I sat back looking at my newly-painted beige kitchen and realised that the reading Marie had given me all that time ago had turned out totally true. She had described this cottage and all of the names that had come to help me get the cottage and gardens sorted. She had described the beige kitchen, the dodgy pipes, and the windows did indeed stick. I knew I was on track, but what next? Something still didn't feel complete. It didn't really take that long to know what it was.

Chapter 29

The Final Battle

There are times when your loved ones up above do a little something to let you know they are there or to heads you up on what is coming. I was having the usual up and down days with a feeling of going no further forward. I knew something was about to happen though as my granddad Fred had paid a visit.

Wednesday 19 April 2017
Yesterday I found my candleholder on the wall in the sunroom across by the window on the floor. It had been placed right next to my granddad's Rosary and Snowflake Obsidian! Well, Snowflake Obsidian is to balance depression and negative emotions! I was contemplating going back to the doctors after my emotional explosion in Grenada, but don't need to anymore! Thanks, Granddad! Around 7.07 pm whilst Jay was downstairs the TV turned itself off! Another sign to say they are with me! I'm blessed! Happy days. This year is going to be huge and thank you, Daddy, for telling me it was going to be OK in 2017. I AM BLESSED!

Simple little signs and synchronicities like these kept me going. They charged my positive power battery up which would last for a number of days. They always knew when to pop in and give me a 'chin up' sign. I remained quite positive as I kept feeling I was waiting for something to happen. The suspense and excitement seemed to hang in the air.

They didn't disappoint.

Monday 8 May 2017
Life takes so many twists and turns. I have amazing news! Got an email from Tracie Cooper at Spirit & Destiny *magazine. She's asked*

me to do a column, "Diary of a Psychic"! It's boosted my confidence as
I was feeling a bit shitty.

I couldn't believe that I had a second column. If there was any
doubt about me changing my career to mainly writing, then this
certainly was the way to show me that I wasn't wasting my time.

Very slowly men were coming in to decorate and improve
the cottage when I could afford it. That was the only thing I saw
progressing. I had put my fiction book out to agents and just
got one 'no' after another, which did knock my confidence so I
decided to give the submissions route a rest for the time being as
I was too fragile to keep taking the rejection.

One thing that did happen which changed my life significantly
was a phone call I got from a nutritionist. I had randomly sent an
email weeks ago asking about how diet affects M.E. and fibro. I
then completely forgot about it.

Sunday 11 June 2017
On Friday I went to Jay's as I couldn't bear to be in the house. I cleansed
it and then left. Alex the nutritionist called me as she had missed my
email until that day! Angel led? I started the diet the following day.
No sugar, no caffeine, no gluten. Because I have been so weak and
vulnerable I need to get control back. So the diet was the first step. If I
get well I can get a life back and control my destiny. Not just sit back
and rely on people.

The diet withdrawal has been horrendous. I have done nothing but
sleep, have a permanent headache and have been completely weak but
I must persevere. I have no choice. I have just ordered some sugar-free
recipe books and chai tea! I hope I like it. I must get well. I beg the
Universe that this is the successful step I must take to recover. My
redemption has surely been met. I must focus, be kind to myself as the
sugar and gluten die in my system. I will force myself onwards with
this diet as I believe the week before last was the final closure and a
proper kick to get my final healing stage done. I cannot keep going up

and down all of the time, things have to change.

Sunday 18 June 2017
I am fighting a massive battle. My body is trying to adapt using protein as a source of energy rather than sugar. It is horror! I feel very fat even though you are supposed to lose weight. I am dizzy, weak and sleep a minimum of fourteen hours a day. Thank God the babies are with Jay in Weymouth as they would be so bored and unhappy. It is my last ditch attempt at health. If this doesn't work then nothing will. I have ordered all sorts of weird and wonderful foods in order that I make this diet for life. I need all of the celestial help that I can get.

Many things are dying, passing and hopefully exorcising themselves from my body, mind and spirit. I can take being weak and ill no more. I am done with it. I will make this my last battle that will win the war. I need help and invoke:
Archangel Raphael
Archangel Azrael
Archangel Uriel
May you be by my side to dissolve the illness, rid me of heartache and give me the strength to move forward sorting out everything that has kept me blocked. All the cards have been right. All the dreams and signs have been right. Give me my health. Give me my life's spiritual missions and writing and spreading the word.

I am completely resting and allowing this battle raging within me to be victorious. My redemption surely is complete?

I have found a lot of truth in an online prediction site. This is for the following week!

"The happy home. Ten of cups, all to do with home and people in it. It also represents your own personal happiness. You seem at a crossroads at the moment, it is around the 'home' you have a 'yes' or 'no' decision that needs to be made. You are the only person who can decide but the High priestess showing near the latter part of the week, you well and truly believe that you have reached the end of your tether. There is no more. You have no more to give. Well,

that strictly isn't true. You are drained of your emotion, your health might even be suffering as a result of stress. It will pay, dare I say to pay the predator off. You will be able to relax, you will be able to sleep at night. Money can be earned but your health is far more precious, more than gold.

Archangel Raphael will stand close by."

The tarot scopes on this website were never wrong. I needed to concentrate on my health. It wasn't surprising that Archangel Raphael was my angel for the week when I had invoked him. That's how you get acknowledgement that they have heard your prayer. You will find another source where their name is mentioned, or something out of the ordinary will happen where you know they have heard your prayer.

The 'yes' or 'no' comment was interesting. What decisions would I be making about my house?

All I knew was that I had to change the physical 'inside' of my body through diet. The inside mental health and spiritual living improvement was a working project; the least I could do was feed my body with goodness. Within a couple of days, my tummy upsets and nausea completely stopped. It was obvious that I had an intolerance to gluten. I found sleep more restful and noticed, as the withdrawal dissipated, that my energy levels started to even out without the sugar. I also started to find that naturally sweet things such as fruit and even cucumber started to taste like candy. My palate was changing as well.

The only thing that was puzzling me was that my tummy felt large all of the time. I felt like I was putting on weight where I had been told by the nutritionist that it would drop off! I was doing nothing wrong. Not a grain of sugar or gluten had passed my lips. The last thing that I needed was to put on weight! The nutritionist was not great at follow-up calls and kept ignoring my emails when I repeatedly asked why I was putting on weight. I was drinking fresh cow's milk literally from the farmer and everything I ate was organic. It cost a fortune but then I figured that it would be worth it. Just for the record, the price they put on gluten-free foods is disgusting. You pay triple price for everything. Again though, I saw it as an investment for the future. I don't know if it was the diet or the fact I was doing something to help myself, but I sensed an electricity in the air like when you are waiting for a train to arrive. I could feel a sense of change but I couldn't work out what it was. I kept getting butterflies in my tummy as if I was looking forward to something, but then when I tried to think of what it might be, I had no idea.

It kept burning away, this sense of apprehension. All I could really concentrate on though was this new diet and lifestyle.

The last battle had commenced, but all I yearned for was to win the war.

Because of the columns being offered to me, I started to realise as I looked back on the last couple of years that when I needed things or asked that lot above for anything, it seemed to deliver itself. I started to regularly ask for things and affirm things as I had a clear knowing that the Universe was in sync with me and was indeed bringing me things that I needed for the greater good. I had never been a great believer in cosmic ordering and karma, but by recent events, my head had been turned and I was now 'ordering' my requirements regularly. If I wasn't asking for things I was writing affirmations to reinforce positive living. I realised that I had set up a very comprehensive self-help guide to spiritual living. This then gave me an idea. I created the PRISM LIVING course. It was a seven-week online course for people to take. It contained all of my tips and advice on positivity and how to incorporate angels and the spirit world into your daily lives. It was a great success and also a fantastic feeling to know that I could still help people from my bed.

The weirdest thing happened which also ended a phase from my past. After starting this way of living I got some news.

Remember Dick, the one who ran off with all of my money? Well I got a phone call telling me that he had been arrested for ripping off old-age pensioners for thousands. Looked like this karma lark worked! I did understand though that karma isn't waiting for revenge on the person that has wronged you. I learned that if you stay in your own positive energy and they stay in theirs, their actions and deeds will definitely come back and bite them on the bum. We can bask in our glorious crystalline ocean, they stay in their filthy boggy swamp. Who ends up the winner?

Saturday 1 July 2017
Amazing event this week! Dick was arrested for thieving off old grannies, £15,000! So I am getting my closure on that! Karma has been dealt. I should feel grateful. Perhaps it's another closed wound, something else to move on from. So many amazing things have been happening this year. It is truly remarkable.

I had yet another interesting message from that tarot scope website:
"Cheated, deceived by people or a person close to your heart. You had given them the benefit of the doubt, you had hoped that situations that involved you and them would have started to move in the right direction but bam, bam, bam. Life has not been easy but it seems as if you have an inbuilt reluctance to consider other options. Your way is the right way and you feel that if you hang on in there long enough, you'll be able to prove to everyone that you were right all along.

Over the weekend, take control of your life and focus on what you're going to do next and that is something that will work for all."
TO THE UNIVERSE
Thank you for all of my writing opportunities so far.
PLEASE HELP MY BODY TO CONTINUALLY RECOVER.
Thank you for everything so far this year re: The diet/people/home/ friends/babies (dogs).
PLEASE BRING THE RIGHT PERSON TO COMPLETE MY HOME/DIY ETC.
Thank you for my beautiful home!

PLEASE BRING ME MORE OPPORTUNITIES TO BRING MY KNOWLEDGE TO THE MASSES.

I thank you for my columns in Fate *and* Fortune *and* Spirit & Destiny *and the inspiration for PRISM LIVING.*

I ask the angel realms to continue to bring blessings upon me, Teddy and Mia. I ask that I am surrounded by love only and quick to see if that's absent. I acknowledge my downfalls in life have usually been due to the wrong men and relationships. I therefore ask that self-love and self-protection is stronger in your love. I only wish to bring your word and that of the Spirit World to everyone that needs it. I ask for you to help me reach as many people as possible please!

With money, I only ask that I am comfortable, can afford everything to complete this home and be able to look after myself.

The rest whatever the future may bring in love is welcomed.

Thank you for supporting me and listening to me. I just ask that at some point soon in human time you show me a sign that you have heard my respectful plea on this evening.

Thank you.

Saturday 29 July 2017

Dad came and visited my friend Tracy last night. He said to her to tell me that I haven't finished with 'me' yet. That nothing will flow until I clear myself out. Christ knows what I need to do! All I know is there are still demons lurking. There are still some boundary and self-esteem issues. I also think I might do a non-fiction book on my soul journey starting from the accident, I just feel it is what I should be doing first, I don't know why. There was a toad that sat in the door earlier. He just stared at me. I googled the animal totem for a toad and it said to solely concentrate on oneself and let nothing else get in the way. Point noted.

Last night I had that recurring dream. The one with the pine trees leading to the beach with the swimming tubes and giant swans. What the hell is that all about?

But then one fine day, the answer came to what Dad was talking about in the reading.

There was one more thing that I had to do in order to end my journey.

Chapter 30

Trust the Universe

As I mentioned earlier, you can do nothing wrong by cosmic ordering and asking the Universe for things. Why don't you try it? I started to regularly ask for and affirm things as I had a clear knowing that the Universe was in sync with me and was indeed bringing me what I needed for the greater good. If I wasn't asking for things, I was writing affirmations to reinforce positive living.

My mood was starting to become more light and positive as the days went by. I was noticing the birdsong more. I would smile at the smallest of things. I started to feel grateful for my life. I started to actually be proud of myself and love me for who I was, plain old Nicky fighting a cruel disease.

I also sensed a certain freedom just being 'me'. It was invigorating. I had nothing to offer anyone apart from my love and loyalty. I was starting to feel the chain mail of my armour falling away with each positive thought and action that I did.

I was also proud of myself for maintaining a diet lifestyle that was good for me. I started to research all of the health supplements that would help me as well.

We all have different bodies and types of symptoms, but I would like to list what I started to take and still do take daily as this may help a fellow M.E./Fibro sufferer.

1. **Glucosamine Sulphate with Chondroitin** – Feeds the joints, has a vital role in feeding cartilage.
2. **Magnesium** – Orally taken it helps cell, nerve, muscle, bone function. In a bath (Epsom salts) it relaxes your muscles and eases stiffened joints.
3. **Cod Liver Oil** – Autoimmune deficiencies, relieves joint pain, and alleviates depression.

4. **Vitamin D** – Helps the body absorb calcium, prevents bone loss.
5. **Busy B's** – Promotes nerve and blood cell growth.
6. **Vitamin C** – Repairs bone, cartilage and teeth. Produces collagen to make skin, tendons, ligaments and blood vessels.
7. **Turmeric** – Improves depression and works as an anti-inflammatory and antioxidant.
8. **Dried Sage** – Helps with hot flushes and temperature disorders. Alleviates digestive problems. Helps with depression.
9. **Vitamin K** – Helps to absorb magnesium into your system.

The magic number nine, an angel number of goodies to take!

Please always check with your doctor if you plan to take any supplements to ensure that they do not interact with any medication. You will know pretty quickly if your body doesn't like any of the supplements. I found if anything went into my body, including food, that it didn't like, it took minutes to be purged, literally!

I was mindful of what foods were high in particular minerals and vitamins. I would eat these and also put them in juices and smoothies. I invested in a food processor and a NutriBullet so I could make organic foods from scratch, and nutritious shakes and smoothies full of goodness. I would add cinnamon to the smoothies as I found this to be an antioxidant and anti-inflammatory.

I also started taking regular Epsom salt baths with lavender oil added. They were so soothing and took the edge off of the pain quite noticeably.

I didn't really care at the time if they worked or not. The fact that I had some control over this condition helped me to cope. I felt that I was actually doing something to help my health and energy.

Despite all of my efforts I went down with a head cold. I had to visit the doctor's surgery and no doubt picked up someone's germs.

This cold, however, was a fortunate event. I was sleeping most of the day as I knew my body was struggling to cope fighting the germs. I just did absolutely nothing apart from sleep. If you try and fight it, you end up prolonging your relapse. The reason that it was fortunate was because the dreams I was having were well remembered when I woke up. On my dad's birthday, I dreamt of standing by the sea and smiling. The emotion was so strong that when I woke up, a certain mindset had shifted within me.

Things were about to change on a major scale.

Sunday 27 August 2017
On Tuesday I went down with a head cold and now sleep like a bitch as my body is obviously struggling to cope. I feel isolated and on waking up from a dream today, for the first time I seriously doubt my move here. I'm miles away from any shop and am not close to anyone to ask for help.

I need a plan.

I need to get this house finished.

I need to get a book out.

When I know my financial status I will move back to Devon in a house that's done. Has a nice garden and sea views and near the fucking shops! No more being in the middle of nowhere, it just doesn't work when I'm ill. I am totally alone and have no one really close. I just can't believe how alone I could be. At least in Devon there are beaches. At least I can get a lovely sunny home by the sea.

That is my next goal.

I adore this house but it's too far from anywhere and anyone.

If I lived in Brixham or nearby I know more people and can get on to the beaches and in all the pubs and restaurants.

A nice bright house!

I HAVE TO GET A BOOK DEAL!

I have to!
Archangel Gabriel please steer me well and help me. PLEASE!
ORDER:
SEA VIEWS
NICE GARDEN
EN SUITE/NEAR BATHROOM
NO MAJOR WORK
NEAR HARBOUR OR ALONG THE COAST WITH VIEWS
AIM TO HAVE FOUND A HOUSE SPRING 2019.

I didn't realise it at the time, but my dad had given me a present on his birthday. I was totally up for moving back to Devon. I knew it would be hell packing up and moving again but there was a driving need in me to have to do it. I can't explain it, I just knew that I had to move.

The cottage had served me well, as had the cemetery cottage, but I felt that I needed to re-enter the world again, being alone in nature was now not enough. Glastonbury had also been a major part of my healing. On any day that I felt well, I would go to the White Spring and meditate. I would then sit there for as long as I could absorbing the mysterious energy in that cavern. I had been called to that area for a reason, but now it was time to move forward.

Incredibly I had made £70,000 equity on the house which in normal life was impossible, but I had the angels on my side. I was still very scared to make such a big change so I decided that I would pull three angel cards. I would make the decision on those cards as that was the faith I had gained through all of the suffering.

Three cards were going to make a decision on my next life event. Now is that absolute faith or what?

PAGE OF FIRE
Situation: An exciting opportunity comes your way! The angels

guide you to wholeheartedly embrace this new endeavour. It may seem like a challenge but it's one you are ready for. Dazzle people with your originality and ingenuity.

Good news. Creativity. Project. Believing in yourself.

Moving and book!

NINE OF AIR

Positive thinking is essential right now. Your own obsessive thoughts are the true culprit here behind the trouble you fear. Release your guilt and realise that regret is a wasted emotion. Turn your attention to the amazing possibilities for the future and leave the past behind.

ARCHANGEL AZRAEL

RELEASE

Time to move on because this project or phase of your life is now complete. There's no benefit in remaining in this situation. Instead shake off the old, and welcome the new! You may experience a sense of relief at this ending, or maybe some sadness. Either way it is time to leave that which you have outgrown.

Take your time adjusting to this change in your life. It's not necessary to rush ahead. Be kind to yourself during this period of transition and seek the support of family and friends.

Azrael heals your heart when changes and losses bring grieving.

Move forward fearlessly and let go of the past.

The word 'family' stuck in my throat as I read the last card. I had none; I still felt abandoned by my brother and sister. They knew I was very ill, so how could they possibly still leave me alone knowing that? What had I done that was so bad that they had forsaken me?

Is that something I needed to clear? Is that what Dad meant in the reading? Or was it just the move that I needed to do?

I also felt very worried about the 'sadness' bit. Perhaps it was the sadness of leaving the cottage. I knew that I would miss my spiritual visits to Glastonbury as well, but surely I wouldn't be that sad?

All these questions were answered within the year. I also didn't realise how much Archangel Azrael would be in my life in a matter of months.

Needless to say as soon as I read the third card, I phoned up the estate agents and put my house up for sale. I didn't need to think about it, the cards had said it all.

That evening I packed my first box up. I knew I had months of packing as I couldn't manage it in big hits. I felt excited but also terrified. What if I had made the wrong decision and the cards were just coincidence?

Despite my silent fears, it appeared that my writing career was being boosted yet again. On 27th September I got an email from one of the team at Bauer Publishing who I write the columns for. My column "Diary of a Psychic" was now going to be included in the Australian launch of *Spirit & Destiny*. I was now an international columnist. The first column was to go out in January 2018. I felt that yet again I was being reminded that I had to stay focused as a writer.

Saturday 14 October 2017

LOVELY DAY! The last three weeks have been excellent and manageable. Is the diet kicking in? Been to Mum's which was heart breaking as nothing changes there. Joe has been diagnosed with lung cancer. They are not operating so it doesn't look good. I tried to sort everything out I could.

Brixham was amazing. I want to be in Brixham but the first two viewings there I didn't like the road. I am not going to stress though, I trust the process implicitly.

Lindsey is here and we went to Glastonbury today.

In the White Spring I asked for strength to move forward and take on my new transitional stage. We then went to the Goddess Temple. Wow! What a meditation! I was walking along a path barefoot. I had a long white robe on and long dark hair. As I walked along I stroked a lion (inner strength) and then saw my wolf that has returned to me. White with two black markings on the face. I then had a white pigeon that turned into an eagle on my shoulder. I was in a glorious enchanted garden but then I walked into a cave. By a fire was Catherine as a crone. She showed a Labradorite and a Ruby which I must wear. I then moved on and saw Lindsey's dad giving me a watch that said 5.25. I then walked out to the fountain. I swirled the water and asked about me.

All I saw was APRIL and AUGUST. I then came around.

My four cards were:

Doing things for the earth.

Coming to the end of a phase.

Being given the strength to move forward.

Saying goodbye to an old life.

I knew that I had to get a Ruby so I and Linds went to my fave crystal shop.

The only one in the shop was a crystal pendant, really pretty, so I bought it, very naughty!

But, its properties are to get rid of exhaustion and strength to move forward, saying goodbye to an old life! It's a power stone! Happy days!

When we walked up the High Street a white pigeon flew down right in front of me and landed. It then took off and flew within inches of my left shoulder.

Gorgeous synchronicity.

All in all a very special day. I have now got my wolf back so I am ready to power forward. I have also booked my first eve of mediumship in Devon! Can't believe it. I just have started to feel so different! Long may it last!

Amazingly Linds called her mum and asked her to dig out her dad's old watch. Her mum went and got it, and the time on the watch had stopped dead at 5.25. I was so thrilled! It was a lovely bit of evidence that also backed up the rest of my meditation. I was totally in sync with the spirit world, the angel realms and the Universe. I loved living, breathing and digesting every synchronicity and sign. I just regretted not doing it earlier. They had been there all along. It was me that had blocked them out in the early days. We can but only learn and move on, we must never regret anything.

The Ruby and the Labradorite did not leave my body for months.

The decision to move had brought a definite skip in my step. I had something to aim for again. The boxes started to multiply as I packed one or two a day. The realisation that I was actually moving hit me with a feeling of apprehension and fear, but I knew I had to trust the angels and the Universe.

My health definitely felt better. I knew that the diet was helping me to feel stronger. I was experiencing less pain on more days of the week, was sleeping soundly and could actually stay awake all day! I had no digestive issues any longer which was such a relief. Everything seemed to be going along nicely. There were people viewing the house but I heard nothing back after each visit. This didn't worry me though as I knew that my movement would take place April and August next year.

I had lots of time to get packed up and ready. It wasn't long before I was due to go back to Devon to try an evening of mediumship at Paignton. With this newfound energy I wanted to see how I would fare linking up to spirit people for an evening. I was excited but also exceptionally nervous. I had not done an evening like this for years. Was it going to work? Was I going to fall flat on my face? Was I going to embarrass myself in front of a whole audience? Was I going to be as good as I used to be? Would I ruin my reputation? All of these ego-based thoughts rented my head.

The evening sold out really quickly so I knew that I had to deliver to all of these expectant people wanting to know their futures and hear from their dead loved ones.

Funny how life takes its twists and turns.

I was in for a ride that I never expected. It was going to bring exceptional pain but exceptional joy.

To think that I was worried about an evening of mediumship makes me want to laugh now, as I now know what was coming.

Chapter 31

The Reunion

The evening of mediumship went better than I could have ever imagined. Because I had been away for so long, the spirit people were lining up to get a message to their loved ones in the audience. I could see their shadows on the walls all around the room. I could feel their apprehension and desperate need to use me to bring words of comfort and evidence to all of the people they loved stuck down here on the earth plane.

The second half was a lot tougher. I could feel my energy leaving me, my legs started to shake with the effort of it all. I could feel my throat straining to get one spirit person through after another. The pain started to snake its way through my back and neck as I trundled along to the finishing line.

I am my own worst critic. The audience was elated, and as I walked out of the hall to the sound of rapturous applause, I thought the knotted feeling in my stomach was that I hadn't done well enough. I checked my phone and had a call from my stepdad Joe's daughter. My mum had had a fall that evening and had broken her hip. That explained my knotted stomach.

I had a day's rest then drove to Hayling Island. I drove in a zombie state as the show had totally exhausted me. My heart kept palpitating. I had a sense of doom but I didn't know why. It was only a broken hip, nothing life-threatening. I was also terrified as I had been told that my brother was also coming from Essex to see Mum. I had not seen Richard for six years. We had parted on bad terms. I didn't know if he was going to ignore me, shout at me or had got to the stage of a truce. The closer I got to Hayling, the worse I felt.

I arrived at my mum's house and couldn't find the spare key. Luckily there was a window ajar at the back of the bungalow so I crawled through there. The familiar scent of my mum's bedroom brought a lump to my throat. The fact that she wasn't laying there as was usual for her left me feeling desolate and scared. She had been pretty much bed bound for a while, her mobility not great. I had been asking social services for care to be provided for both my mum Evelyn and my stepdad Joe as he had had a stroke and was battling lung cancer. I was perpetually ignored or sent to another department to no avail.

I then heard voices in the back garden and my stomach lurched. My heart was banging through my ribcage as I saw the outline of my little brother.

He looked at me through the window and said, "Alright?"

I could see in his eyes that he wanted peace between us. I was too emotional to answer. As he climbed through the window I grabbed hold of him and stood there embracing him for a long time. As I breathed him in, visions of us playing as children in our bunk beds fired through my mind. Protecting him from the abuse monster during our childhood, him holding my nephew Tyler only a few days old flashed into my head. I sobbed and sobbed as we clung on to one another. How had we come to this juncture? After everything we had endured in our lives, the loss of my dad, the loss of my mum's spirit, the abusive years, why had we been so stubborn?

All I could muster was, "I'm so happy to see you and I am so sorry."

Why had we been apart for so long? Why had he distanced himself and refused to see me or talk to me? These were questions that we had to address at a later stage. I then saw my sister-in-law Louise, and then in a shallow breath I gazed upon my nephew Tyler and niece, Jess. Memories of me babysitting Tyler came reeling back. The thought of missing out on so much of his little lifetime brought more tears to my eyes. He came up to me and hugged me saying how much he had missed me. The last time that I had seen him he was four years old.

Jess was slightly more apprehensive. The last time that I had seen her was when she was a few months old. She was only six and so I had missed all of her life. She did, however, give me a cuddle. To feel her in my arms was nothing short of pure joy. I vowed I would never be apart from these beautiful children again.

I felt an enormous sense of relief as we started to discuss Mum. The loveless six-year void started to close as we chatted and laughed.

When we got to the hospital, I could see my mum was elated to see us all together. There were two things she said that she wanted to see before she died. One was to see us all together again. The other was that she wanted to see me settled down with a lovely man who would look after me. That's all she would ever say. She was a nightmare, my mum. She refused to talk about her wishes for her funeral, she refused to address any of that sort of subject. Her usual response was, "Don't be so bloody morbid!"

My mum had grown a protective shell after my dad died. She then endured the physical violence and the mental cruelty by the animal. By the time she met Joe, him not being anywhere close to death and not a violent animal, she found a form of happiness. They lived in Spain for several years and then came back to England, setting up roots in Hayling Island where Joe's family lived. She would never open her heart to any of us. She would never discuss her feelings, fears, hopes or dreams. She disappeared into a safe space in the latter part of her life, watching television, drinking alcohol and smoking heavily. It was heartbreaking to see.

Whenever I tried to encourage her to get out and about she blatantly refused. The only time you would see her true feelings was when she was drunk. I would be told by her that she was sorry for the pain I went through by the animal. She would say how much she missed Dad. She would say that she wanted me to find my soulmate and be happy. Then she would check herself and change the subject.

Despite all of this though my mum was a very witty woman. She would talk to anyone and was fearless. Her dry sense of humour made her hilarious. She would tell me off for swearing but could take on a sailor any day of the week! She was brave, fragile, beautiful and stubborn.

As we all entered the room, the first thing she said was, "The tea is shit in here!" She was fully made-up, hair done and was restless; she wanted to go home. I smiled with a huge sigh of relief. It reminded me of when she had had her breast removed years ago. I had warned my sister, Sarah, that she would probably look awful as she had had her first round of chemotherapy. When we got to the hospital she was fully made-up, hair done and moaning that she wanted a glass of wine. She adamantly refused to go down to the operation without her make-up on!

Joe was there sitting by her side. He looked like a shell of his old self. He didn't talk a lot or engage with us. I could see that somewhere along the line he had lost the will to fight.

We all found chairs and started to amiably chatter and have a laugh. I love photographing anything. I love the nostalgia as I look back at photos imprinting a space in time. I took a photo of my sister-in-law and the kids across the room from my mum.

As I took the photo, I heard the name, "Azrael."

I shivered as I heard the name. Amongst other things, he is the Archangel who presides over people who are passing over and the family surrounding them. I felt physically sick. I then gasped as I looked at the photo. The whole picture was blurred with a thick blue and white mist. It looked as if I had taken an out-of-focus picture surrounded by a thick cloud. I immediately took another photo, but the mist had disappeared.

I had an immediate sense of impending doom, but refused to give it life. Why would Azrael be in the room with us? I swallowed it down, forced a smile and continued to sit in the chatter-filled room finally amongst family. I had waited years for this reunion, but it felt bittersweet. A small discarnate voice nagging away in the pit of my stomach wouldn't shut up.

My mum was severely underweight, but apart from that she was her old cynical, dry, funny self. After visiting hours we went back to Mum's. Joe started to drink and had started smoking again. He sat watching old films and made it clear that he didn't want to talk about anything. The news of his lung cancer seemed to be the final nail in his proverbial coffin.

The following day before visiting Mum we all headed to the beach. I felt a sense of belonging as I watched Tyler and Jess run in the sand. The night before, Tyler had insisted on sleeping with me. We talked to the early hours catching up on everything. I learned that he was exceptionally psychic and saw spirit people quite a lot. I was filled with a sense of kinship, the psychic legacy was being handed down to the next generation. Jess warmed up to me very quickly. Our obsession with fairies and unicorns sealed the deal. She is an elemental. A soul that adores animals and the planet. She is completely convinced that there are fairy realms and now is a vegetarian. Yet another special soul in our family.

I had decided to stay at my mum's. I needed to arrange care and sort out sheltered housing. There was no way my mum and Joe could cope alone anymore. On good days I could feed them, clean the house and start sorting out their lives. Rich and Lou left with the kids a couple of days later. A part of my heart went with them as I waved goodbye.

Before they had left I had whispered in Rich's ear, "Promise me, no matter what happens we will never be apart again."

He nodded and said, "Of course, stupid!"

I knew that we had to discuss our estrangement, but it was the wrong time.

The following day I went up to see Mum. One of the doctors who was particularly handsome popped in whilst I was there.

He came with grave news. My mum was initially flirting with him asking him to join her on the bed, but as he spoke his fatal words, it was the first time I had seen my mum truly scared.

They had found cancer nodules on her lungs and liver. They weren't huge but were still there, promising a future of more chemo and misery.

My mum cried for a few seconds as she gulped the words out, "But we can get rid of them though, can't we?"

The doctor assured her that all questions would be answered by the oncology doctor. Isn't it amazing how mere words can bring shock to the soul? I felt like I had been hit by a train. I knew that my mum wasn't going to make it even though the doctor had said that the nodules weren't life-threatening in any way.

That night for the first time in five years I spoke to my sister Sarah. It felt like I was talking to a stranger. I spoke with the children as well, Faith, Grace and Harry. My heart yearned to see them in the flesh. Nothing was discussed apart from Mum's predicament. All of that could wait. The time would be right for that conversation, the conversation of the 'hows' and 'whys' we had denied each other sibling love.

Mum was discharged a couple of days later. The first thing she did was drink a large glass of cider and light up a cigarette. I realised in that space of time that she really didn't want to fight. At night I would cry silent tears. She was slipping away and there was absolutely nothing I could do about it.

The next days were filled with occupational health workers, social workers, oncology doctors, assessments and care teams. I was getting more exhausted by the hour. Finally when the care teams were in place I had thoughts of going back home to rest. I also had to get a hold on the status of my moving. I assured my mum that she would now be well looked after and that I would be back soon.

I will never forget these words.

"Please don't leave me, Nick, please stay," Mum pleaded.

I assured her that she would be fine. I needed some peace and quiet. I felt so guilty on having to leave. I also felt torn as my mum had never shown weakness or begged me to stay before. I knew though that if I stayed there I would go downhill; my body couldn't take much more. I knew Rich was going to go to see them and that the carers were there three times a day. She would be fine.

How stupid was I to leave.

Saturday 18 November 2017
The roller coaster is never ending. Soaring and dipping leaving me lost and found. Mum had a fall the same day I did my show on 2 November. The show was a blast. I worked quite well but the second half was a lot harder. Mum broke her hip so after a day's rest I went straight over. In true fashion Joe was smoking and drinking. Mum looks like a bag of bones coloured in black and blue. It's heart breaking to see. I got everything sorted, social care, etc. and to be honest it killed me. I'm back at home now and haven't left my bed for three days and have flu symptoms. I have had no viewings. Just one for the 26th November.

Sometimes I get down, other times I have to convince myself that I have to trust and everything is as it should be. What do I want when I move?

ORDER:
Walking the dogs straight from the house.
Bedroom near toilet/kitchen/garden
Small garden
Near shops/facilities
Nice views preferably sea views
Parking
MARCH/APRIL seems the month, if nothing happens after that then I'm going to start doubting my motives.
But this has to be right?
I need to be near people and shops. The way Mum and Joe are going,

I don't think it will be too long. I met Tyler and Jess. Beautiful children. Made my peace with Richard. So at least something has come from all of this. It appears nothing much has changed in all of these years.

I tried not taking LDN, but I could feel the pain snaking its way back in after three days so I went back on it. Within half an hour, the pain started to go.

I have no other arsenal. I just have to wait for this illness to leave me.

I have been very grounded whilst being at Hayling. Feeling nothing but anger, frustration and exhaustion. So I thought I should pick some cards.

STRENGTH

ARCHANGEL ARIEL

You are stronger than you realise. You can definitely handle your current situation. Softness and compassion are needed. Patience. Forgiveness. Courage of your convictions.

Ariel helps out on earth needs, home, food, clothing, desperate times and finance.

QUEEN OF AIR

Your clear decision-making abilities are needed right now. See through hidden agendas. Remove things/people that no longer serve your greatest good. Still, try to see the underlying humour.

THREE OF AIR

Something has occurred that makes you sad. Trust it will pass and you will see this situation's purpose in life. Take time to heal. Remove painful memories and move bravely forward. Don't hold on to past disappointments or conflict. Forgive yourself for choices you might have made differently. You did the best at the time. Allow yourself to move on.

Misunderstandings. Loneliness. Relationship concerns. Painful revelations.

Those cards could not have been more accurate if they tried.

Chapter 32

So, This Is Christmas

For the next couple of weeks I was completely bed bound. I had noticed that pushing your body with this condition is really not a good way to go. Your immune system hits rock bottom and you tend to pick up every single germ going. Every morning I would wake feeling positive, but as soon as I started to move about symptoms of a flu nature would wrack through my body.

I had no choice but to rest.

I phoned Mum every day and got the usual, "Yes I am eating, yes I'm having plenty of juice, yes Joe is alright, and yes the carers are OK."

Why she didn't tell me what was really going on I will never know.

I had explained that I was really weak and had to rest; she said that she understood.

For the first time after many years I was going to have a family Christmas. The plan was to pick Mum up at Hayling a few days before Christmas and take her down to Richard's in Essex. We would then have Boxing Day at Sarah's house where I would finally see her, my nieces and nephews. I didn't care how ill I was, I was going to bloody well get her and me to Essex if it killed me. The closer to the date, my mum started to change her mind. I started to get really pissed off with her as I thought she was just being her usual agoraphobic self. It never occurred to me how ill she really was as she didn't hint at any problems at all. Besides, if there were any major problems the carers would have let me know.

Around the 19th December, I kept calling Mum's house and the line kept ringing. I thought that she had left the phone off of the charger and it was flat. To be honest I really did have the hump with her as I thought she was avoiding me. After ringing her time and time again with no answer, I thought, 'sod her'. I will go down to Essex on my own. I left a message on the answerphone saying that I was going to Richard's and I would see her the day after Boxing Day. I had arranged home-delivered dinners for them, and knew that when she wanted to talk, she would phone me.

How many times in your life have you let your ego make your decisions and then felt that heart-smashing regret afterwards?

I felt a little relieved if I am brutally honest that I didn't have to go to Hayling and then drive to Essex. I was beyond exhausted so just concentrating on one long drive was bearable.

It was an absolute joy to see my brother again. To hear the normal sounds of a family unit hit me with such intensity. Watching the kids eat their breakfast, the jokes, them clattering about upstairs playing in their room gave me a sense of such comfort.

On Christmas Day I was determined to have any other normal day like any other family member. Lou passed me a glass of Prosecco at midday, and I drank that glass as if it was a challenge. Alcohol had not passed my lips for years. I felt my body burn as it entered my system. LDN is not a great mix with alcohol because it makes you go slightly hot in the face. I was determined to be normal, so when the second glass came, I sipped away ignoring the heat creeping up my cheeks.

At 1pm I had a niggling feeling and knew that we had to call Mum. I had still not heard from her, and had moaned at my brother that she was a stubborn old cow that just wanted to stay in bed, drink, smoke and watch *Death in Paradise*, her favourite programme.

Rich wanted to wait until we had dinner but I just couldn't shake this intensely dark feeling.

"Rich, I am not being funny but we need to ring Mum now!"

"Nick, let's just wait until after dinner," Rich reasoned.

"No, we have to phone her now!"

I called her number and to my relief my mum picked up. As soon as I said hello all I got back was breathless moans and unintelligible speech. I started to panic. I had her on speaker phone. As soon as Lou heard her, she dialled 999.

I was so shocked and angry, she sounded horrific. Where the bloody hell were the carers? Joe's daughter was supposed to be going round there, why didn't she say anything?

The next we heard was my mum had had a cardiac arrest when the paramedics moved her. She was resuscitated and taken to the hospital. If I hadn't phoned when I did she would have been laying in the bed dead. We then heard that both Joe and my mum were in A&E, and that we should get there as soon as possible. What the hell had happened?

My brother called my sister. Within twenty minutes, our Christmas dinner not even touched, I stood outside Rich's house numbly awaiting the reunion with my sister.

Sarah got out of the car and I hugged her. It was surreal. We were crying, panicking, scared. Our past was left unspoken as she got into my car and we started the trip to Hayling. I had had two glasses of Prosecco and felt guilty, oh so very guilty. I could be over the limit but worst of all I had not gone to see my mum. I had assumed that she was OK and had left her. With each mile I drove, more guilt ripped into me.

I cannot even begin to describe the feelings that reeled through me when we arrived. Both Joe and Mum were on oxygen, couldn't speak and looked on death's door. It had turned out that they were pretty much starved, dehydrated and would have died if left for any longer. We were all raging. The A&E doctor had put an immediate safeguard against the carers. She was disgusted at the state of both of them.

I can remember so clearly Sarah, Rich and I sitting in the hospital car park on Christmas Day eating vending machine crap and drinking shitty tea for our Christmas dinner!

We sat with both of them for hours. They were both so disorientated and breathless, we couldn't communicate with them. I said a prayer in Mum's ear saying that Raphael was with her as we left. Some heads were going to roll for this.

When we got to my mum's house the second shock was about to take place. The bin was filled with rotten food and soiled incontinence pads. There was a bin bag next to where my mum's pillow was, filled with faeces and incontinence pads and an overflowing needle bin. The mattress was dripping with urine on to the floor. In the fridge all of the delivered meals were in there rotting. The milk had gone off over a week ago. It was disgusting. The last few weeks of my mum being in her own bed, she was surrounded by filth. I noticed from her medication that she hadn't taken anything for over a week. As far as I was concerned the pathetic care system had failed massively. I did not get one call from them at all. The anger and the guilt were overwhelming.

That night after cleaning everything up, Sarah, Rich and I had the inevitable 'What the hell happened all those years ago' chat.

It turned out that Dick, my ex, had been stealing money from my company. Sarah and Rich had found out. I was ill in bed after the road crash and was told by Dick that they didn't want to see me. He convinced me, which he would as he is a con man, that they no longer wanted to work with me and had had enough of me. I believed this as it just corroborated what I already thought about myself back in the days of my low self-esteem.

Sarah and Rich were amazed as they had been banging down my front door asking to see me at the time. They in turn had been told that I wanted nothing to do with them and never wanted to see them again. Dick had taken my phone, so they had no way of contacting me. He manipulated us against each other so he could get away with stealing the money. Bearing in mind he had also cashed out all of my credit cards, he knew that the game was up; time to move on leaving a family broken in his wake. As we were already splintered from our past, time marched on alongside our loathing and betrayal of each other.

I could not believe the things he had said to my little brother and sister. The lies so easily planned and executed. He had even sent awful messages to them pretending that they were from me.

We spoke for hours into the morning making our peace, reaffirming our sibling bond.

It felt good. It felt like this incredible weight had been lifted from my struggling shoulders. It was a release that I never knew had been such a weight on my soul. Finally we were together again. It was just a tragedy that it was because Mum and Joe were in hospital. All I can add is if you are in a similar predicament, call whoever you are estranged from. Bridges cannot be built without that first move from either side.

The day after Boxing Day I drove back to Essex with Sarah and Rich. Mum was stable in a ward. She still couldn't speak and was struggling for breath. My auntie June and cousin Leslie joined us as we sat around Mum, all silently shocked by the state of her. She had deteriorated so badly since I had left her. I wanted to strangle the carers; who the fuck leaves human beings in that state? We had already put a complaint in to the local authorities; we needed answers.

I will never forget as we were about to leave. I told Mum that I would be back in two days. As I told her I loved her, I whispered into her ear, "Don't be scared, Mum. Dad is with you and all the rest of them, and so are my angels. I love you."

She looked into my eyes smiling and just winked at me. I will never forget the look she gave me and that wink for as long as I live.

Sarah had a cold during this whole time. It came as no shock that when I was driving back down to Hayling after two days I could feel myself get a fever. My chest was aching with every breath. I had a sore throat, my head was banging and every inch of my body was mutinously limiting my every move with gut-wrenching pain.

When I finally got to Mum's I knew that I had to go straight to bed. I called the hospital to ask them to tell Mum I would be there tomorrow as I wasn't very well. They said not to worry as she was moaning about the tea and was comfortable. I smiled at this and thought all was OK.

The following day I could hardly breathe. The pain in my chest and body was excruciating. It was the 30th December, and yet again I knew that I would be seeing the New Year in alone and ill in bed.

I knew the staff at the local surgery who kindly got me in to see the doctor within an hour. I had bronchitis and a throat infection. My body was in such a weakened state that I couldn't walk very far before I would collapse. I was in a bad way with no one to help me.

I was seething with self-pity, anger, fear and frustration. My mum was lying in a hospital bed, I was a few miles away and couldn't get to see her. I cried on the phone to the nurse when I explained my predicament. He was very sympathetic and said that it wouldn't be a great idea anyway for me to go to the hospital spreading my germs to all of the patients. He stated that Mum was comfortable and that she knew I was poorly and not to worry.

Monday 1 January 2018
I wanted to read my entry for last year but haven't got it. I wonder what I asked for and hoped for?

I cried as I watched Big Ben. I'm sitting at Mum's on my own whilst she is in hospital. I don't know what is going to happen and I don't know what is happening with my move either. I caught Sarah's cold and feel like total shit so I'm not exactly in the right mood or energy for positive cosmic ordering. I think it's also the thought of another year gone by of illness. I achieved a column in Australia and with Spirit & Destiny *and made money on my house. That's it. Oh and went gluten-free and I have to say restricted sugar as I have been eating things with sugar in. It's hard to maintain it when my arse is here, there and everywhere.*

My horoscopes keep saying creating, writing, publishing and successful career moves this year. We will see.

I hope I find the most amazing house imaginable that I just can't wait to move in to. I hope I get a grip on my health and have better days socially.

I really hope that I get out there as a writer. I hope that Mum ends up comfortable and happy somewhere.

I haven't seen many signs or synchronicity.

At the moment I call upon Archangel Azrael to preside over Mum, Joe and us.

I also ask Archangel Michael to protect me from stressful situations and people and to give me the strength during this year of transition.

Networking, improved social life and lack of isolation have also come up on my horoscope, so hopefully that will come into fruition.

I desperately hope that this time next year I'm sitting in my new home smiling, knowing that I have found a forever home. Movement has been the presiding factor and I need to find my roots.

Perhaps then I can attract more solid things in my life.

It can't get much worse so surely things can only get better.

MY WEBSITE TAROT READING

PAST

Mastery of all the suit of cups. Art, beauty, intimacy, love.

Ability to express love and nurture others.

PRESENT

Feeling vulnerable. The ability to defend yourself in a difficult situation. Need for caution and examination.

POSSIBLE FUTURE

Expectations of reward. Waiting for a material harvest, be it a creative project, personal relationship or both. Financial reward. Nurturing others.

OVERVIEW

Dissent that may be the psyche or personified by people around you. Conflict for the sake of conflict. Losing sight of what's important over petty decisions.

Great...

Then I asked when I'm moving.

Constructive and pragmatic building. The ability to transform talents into material goods or business success. Cooperating with others to create such an adventure.

Wisdom gained after struggle. End of a difficult situation. Experience is the best teacher, for better for worse. Sharing your knowledge with others.

Cutting through confusion. Being able to defend oneself brilliantly. Focus/clarity of understanding.

The forces of worldly prosperity. The ability to create wealth. Real estate transactions. Investments, money or emotional. Steadfastness.

Great satisfaction. Prosperity and the construction of a home. Joy and pleasure.

New knowledge that will help one grow and move beyond current limitations. Travel in order to gain distance from difficulties.

OVERVIEW

Important decisions or news. Movement into the next phase of life. Time for a major and necessary change in life – often welcome but frightening because of its magnitude.

We shall see. Just need a sign to back up these messages.

SQUIRREL

One ran out down the road in front of me. Then I saw one hanging from a tree right in front of me the same day. Googled animal totems.

Have more fun, take life less seriously.

Get ready for major changes.

New job, new move. Start preparing!

Lighten the load of previous worry, thought and stresses.

There for the grace of God go I...

So it appeared that I was going to do well with my work and would have my new home. I stayed in bed calling the hospital a couple of times a day. Mum seemed fine, so I didn't feel too guilty that I was stuck at her home only a few miles away and not able to see her.

Then your world shifts, the goalposts change and everything you see as familiar turns into a dark shadowy stranger.

At 8.33am on Wednesday 3 January, the hospital called. I was told to get up there immediately.

Chapter 33

The End of a Season

Azrael heals your heart when changes and losses bring grieving.
Move forward fearlessly and let go of the past.

That was in my head as I put the phone down. It was one of the cards that I drew on my dad's birthday on the 27th August. I knew then that my mum was dead.

I started to panic. I called Joe's son-in-law as I wasn't fit to drive. I pushed my boots on, still in my pyjamas, and waited for him to arrive. The drive to the hospital was surreal. I was in denial hoping that my instinct was wrong and I would find her up drinking tea moaning about how shit it was. My whole body was tingling so I knew that I wasn't alone. My spirit family were there with me.

The cliché of running to the hospital room to find the bed empty came into play, and before I knew it I was being ushered into a private room.

I screamed out, "Don't bother giving me the agony, where is she?" albeit rather aggressively. I was beside myself. I had missed her passing. I had stayed at her house ill and had not been with her for the last days of her life. The guilt consumed me as I burst the door open to her room.

She was still warm as I cried out,

"No, Mum, why didn't you wait?" grabbing her hand. She had passed at 8.42am as I was on the way to the hospital.

This is going to sound weird but the first thing I did was take off her silver bracelet as it was still warm. I put it straight on and said to her,

"Mum, I know you are still in the room with me. Listen, when you are ready tell one of my medium friends that I took your silver bracelet off with the dangling heart, so I know that you are safely up and with Dad."

I told no one about that. I wanted the proof when she was ready.

I called my brother and told him. I didn't tell Sarah over the phone, I wanted Rich to tell her face to face.

I then sat there numbly looking at my mum's tired face. That blessed time I had with her for a few hours alone was the perfect opportunity to tell her everything that I wanted to say. I kept her hand warm so that Sarah wouldn't feel how cold she was when she got there.

The pain that ripped through my heart was tangible. I thought of my mum's life. She had lost her soulmate, been punched and beaten for years, settled down to a nondescript life and then had died.

I cried for her, I cried for my family and I cried for me. We were now orphans. Yet another family member residing in the spirit world. There was just my auntie and uncle left along with my cousins that was it.

Joe's son-in-law came in and said that the CD player in Mum's car had just turned itself on. A CD had been stuck in the player for five years and it was totally broken. It then, to his shock, came on by itself and played *Mirror in the Bathroom*.

I could see no relevance to that, but as soon as he said it, my friend Nick phoned and said she had just filmed the weirdest thing. Her bathroom mirror started flashing like disco lights. This was impossible as it was just two lightbulb tubes under a mirror. The bulbs, however, were flashing in different places along the tube. When I saw the footage there was also a massive orb that floated from the mirror.

This was my first sign from the spirit world that they were with us.

I honoured their effort but when it's raw you don't give a shit about the spirit world, you just want your mum back. Sarah and

Rich arrived hours later. It was a scene of misery and disbelief. Why had she died? What had she died from? The anger then kicked in along with the guilt. Knowing the stages of grief I was monitoring my feelings as they came. I knew there were plenty more stages to come.

My Auntie June then turned up with my Uncle Bob and my cousin Leslie. We all sat around Mum saying our goodbyes. The hospital was great, they didn't rush us at all.

I placed a selenite crystal on my mum's solar plexus. It's an angel stone. I wanted to help the link between Azrael and my mum's soul. I wanted her to be met by Dad, Nan and her favourite Aunt Rene as she was taken to Jeremiel.

I explained the process to the rest of the family.

It was later in the afternoon, as I looked out of the window to the bleak grey building opposite, that I felt the surge.

It's like going over a bridge in a car when your tummy turns over. The tingling started in the bottom of my spine and surged up to my scalp buzzing my crown chakra.

Her soul was leaving the building.

I quickly turned around and was so shocked when I looked at her. Her face looked empty, bereft of any soul. She had waited for everyone to be there; her soul then went home. She had now transitioned; the only thing left was skin and bones. I knew it was time.

I said to everyone, "Right, that's it. I think it's time we left her now rather than sitting around her."

As I said this everyone looked up as one of the ceiling lights that was over Mum's body blazed to a magnificent brightness. It then dimmed down to nothing, and went back to normal.

"You all saw that right?" I asked. "That's Mum's sign to let us know it's time to go, she is OK."

Everyone silently nodded still looking at the light.

We said our final goodbyes and listlessly left the room with much reluctance. The physical parting had taken place, the next challenge would be dealing with the parting emotionally.

We don't get much chance to grieve in the early days when people pass as it's all about the legalities and sorting their affairs out. So we all robotically went through the motions. I drove myself on day after day stuffing painkillers down my throat. My solace was being amongst my siblings. We pulled together and supported each other.

With this physical death my mum had left a legacy of sibling reunion and unconditional love. It was something that we never really had. Isn't it funny how such tragedy leads to something quite precious?

The police got involved. They had to investigate if my mum's death was caused by manslaughter through neglect by the care people. They decided that it wasn't a criminal matter, but because of the circumstances Mum had to go under the coroner. This brought more pain as I knew exactly what her body would go through. I had seen many post-mortems in the police. I tried to block it out, but in my heart I knew she was up in heaven, no doubt drinking and smoking and laughing with all of our lot and nowhere near a morgue.

I must say the grieving was easier, as we are all psychic in my family and know the spiritual journey that a soul takes. Our esoteric knowledge brought a massive comfort to us all.

As with family and difficult people we weren't allowed to see our stepdad. So we were grieving the loss of two people.

On Sunday 14th January we went back down to Hayling from Essex to clear Mum's place as no one else was going to do it. We tried as hard as we could to make each other laugh with all the memories that clung to her belongings. You find yourself keeping absolutely everything in the beginning as you know that they had touched it or used it at some point. Pain soared through my heart when I saw the things that Mum had kept. Under the bed there was a little box containing the first bits of pottery that Sarah, Rich and I had made. I had no idea that she had kept them all these years. She never told us she had them, she never really shared any sentimentality with us. It was her way of coping.

Mum didn't have a proper life insurance so we were panicking about how to pay for the funeral. Luckily we sold some furniture and white goods that could all go into the pot.

As I looked at the empty bungalow, I knew that we had all entered into the change of an era. The end of a season was upon us. As in nature, life dies to create new seeds. Those new seeds would be the beginning of our lives, a family reunited, to grow strong and be nurtured by each other so that we could blossom.

As I got in the car that was full to the brim of crap, *Bridge over Troubled Water* played on the radio, just after the police phoned. Dad was with us.

The drive back to Essex was contemplative. We were also exhausted and drained of any emotion.

As we arrived at Rich's I stayed in the car as the detective on my mum's case was giving me an update. As I put the phone down, yet again unbelievably *Bridge over Troubled Water* played on the radio. Dad must have been in the car with me for the whole journey home.

That was when the flood gates opened.

I drifted back to the day when I was nine. Auntie June came into my room and told me Dad had gone to heaven. I then saw Mum's face battered and bruised from the animal. I saw us driving to hotels with Rich and Sarah as little mites to escape his overeager fists. I saw me crying in a hospital bed in a neck collar after he had punched me down the stairs. I saw my mum lying dead on the hospital bed. Flashes of trauma played out like a movie in my mind. My God, did I sob my heart out. I walked into Rich's and Lou just rocked with me as I let out all of the pain of our family history.

A little later I wrote in my journal. It is what all bereavement counsellors suggest you do.

Sunday 14 January 2018

It's finally happened. The dreaded transition. Mum passed on the 3rd January. The carers are being investigated. It sunk in when I was back at Rich's. When the DS called me, Bridge over Troubled Water *played and then again when we got home. That's when it broke me. To think of what's to come is unthinkable. Mum, I'm so sorry I didn't come to you on the Thursday. I didn't realise how ill you were and I was a little upset that you weren't coming down for our first Christmas together. I had no idea how ill you were. I feel so guilty that I wasn't there and the carers weren't doing their job.*

I'm also sorry that I didn't force myself to come and see you when you were in hospital. I felt so ill, I had no idea that you were going to pass and I can't bear the thought that you were there for four days without seeing us. Please forgive me!

I knew you were gone on the way there. I truly hope that Dad and Nan were there to take you up.

I hope that you are not angry for the police getting involved. I hope that you are not upset by it. You can see how pathetic people have been so I hope you understand.

I please invoke Archangel Raguel to remain with us all through this desperate time.

I please invoke Archangel Raphael to bring showers of healing upon us all.

I ask Archangel Azrael to remain close by whilst we go through the horror of what's to come from the authorities.

I hope you are resting, Mum, and are being cuddled by Dad, Nan and Aunt Rene.

Please keep sending synchronicity and signs to help us through as that is very important.

PLEASE let us have a successful result if we are to go through with this.

PLEASE let there be a happy ending.

Don't let us feel alone, let us get some form of connection as often as possible.

Sorry for all of these asks but you will soon forget the human condition and our need for physical signs.

I hope you feel happy that it's all over. I hope everything we have planned for the funeral is how you would like it.

If there is anything else you would like either you or someone else can bring your wishes to my mind as an idea or in dream state.

It has hit me as I write this today that it will be the last day I will ever set foot in your home again.

I see you now as very young and pretty and I hope that's how you are seeing yourself in the image that you create.

Gabriel, I would also appreciate your help in inspiring me for Mum's speech at the funeral. I'm very concerned as I truly want it to be perfect.

I'm trying to focus on the end of this chapter. Being happy being by the sea.

I will never forget you as you know.

I always saw you as a very brave, but insecure, withdrawn woman emotionally. I hope that is finally released in your new life.

I hadn't seen you truly laugh or genuinely smile for a very long time, so I hope your beautiful smile has returned as you make yourself at home up there.

Come to me when you are ready. Let me know that you are OK or use one of our lot's energies up there to present yourself.

I feel so deeply sad and need to let go of the guilt of not seeing you on the days you had alone before passing. Of that I am truly sorry, I truly am.

Love you, Mum xx

I pulled one angel card after this entry. It was Archangel Jeremiel. The angel that receives human souls in Heaven and reviews their lives. I knew that she was safe in his arms.

And that is how spiritual people cope with physical death. Each day is taken one at a time, full of prayers and conversations with spirit family. Looking for synchronicity and of course the love of supportive friends and family.

I was reading over my journal from last year and I read about the angel who was wrapping up a ball of light and had tagged it the 19th January. On the 19th January we had finally completed everything we needed to get done. I also had been told that Mum had died of a burst ulcer, which was the only non-life-threatening thing she had which no doctor had found or treated her for. It was obviously her time to go. So that day marked the finality of Mum's passing. We just had the funeral to go.

Unbelievably people were placed in front of us so we could afford a fantastic funeral. Holli, my sister's best friend, was there looking after Mum as she worked at the funeral home. She helped us out a lot. My friend Jo asked her sister to do our flowers, which she did magnificently and at a very low price. We found a great social club for the wake, and my two favourite people Trevor and Patrick who run the Dartford Spiritualist Church kindly provided us with the most beautiful spiritual service for nothing.

Gabriel provided me with the words to create a poem, "The Seasons of Mum".

It wrote itself and I know Mum would have loved it.

Three weeks later my Uncle Ron died and so the grieving began yet again. He came to me though on the night of his funeral. I could not attend as I was so exhausted. I had gone into a big M.E. crash. We spent a lovely time in Spain talking about nonsense and I got my closure.

Endings in life always lead to new doors being opened and new beginnings.

It would be interesting to see what was coming next.

Would there ever be a fairy tale ending?

Chapter 34

It's All In the Cards

It was Sunday 28th January and I was very tired. I spent most days at Rich's in my pyjamas doing nothing, allowing my body to rest as I knew that I had a long drive back to Somerset.

As I drove back home to Somerset, I realised that it was the anniversary of my dad's death, the 5th February. I walked into the house relieved that I could be in my own peace to heal and prepare for what was to come.

I walked straight into my bedroom and sensed the quietness. I have a large clock that ticks away near my bed. It wasn't ticking. It should have been as I had put a new battery in it before I left in December. I looked up and gasped. The clock had stopped at 8.42, the time of my mum's passing. I smiled and left that clock for three days before I changed the battery.

The signs keep you going; the synchronicity lets you know that you are not alone and no one dies, they just move on.

The estate agents had done absolutely nothing with the move, so I was no further forward.

Angel cards were my solace during those quiet days of healing.

Tuesday 6 February 2018
Card one

Memories from your childhood have resurfaced for a reason. Perhaps there's an old issue you still need to resolve.

New acquaintances may feel like old familiar friends because of karmic connections.

The effect of children on this situation could be important. Childlike innocence or a lack of guilt is also indicated.

Inheritance. Gifts. Reunions. Romanticising the past.

Card two

This is a successful time. Your projects will go well. Your talents and skills will bring rewards for you and others. Accept the opportunities offered to you and have confidence that you will succeed!

The Midas touch. A captain of Industry. Financial security.

ARCHANGEL AZRAEL

The end of a phase or situation. Spiritual transformation. Time to move on.

This card signifies that it is time to move on because a phase of your life is now complete.

There's no benefit in staying in this situation.

Instead shake off the old and welcome the new. You may experience a sense of relief at this ending, or there may be some sadness. Either way it's time to leave that which you have outgrown. Take your time adjusting to this change in your life. It is not necessary to rush ahead. Be kind to yourself during this period of transition and seek the support of friends and family.

Inevitable positive changes. Facing your fears. Relationship transitions. Spiritual education.

My God the cards never cease to amaze me. They have basically covered Mum, my move, my reunion and my book. Exactly what I asked before I even pulled them out.

Don't you just love it?

I continued to remain in bed; I was in permanent pain, the symptoms of M.E. and fibro ripping through my body and affecting every system going. I had dark days but had learned to pull myself up with positivity and affirmations. Every time I pulled the angel cards they said the same thing: positive change, success in creativity, abundance, new opportunities and rapid advancement. I clung on to those cards as I had nothing else to cling on to during the days of my crash and grieving. M.E. is very clever. It knows when you are down, it knows when you are stressed or upset, and it then jumps in and completely annihilates your body.

Richard was starting to seriously think about becoming a full-time medium. He was getting more aware by the day of the angel realms and the spirit world. He was getting messages in meditation from his guides pushing him to work for them. He also had been given the gift of health intuition. He phoned me again and again telling me to ditch dairy, that it was the last part of my health transition. I did not want to give up yet another part of my diet. I sulked and refused to do it. He and the family had come to stay; his nagging was relentless. On the morning of them being due to arrive, I heard a crash in the living room and saw that someone had thrown the fire poker across the room. They were obviously excited that Rich and the family were coming to see my home!

I eventually gave in and went dairy free; it is one of the best things that I had ever done. The nutritionist from way back had failed to identify why I wasn't losing weight and why I was so bloated and lethargic all of the time. She had made me drink milk and have cream, and use these fats for energy. This, according to Richard, was the last thing that I should be putting in my body.

Within two weeks I had lost nearly a stone and my tummy was no longer bloated. Rich had been totally right.

I started to feel better. After two months in bed, I felt I could get out and about.

I went to Devon and found the loveliest house sitting on a clifftop overlooking Brixham High Street. I was so excited. I couldn't put an offer in though as I hadn't sold. Time was ticking by and I was getting impatient.

On Friday 6th April I had a little wobble at the spirit world. Yet again I was sitting in my bed feeling the familiar downfall of my positivity. I had no one ordering my PRISM LIVING course anymore. I thought it would fly out of the window as it is a perfect guide to help people cope with depression and find a way to live in positivity and live life down here spiritually. I felt like I was bashing my head against a brick wall. I had so much to give to help people but I couldn't do bugger all sitting in my bed.

As I ranted away I heard a voice say, "Teach!"

"Oh really, and how am I going to do that sitting in this bloody bed!" I snorted resentfully.

"Teach!" the voice boomed again.

"How?" I shouted at the top of my voice.

My phone then beeped, I looked down and a YouTube video started playing. I thought this was weird as I wasn't even subscribed to the channel the video was playing on.

It then dawned on me.

"Are you having a laugh? You want me to go on YouTube?"

"Teach!" the voice said again.

I rolled my eyes. No one was interested in my course. I had had no's from agents for my fiction book *Earth Walkers*. Everything I tried seemed to be failing miserably, I didn't need to be a failure on YouTube either!

But the thought and the feeling that I should be doing something bit into my conscience hour after hour.

I decided, yet again, to pull a couple of cards.

Card one

Don't give up. Protect that which you have created and believe in yourself.

You've put a lot of work and energy into this situation. This card comes as a sign for you to actively protect what you have created or earned.

Have courage, believe in your ability and the right to defend the fruit of your labours. Strengthen your resolve and don't give up.

Being prepared. Physical strength. Feeling of paranoia. Tiredness.

Card two

The Hermit

Archangel Raziel

Benefit from the downtime and listen to your inner voice. Meditation! Learn to love your own company. There is a difference to being alone and lonely.

Spiritual teaching – wisdom to impart on others.

Sharing wisdom is part of your spiritual journey, especially right now.

Becoming a mentor, self-discovery, evaluation of plans, spiritual quest.

Raziel gives sage advice and guidance for your esoteric concepts. She also helps interpret dreams and past life memories.

Bloody hell, the cards always reflected what I needed to do! Spiritual teaching... Sharing wisdom... Bugger it!

So, ladies and gentlemen, the birth of 'The Bedroom Guru' took place that night.

I sat looking like shit and spoke from the heart. I asked Raziel to inspire me and I came up with all sorts of spiritual teachings and guidance. Within days I started to get comments on Facebook and emails telling me how much the videos on YouTube were liked. People started to subscribe to my channel and I enjoyed imparting my wisdom. I even helped a woman who had days to live. I explained the process to her and guided her on what would happen next. How precious is that? My online presence started to grow from these videos. I was back in the running. All I wanted to do was help people, and eventually help them through my books.

If that lot up there want you to do something, they will press you until you do it!

I spent most days packing and sleeping. I was waiting for the sale of my house as I desperately wanted the house in Brixham.

But I found if I was making a mistake or taking the wrong path, the spirit world put an instant stop to it. It seemed more powerful than ever before. I was totally in their hands and knew that they had my back every ounce of the way.

Monday 16 April 2018
Today is the day! I have sold my house and my offer was accepted on Cavern Road! I have a new home!

It's the beginning of a new adventure. It's the beginning of a new life!

Once more into the breach!

Incredibly, though, the powers that be got involved.

Saturday 9 June 2018
Fuck me time goes quick. Not written for ages. Most probably because I have done nothing but pack and sleep. To what end I don't know. I have lost Cavern Road TWO FUCKING DAYS before exchange. They have backed out. I'm sick to the stomach. Everyone is saying it's the Universe's way of it being wrong, well what the fuck was it put in my path in the first place? Am I supposed to be in Devon? So I have nowhere to go, wasted £375 on searches and back to square one sitting surrounded by boxes. They said I would move the 3rd August but to WHERE? They better find me something soon.

Mum came to Holli in a dream angry about a move a couple of days before the people dropped out. So I hope she now sends a message of what happens next. Or comes to me for Christ's sake!

Is Brixham wrong? I just don't know. It's there or Essex and that's defo not going to happen.

Let's try two cards.

Card one
Too much going on at once. Need to make a decision. Consider a more playful approach. You are doing too much. You may be experiencing financial instability or have too many projects on your plate.

You're feeling stress, yet you're managing to maintain status quo on home/work. Consider career change, keep current job but slowly transition.

Card two
The situation that you are enquiring about needs a decision

from you. Stay open to creative ideas or new perspectives. If you're struggling to choose, consider a playful approach. If you lighten up you may easily find the answer.

Dealing with change. Balance your budget. Ability to adapt.

So with these cards in mind, I did indeed lighten up. They both incredibly had the words "playful approach" in them.

I drove down to Devon asking Mum and Dad to help me make a decision. I lightened my energy and stopped putting pressure on myself. My buyers, thank God, were willing to postpone the completion date in order for me to find somewhere.

The times that I tell students and people to trust, you think I would adopt that attitude straight away. But no, I still got into a state if things weren't going the way they should.

Oh how they must laugh up there! What was to take place was truly unbelievable. They had it in the bag and I had no clue.

Chapter 35

The Last Leg

On Tuesday 26 June I was in Devon. I was looking forward to viewing some more houses. Luckily my pain and exhaustion levels weren't too bad. I asked my friend Gaynor to come along with me on the viewings. There were a number of reasons why I expressly chose her. She is straight down the line and says everything how it is. She always sees the practical elements of everything rather than the rose-tinted glass ones. She is also a numerologist and tarot reader. What harm could it do to bring another psychic along?

We went and looked at one house after another in Brixham. They were all wrong. I was getting more and more despondent.

"I can't see you here in Brixham, Nick," Gaynor said during a coffee break. "It all just feels wrong, plus you got all these bloody hills everywhere. How are you going to cope with that?"

I was letting my ego decide the house, I realised. I wanted the perfect fishing cottage overlooking the harbour so I could hear the sea. The problem with that was they had multi floors and nearly always no parking.

In my silent response, Gaynor grabbed my phone and started looking at the local houses for sale.

"What about this one?" she asked showing me a picture of a bungalow.

"It's a crappy granny place with only two bedrooms, Gaynor, it's not big enough!"

"Not big enough? How much bloody room do you need? Phone it up now."

This conversation went on and on. I refused to even think of the viewing the place.

Just then I got two emails. I couldn't believe what I was

reading.

One was from an old student of mine, Anna, who is an incredibly gifted medium. It basically went along the lines that my mum had popped in during a meditation to speak to her.

My spine tingled as I read on.

"She's saying that you took a silver bracelet off of her just after she passed…"

My eyes welled up. My clever mum had done it, and she had passed on our secret message to another. She was safe, well and ready to talk. Anna went on to describe our first dog that was running around with Mum, and that she was up there with Dad. She then said,

"Your mum mentioned the name Tyler. She was saying that you always told her off for smoking. That you swam with dolphins. That you are having head pain at the moment and digestive issues are sorted. Someone has just hurt their right ankle. Your mum's death hasn't been resolved and there's paperwork to be done or some sort of legal action, dig deeper. You are going to be on stage bigger and better than before. She did also say, go for the address with the 'B' name as it has a great feeling. She said she would be visiting soon."

I just couldn't believe what I was reading.

My brother had just gone over on his right ankle and had sprained it badly; his son is called Tyler. There was a massive investigation going on about my mum's care, perhaps I needed to seek counsel. The house address beginning with B, that was interesting.

I felt so happy that she had finally made contact; it was a bright release of grief as I reread the email.

I then went to the next email which was from my friend Julia who is also a fantastic psychic.

She pinpointed a lot of brilliant facts but the one that made me sit up and take notice was when she said,

"The house you are getting is near where you used to have a house and one that you looked at before."

That was Goodrington. I had my mobile home there before it was repossessed. I had also put an offer in on a bungalow in Goodrington but then withdrew the offer after I saw what the neighbours were like.

I looked at the bungalow that Gaynor was still showing me on her phone.

"Bloody ring it!"

I looked closer at the bungalow, the road name began with the letter B.

It was also in Goodrington.

The tingles on my head made me pick up the phone and call the estate agent. There would be an agent there in twenty minutes. My pulse quickened as we made our way to Goodrington.

As we pulled up in the road, I started to tingle all over. We parked up and saw a 'For Sale' sign outside a most beautiful bungalow with majestic steps leading up to the front door, sporting a magnificent palm tree in the well-manicured front garden.

"That can't be it?" I said to Gaynor as the pictures did not give it justice at all.

As I said this the rear sensors started beeping. We both looked back but I realised I had turned the ignition off so it was impossible for the sensors to operate.

"What the fuck!" Gaynor exclaimed as they started beeping again.

I started to giggle; this was great.

"Is there someone making that bleep?" she called out.

The beep changed to two beeps.

"Are you wanting to tell us something?"

Two beeps.

"Is this the right house for Nicky?"

Two beeps.

Then, silence.

"I know I am being sceptical but could you beep three times

if this is my new house?" I asked.

Bugger me, I held my breath as the sensors beeped three times.

I couldn't believe what I was witnessing.

"Jesus, Gaynor, I think this is it!"

We both said thank you to whoever had been beeping the sensors and got out of the car excitedly.

The road itself was so pretty. All of the gardens were immaculate, full of exotic plants and palms. To my left I could see green fields and woodlands with lakes at the side. "That would be my view," I thought.

I then realised in this peaceful road that I could hear the sea. I was just across the road from it and Goodrington Beach. Seagulls barked overhead which just added to the tingling sensation that was vibrating through my body. When I walked up to the bungalow the sun made the granite stone walls glint in the light. It sparkled like some mysterious house in a fairy tale. I knew that I couldn't stop smiling. The outside of the house was immaculate, and also detached. It looked simply beautiful.

I stood impatiently waiting for the estate agent and couldn't believe my eyes when he arrived. It was Lewis; he had been the same estate agent who had kindly tried to help me find somewhere to live when I was homeless.

"What are you doing here? Oh my God, I can't believe this!" I exclaimed.

"Hi, Nicky, I moved office. How strange to see you here after all of these years!"

I knew this was just another synchronicity. At the beginning of my struggle he was there, perhaps he was there to mark the end of my journey.

The bungalow was just as immaculate inside as it was outside. It was bright and sunny with large rooms and had everything I needed.

I stood in the kitchen thinking hard as the house really was at the end of my budget. I couldn't afford the asking price and all of the removal costs. The more I walked through the rooms, the more I fell in love with it.

The rear garden was gorgeous, with different sunny patio areas and an abundance of pretty flowers and shrubs in the raised flower beds. The lawn was the perfect size. I knew that I could maintain this garden easily.

It then hit me as I sat in the back garden that I had sent an order out for my new home a month ago.

Near the beach/nice views – tick.

Place to walk the babies – tick, it was directly opposite.

Bathroom near the bedroom – tick.

Kitchen near the bedroom – tick.

Near the shops and facilities – tick.

My order had been delivered.

I then realised that if I had bought the house in Brixham it would have been a massive mistake. The bathroom was nowhere near the bedroom for when I needed it on bad days and neither was the kitchen. There was nowhere locally to walk the dogs and I would have had a long hilly walk to the shops or would have to drive. I certainly was not near any beach without having to drive. There was also no parking at the house. I realised that I had made an impulsive decision just to fit in with my ego by wanting a place near Brixham Harbour. I could now see clearly that that place was totally wrong for me. Thank God the Universe had stopped me.

Gaynor was so excited; she adored the house and kept telling me to put an offer in. She then noticed that the number on the house added up to 11. The master number. It represents your soul mission and your life purpose. The post code added up to nine, another angel number.

I closed my eyes and felt the energy of the house. It felt warm, calm, light and welcoming. I then saw a lady smiling sitting in the lounge in my mind. She was slim built, glasses, short dark hair and was dressed very smartly. She said her name was Dorothy and it was her house. She was beaming at me. I took it as a blessing that she wanted me to have the house.

I then realised that I had to be honest with myself. This little bungalow was perfect for me. It needed no work, was immaculate inside and out, and wasn't too big to look after. I had to face facts, stairs were not good for me and neither was a big rambling house.

It then hit me as I took a deep breath.

I had made a decision.

I was home.

I put an offer in then and there.

The estate agent was a little dubious as he knew the sellers did not want to drop the price since it was their mum's house.

Amazingly after an hour of torture, they accepted the offer £17,000 under the marked price.

I remember jumping for joy and also crying with relief. This was my home, and if Gaynor had not been there and I hadn't received those emails, I would never have looked at it.

When I got home that day, I received an email from an investment company. I had forgotten about an old savings plan that I had in the police. They informed me that my plan had come to fruition. I had an extra £6,000 in my bank account. I could not believe my luck.

I could get a new bathroom and something that I had always wanted, a whirlpool bath to help ease my pain.

I picked one card that night to make sure I had made the right decision about the house. I could not take it in. Archangel Michael had been my guide finding the first house; it looked like he was presiding over this one as well.

Tuesday 26 June 2018
I just asked if I was getting the right house.
    ARCHANGEL MICHAEL

THE WHEEL

The Archangels sent you this card because of the positive changes in your life. Expect and enjoy beneficial new opportunities as they present themselves. This is an optimal time to make big and small changes. Take the leap with the knowledge that everything will work well for you.

Old blocks are lifting and everything now moves forward quickly. If recent events shook your faith, now see how they were actually positive for you. Rapid advancement is likely now. Good Luck. Balanced Karma. A miracle. Destiny.

Archangel Michael is the supreme protecting angel who works beside you through changes, giving you courage, strength and self-confidence.

Call upon him whenever you'd like specific guidance about your next step, especially if it's connected to your life purpose or spiritual path.

And... Breathe!

Archangel Michael, I ask you to guide me through my move and to stay strong throughout. I ask you continue to remind me of my true path.

The book is next!

The best days ever are coming!

That night I looked at the map that surrounded my new home. I couldn't believe that when I looked at the area and district it was called St Michaels.

I later discovered on talking to the seller that her mum was indeed called Dorothy and fitted the description that I had seen in the lounge. Dorothy was obviously happy for me to take over from her in this wonderful home.

Could the end of my nightmare finally be over?

Could I possibly experience complete happiness and peace?

I just had to stay focused, go with the flow and see what came out in the wash.

Chapter 36

The End of an Era

Some would say that our condition is all in the mind. I have had a few people say that to me over the years. Just for the record that is an insult. This disease is real and finally we are getting our voice heard in Parliamentary debates, so hopefully we will receive the acknowledgement and vital care that is needed.

I can say that when we are happy and stress-free our body does indeed run a bit more smoothly. But that certainly doesn't mean we create our own illness by being stressed.

I must add, however, that I had a new spring in my step knowing I had found my new home. Positivity and life goals are vital to chronic illness sufferers. I had more energy and vigour. I was completely happy and tranquil. This could have been because of the weather improving or the fact that my diet was exemplary. No matter what the factors were, I was feeling good.

I paced myself every day as I packed up my belongings making sure not to overdo it.

I found that positivity far outweighed any negativity. I found the deepest joy in the most simplest of things. I spoke with the angels and my family in the spirit world every day. I had total faith in them; they had delivered time and time again. There was a shift in my energy and it felt good. I no longer worried about anything. I found that I had become patient and at peace with myself.

I was even picking up the phone when it rang, much to the surprise of my family and friends! I no longer wanted to isolate. I wanted to be part of the world and mix with the people in it. I was ready to come out of my cocoon of healing and face the world and all of the challenges that it may bring. I was strong and I had courage. I was complete.

Incredibly the completion date for the move came through for the 3rd August. Just as my lovely lot up there had predicted. The house had sold in April as they had said, so I had no doubt everything would go smoothly in the arms of the angels and the spirit world.

The only fly in the ointment was the fact that the local authority had agreed that my mum's care was thwarted with massive mistakes and failures.

They said, 'sorry and could they use my mum's scenario as what not to do for their new students'.

I felt angry but there was nothing I could do. I tried calling solicitors but none of them were interested in the case, stating I did not have a claim.

I still feel unrest with this situation but it is manageable and certainly was outweighed by the new life that I was about to embark on.

August brought the most glorious weather. If anything it was a tad too hot.

The removal men turned up at 8am sharp on the morning of the 3rd. The babies were at Jay's so that they wouldn't get stressed with the upheaval. There then began a frenzy of packing and cleaning the house as they emptied each room.

As the empty cottage stared back at me, I thanked it for being another stepping stone towards my destiny. I wandered through the rooms and smiled knowing that these walls had shrouded me during my desperate battles for happiness and health. I felt a little sadness on leaving but I knew in no uncertain terms that this was the right move. I could not believe that I was moving again, but this time there would be no vulnerability or fear of losing my security. I knew that I was going home; there was always a part of my heart attached to Devon and Cornwall.

With a satisfied sigh I said thank you to Michael for finding me this place. Without it I never would have had the budget to move back to Devon.

I took one last look across the levels and towards Glastonbury Tor, turned away and walked out of the door ready for my next chapter.

Finally I was in my car driving down to Devon. The enormity of what I had achieved kept rising to spontaneous outbursts of crying tears through a grateful smile.

I felt no great sadness on leaving Somerset apart from the lovely friends that I had met there. I knew I was going to be so much happier in Devon, that's all I could focus on. With each mile, my anticipation levels rose. I had waited so long for this moment.

I finally reached Devon and took a familiar road towards my home. The road has been my favourite for many years as when you hit its apex you are afforded a magnificent view of the bay reaching right across to Brixham.

As I hit that spot in the road, I looked out to the sparkling diamonds glinting off of the azure blue sea and promptly burst into tears.

I had to pull over as I was so emotional.

I looked back on the last six years of my life. I saw flashes of me lying in bed willing death to come and visit me, wanting the horror of my existence to end. I saw me standing on the doorstep in the rain holding dustbin bags, my two dogs crying, wet through either side of me. I saw the mobile home being repossessed, slipping through my fingers. I saw me standing naked in the moonlight begging for help. I saw me being turned away and abandoned by doctors. I saw the tears, the pain, and the loneliness that I had endured. I saw the face of my brave mum still and silent in her death.

I then saw the fight in me, the will to survive and endure. I saw me moving into the cemetery lodge, then into the Somerset cottage, dusting myself off and taking on the next challenge. I saw me starting to listen to what the angel realms and my spirit relatives had to say. I saw me start to trust the Universe. I saw my reunion with my siblings, a void that had now filled a deep dark abyss of blackness. I saw my babies ever present, ever keeping me going. I saw me standing on stage doing my first mediumship show. I saw the will to write keeping me going. I saw me gazing at my new bungalow promising a new beginning.

I saw victory against all the odds.

I may have an incurable condition, but I embraced it, knowing to be kind to myself on bad days. I had the right people around me that respected me and my condition. People would have to love me for me, not what I had to offer, warts and all. If a box set day was on the cards, I would relish it.

I was thankful for the accident. It had, despite the battles, released me from my demons and allowed me to be stripped bare. It allowed me to find the new me, the real me. It allowed me to grab hold of that ever present armour and fling it aside without a second thought. I had never listened to my body so much in all of my life. I had never respected my body ever and now I was passionate in doing whatever was best for it.

I had never thought about what I wanted or had even contemplated putting me first. I did now. I loved my own company, I loved my presence in the world. I found that I was grateful for things that most humans don't even think about. I felt an inner strength that I never knew I had. I had boundaries that had never been initiated in the past. I would never people please again. I had also found courage in making change no matter how hard it would be. Most of all I had implicit faith in the angel realms and the spirit world. I knew without a shadow of a doubt that these celestial beings were here to help us whilst we struggled down here; all we had to do was ask them.

I knew that if it hadn't been for the miracles, signs and synchronicity that the angel realms and my spirit family had brought, I would be dead. There are no two ways about it, I definitely would have ended the pain long ago.

But I didn't.

After taking a big breath, I pulled the car on to the road and carried driving along. I was about to turn off into my road when I looked down to the main road in front of me. I saw, which I had never done before, pine trees lining a barrier between the road and the beach. I drove forward and turned into the beach road. The pine trees then gave way to the railway line. On my right was a water theme park with water slides. To my left there were large plastic swan boats on a lake.

I sat in Goodrington car park and realised with a jolt of recognition that this had been the recurring dream that I had been having for years.

The dream was a promise that all would come good. The fairy tale ending was coming to someone like me who had fought to regain some sort of life. Even though I had been to Goodrington Sands before, I never connected it to my recurring dream.

I sat in the car, the blistering sun was radiating down on the calm turquoise waves. I watched the families laughing and playing with their children. I heard the whoops of excitement as people crashed into the sea. I did not feel one bit of jealousy or resentment. I was happy for them all, knowing that I would embrace that sort of happiness for myself. I pictured me playing with my nieces and nephews on that beach; a swell of love and excitement overwhelmed me.

I had never felt so happy and complete.

Actually I wasn't happy, that was an understatement; I was ecstatic.

If I could pull myself through all of this loss and pain. If I could fight a horrific debilitating illness. If I could change my life in order to find happiness, then I was going to damn well try and help every brave soul on this planet that is touched by chronic illness, pain, loss and darkness through my writing.

Writing.

One of the strongest passions that kept me going through the storm. Not only a passion, but a way in the future for me to reach people in pain, people that are lost and the ones that feel totally alone.

I knew that my next phase of life was to help each and every one of them to find the strength to endure.

I looked up to the sky imagining an angel floating there. I asked them for the title.

That's when I saw it, there by the sea.

M.E Myself and I: Diary of a Psychic.

My first book and my first step to helping the world be a happier place. It would also give me the opportunity to show how a higher power really does exist and really can guide us and help us in our darkest, desperate moments.

I felt excitement surge through me picturing the possibility of people suffering, reading my words of inspiration and finding a way forward. I created a vision in my mind of watching people open their hearts to the angels, ordering from the Universe and accepting their darkness knowing that they could fight it. I watched this hope and faith spread from one soul to another. I would do everything in my power to get my voice out there and help those desperate souls. This was my next goal.

I then came back into reality wearing the hugest smile.

I started the car engine and turned towards my new house.

I had done it.

I was home.

Sunday 5 August 2018

The quietness is deafening in a good way. The cottage was next to the road and I didn't realise how much noise I was exposed to. I awoke to the sound of the sea and the seagulls. I can smell the sea in the air. I am looking in my bright new bedroom and looking out on to eucalyptus, fir, pine and oak trees. I feel so complete it is unbelievable. It's like I have returned to a childhood home. I can't stop smiling! Something has shifted, like an overwhelming sense of release and peace. The fight to survive and endure is now over. I'm exhausted and have pain but it really doesn't matter. The contentment is overwhelming. I keep welling up with the enormity of it all. When I had my first sight of the sea on my moving day I burst into tears. It was relief that finally I have surged through the ribbon at the end of the race.

I look back on every struggle and adversity that I faced in the last six years and I am now proud of myself. I have done it! I have even found out I am living in St Michael's parish! How amazing is that? I now have nothing to do but create beauty in my new home. To embrace my exciting future and all of the possibilities that are to come leaves me breathless.

My seven-year cycle is almost at an end. I know that 2019 will be awesome. I know that I am at the end of my nightmare. I am out the other side and all I can do is now show other people how it's done.

I am so in love with my new home. I am so in love with myself for being a survivor. I have conquered. I have been victorious on the biggest war of my life. All I can do is smile and love my life and the riches that are to come. No more sadness, only light!

All I can tell you is that whatever dark abyss you find yourself adrift in, never give up, fight like hell. Find a higher power, whatever you are comfortable with, and trust that they will see you through. Love yourself before anyone else and the rest will follow.

If I could travel in time and tell the former me that now I would be the strongest and happiest I had ever been and that I lived by the angel and spirit realms through every challenge. That I would be mindful all of the time, meditate every day and love myself. That I would watch my diet, be conscious of my mind, body and spirit most of the day every day – I would have laughed in my face!

You can do this; you don't have to be psychic or have any spiritual belief system in place. The celestial world is sitting there waiting patiently for anyone who asks for help. In their eyes, we are just a soul on a visit to earth and they are our lifeline during the experience.

Embrace your darkness, accept its unwelcome call into your life, because the sooner you accept it and surrender, the quicker you can adapt and own it with strength and courage.

I cannot say that my life is going to be glorious and I am going to have nothing but happiness. What I can say is that whatever hits me from now on, I know I will never be fighting it alone.

I am held in the arms of my spirit family and the angels. There is no safer place to be. x

Chapter 37

To All the Brave Chronic Illness Warriors

As you can see from my story, this isn't an 'I have found the cure' book, which infuriate me as we are all different.

It is also not an 'I have found the elixir to life and chronic illness'.

The only miracles in this book are the ones that were brought from the Spirit World and the Angel Realms. Tough one to swallow, I grant you, but can it really hurt to give it a go? Can it hurt to put your faith and trust in the invisible? What have you got to lose? As you can see, I did not willingly give myself up to these celestial beings. They dragged me kicking and screaming back to normality! So if they could do that with me resisting every step, what happens when you are on board and trust everything they do from the outset?

I still suffer, I still relapse and I still get shit days. The trick is to own your condition and accept it. Acceptance and self-love are the keys to this way of life. Adapt, believe you deserve the best outcome and work towards being the happiest that you can be. I am not only here to share my journey, but for you to reach out to me in any way you want to. I have just added below a few bullet point tips that helped me get through and still do every day:

1. Seriously think about restricting or removing alcohol, caffeine, sugar, gluten and dairy from your diet. All of these substances hinder our recovery.
2. Do not force yourself to do anything. If you want to sleep, sleep. If you can manage a little light exercise, go for it, but don't overdo it.
3. You will be pushed by ignorant doctors, pain therapists

and consultants to do the GET programme (Graded Exercise Therapy). Don't even think about doing this. It will worsen your condition. You move and exercise at your own speed which you will become accustomed to the longer you have the condition. You will 'hear' when your body has had enough.

4. Start looking into essential oils to improve your mood, pain and symptoms.

5. DO NOT let other people judge you or make assumptions on what you are capable of.

6. Bathe in Epsom salt baths, magnesium is essential for us.

7. Get into the sun as much as possible, sunlight provides us with essential Vitamin D.

8. Be kind to yourself, you must take measures to love yourself unconditionally.

9. Allow yourself to surrender to this new way of life, denial will hold you stuck in a miserable existence.

10. Healthily grieve your old life and make efforts to move on from it.

11. Find a higher power to hand all of your worries and concerns over to.

12. Distance yourself from negative people and those who refuse to be empathic of your condition, even if they are family.

13. Encourage your loved ones to learn everything about your condition so that they have a better understanding.

14. Learn to say no to things you can't do or attend, don't people please.

15. Join a supportive forum on social media, you are not alone!

16. Consider taking Low Dose Naltrexone. Information is available at: www.ldnresarchtrust.org.uk.

17. Join an online community and get support at: www. meassociation.org.uk and www.actionforme.org.uk.

18. Don't be afraid to go to your MP if you are being ignored by health services and social services. This is a disability. You have rights to benefits and help. Be a voice.

19. Find things to do that stimulate you whilst holed up in bed which you can manage. Reading, crafts, colouring, watching box sets, jigsaws, blogs, writing. Etc. On a depression day try and watch something that will make you laugh or listen to your favourite music.

20. Pace yourself, make a plan for the day for little things you wish to achieve. If you don't get them done, who cares?

21. Own your illness, try holistic therapies to ease your symptoms, and don't let the illness own you.

22. Use affirmations, CBT and mindfulness to help you get through the darker days. Positivity is a lot more powerful than negativity. Don't allow your negative thoughts to spiral into emotions and behaviour.

23. Surround yourself in things that make you smile. Make your bedroom a haven to be in. Have photos up of your loved ones, be surrounded by your favourite colour and spend as much as you can on having the most comfortable bedding. If you are going to spend all of this time in bed, make it count! I found a heated mattress to be fantastic on bad joint days. A V pillow will support your arms and neck which will lessen bodily stress. Have ample cushions and pillows to support your limbs.

24. Consider using crystals to help your symptoms, google Judy Hall, the author, for crystals that can help.

25. Look into cosmic ordering; the Universe is awaiting your wants and needs.

26. Think about talking to angels and your spirit loved ones; the results will surprise you.

27. If you need help, advice or just a friend, email me at: nickyalan333@gmail.com.

28. If the depression and anxiety get too overwhelming, please reach out to loved ones, your GP, your local mental health team or the Samaritans at: https://www.samaritans.org.

29. This took a lot for me, but don't hide your fight. Reach out and ask for help on day-to-day activities. There is no weakness in asking for help. Try not to isolate yourself.

30. Make enquiries with your local care support office. There are volunteers that will help with daily tasks from cleaning, cooking, dog walking, to cutting your grass and taking you to appointments.

31. You have a disability, you are entitled to PIP (Personal Independent Payment) and a disability blue badge. The Citizens Advice Bureau can assist with this.

32. If you are suffering financially because of not being able to work contact www.stepchange.org.uk. They are brilliant debt counsellors that offer a free service.

33. As you can see in my story you will get intense 'up' and 'down' days for no reason. Mood swings are severe and can happen many times in a day. When the dark comes have people you love with you or try anything positive to get through the black thoughts.

34. Finally, fight with all your might to win. You may never be well again, but a positive mindset is key.

I honour all of you that suffer with chronic illness. We shall all continue to fight, and united we can be a strong voice. Don't be one of the 'Millions Missing', be heard.

I hope that my story has not only inspired you but will fill you with shards of hope and faith as you lay in your beds and dwell in the prison that is your home.

Aim to win the battles as they will all add up to winning the war, and always see your dreams as a reality, just waiting to happen. Xx

Biography

Nicky is a born Psychic Medium coming from many generations of psychics before her. She officially started her psychic work 27 years ago. For 18 years she was also a Major Investigation bereavement trained Detective in Essex Police. Following medical retirement in 2003 and by public demand she has achieved a very high profile in the spiritual industry as a full-time Psychic Medium, Spiritual Teacher, Writer and Angel Expert.

Since 2003, she has been a freelance paranormal writer regularly published in mainstream spiritual magazines. She currently has three columns, "The Psychic Detective" in *Take a Break's Fate & Fortune* magazine and "Diary of a Psychic" in *Spirit & Destiny* magazine, UK and Australia. She is also a resident features writer in *Haunted Magazine* and *Paranormal Chronicles*.

She is noted for her international appearances on radio (winner best show/guest for *Angels* Haunted Devon FM), tours with the late Colin Fry, and TV programmes including *Street Seer* (Gifted channel), *A Sister's Loss* (Sky One), *Live From Studio Five* (Channel 5, with Melinda Messenger, Ian Wright and Kate Walsh), *Come Dine With Me* (guest medium), *Angels* (two seasons with Gloria Hunniford, Glennyce Eckersley and Chris French), and cinema film paranormal documentary *The Birdbrook Ghost Hunt*.

She has carried out European theatre tours, seminars, retreats and workshops to 3,000 strong crowds on the afterlife and angel phenomena resulting in a high social media platform.

She has produced two guided meditation CDs *Soul Journey* and *Meeting Your Guides*. She has a successful online spiritual living course *Prism Living* and helps the public through her spiritual education videos as *The Bedroom Guru* on YouTube.

Since her catastrophic road accident in 2012 limiting her touring, she is now pursuing her passion as a Spiritual Author.

Aside from writing she has a passion for the sea and adores walking her beloved two dogs Teddy and Mia on the beaches of Devon where she now lives.

Thank you for purchasing *M.E Myself and I – Diary of a Psychic*. My sincere hope is that you derived as much from reading this book as I have in creating it. If you have a few moments, please feel free to add your review of the book at your favourite online site for feedback. Also, if you would like to connect with other books that I have coming in the near future, please visit my website for news on upcoming works and events at:

https://www.nickyalan.co.uk
You can also connect with me on:
Twitter: https://twitter.com/@nickyalan07
Goodreads – Nicky Alan: https://www.goodreads.com
LinkedIn: Nicky Alan: https://www.linkedin.com
Instagram: https://www.instagram.com/NickyAlan
Facebook: https://www.facebook.com/nicky.alan.3/
Or why not come along and watch my helpful Spiritual
Education videos on my YouTube Channel: https://
www.youtube.com/channel/UCB1kw1XdNbEUmJQOf7_
M4GQ?view_as=subscriber

Thank you once again for sharing my journey,

May the angels bless you always, Nicky x

**6TH
BOOKS**

ALL THINGS PARANORMAL

Investigations, explanations and deliberations on the paranormal,
supernatural, explainable or unexplainable. 6th Books seeks to
give answers while nourishing the soul: whether making use of the
scientific model or anecdotal and fun, but always
beautifully written.
Titles cover everything within parapsychology: how to, lifestyles,
alternative medicine, beliefs, myths and theories.
If you have enjoyed this book, why not tell other readers by
posting a review on your preferred book site?

Recent bestsellers from 6th Books are:

The Afterlife Unveiled

What the Dead Are Telling us About Their World!

Stafford Betty

What happens after we die? Spirits speaking through mediums know, and they want us to know. This book unveils their world...

Paperback: 978-1-84694-496-3 ebook: 978-1-84694-926-5

Spirit Release

Sue Allen

A guide to psychic attack, curses, witchcraft, spirit attachment, possession, soul retrieval, haunting, deliverance, exorcism and more, as taught at the College of Psychic Studies.

Paperback: 978-1-84694-033-0 ebook: 978-1-84694-651-6

I'm Still With You

True Stories of Healing Grief Through Spirit Communication

Carole J. Obley

A series of after-death spirit communications which uplift, comfort and heal, and show how love helps us grieve.

Paperback: 978-1-84694-107-8 ebook: 978-1-84694-639-4

Less Incomplete

A Guide to Experiencing the Human Condition Beyond the Physical Body

Sandie Gustus

Based on 40 years of scientific research, this book is a dynamic guide to understanding life beyond the physical body.

Paperback: 978-1-84694-351-5 ebook: 978-1-84694-892-3

Advanced Psychic Development

Becky Walsh

Learn how to practise as a professional, contemporary spiritual medium.

Paperback: 978-1-84694-062-0 ebook: 978-1-78099-941-8

Astral Projection Made Easy

and overcoming the fear of death

Stephanie June Sorrell

From the popular Made Easy series, *Astral Projection Made Easy* helps to eliminate the fear of death, through discussion of life beyond the physical body.

Paperback: 978-1-84694-611-0 ebook: 978-1-78099-225-9

The Miracle Workers Handbook

Seven Levels of Power and Manifestation of the Virgin Mary

Sherrie Dillard

Learn how to invoke the Virgin Mary's presence, communicate with her, receive her grace and miracles and become a miracle worker.

Paperback: 978-1-84694-920-3 ebook: 978-1-84694-921-0

Divine Guidance

The Answers You Need to Make Miracles

Stephanie J. King

Ask any question and the answer will be presented, like a direct line to higher realms... *Divine Guidance* helps you to regain control over your own journey through life.

Paperback: 978-1-78099-794-0 ebook: 978-1-78099-793-3

The End of Death
How Near-Death Experiences Prove the Afterlife
Admir Serrano
A compelling examination of the phenomena of Near-Death Experiences.
Paperback: 978-1-78279-233-8 ebook: 978-1-78279-232-1

The Psychic & Spiritual Awareness Manual
A Guide to DIY Enlightenment
Kevin West
Discover practical ways of empowering yourself by unlocking your psychic awareness, through the Spiritualist and New Age approach.
Paperback: 978-1-78279-397-7 ebook: 978-1-78279-396-0

An Angels' Guide to Working with the Power of Light
Laura Newbury
Discovering her ability to communicate with angels, Laura Newbury records her inspirational messages of guidance and answers to universal questions.
Paperback: 978-1-84694-908-1 ebook: 978-1-84694-909-8

The Audible Life Stream
Ancient Secret of Dying While Living
Alistair Conwell
The secret to unlocking your purpose in life is to solve the mystery of death, while still living.
Paperback: 978-1-84694-329-4 ebook: 978-1-78535-297-3

Beyond Photography
Encounters with Orbs, Angels and Mysterious Light Forms!
John Pickering, Katie Hall
Orbs have been appearing all over the world in recent years. This is the personal account of one couple's experience of this new phenomenon.
Paperback: 978-1-90504-790-1

Blissfully Dead
Life Lessons from the Other Side
Melita Harvey
The spirit of Janelle, a former actress, takes the reader on a fascinating and insightful journey from the mind to the heart.
Paperback: 978-1-78535-078-8 ebook: 978-1-78535-079-5

Does It Rain in Other Dimensions?
A True Story of Alien Encounters
Mike Oram
We have neighbors in the universe. This book describes one man's experience of communicating with other-dimensional and extra-terrestrial beings over a 50-year period.
Paperback: 978-1-84694-054-5

Electronic Voices: Contact with Another Dimension?
Anabela Mourato Cardoso
Career diplomat and experimenter Dr Anabela Cardoso covers the latest research into Instrumental Transcommunication and Electronic Voice Phenomena.
Paperback: 978-1-84694-363-8

The Hidden Secrets of a Modern Seer
Cher Chevalier
An account of near death experiences, psychic battles between good and evil, multidimensional experiences and Demons and Angelic Helpers.
Paperback: 978-1-84694-307-2 ebook: 978-1-78099-058-3

Haunted: Horror of Haverfordwest
G L Davies
Blissful beginnings for a young couple turn into a nightmare after purchasing their dream home in Wales in 1989. Their love and their resolve are torn apart by an indescribable entity that pushes paranormal activity to the limit. Dare you step Inside?
Paperback: 978-1-78535-843-2 ebook: 978-1-78535-844-9

Raising Faith
A true story of raising a child psychic-medium
Claire Waters
One family's extraordinary experience learning about their young daughter's ability to communicate with spirits, and inspirational lessons learned on their journey so far.
Paperback: 978-1-78535-870-8 ebook: 978-1-78535-871-5

Readers of ebooks can buy or view any of these bestsellers by clicking on the live link in the title. Most titles are published in paperback and as an ebook. Paperbacks are available in traditional bookshops. Both print and ebook formats are available online.
Find more titles and sign up to our readers' newsletter at http://www.johnhuntpublishing.com/mind-body-spirit.
Follow us on Facebook at https://www.facebook.com/OBooks and Twitter at https://twitter.com/obooks.